THE PERSON-CENTRED APPROACH

The Person-Centred Approach

A Contemporary Introduction

**Louise Embleton Tudor,
Keemar Keemar, Keith Tudor,
Joanna Valentine and
Mike Worrall**

First published 2004 by
PALGRAVE MACMILLAN

Palgrave Macmillan in the UK is an imprint of Macmillan Publishers Limited,
registered in England, company number 785998, of Houndmills, Basingstoke,
Hampshire RG21 6XS.

Palgrave Macmillan in the US is a division of St Martin's Press LLC,
175 Fifth Avenue, New York, NY 10010.

Palgrave Macmillan is the global academic imprint of the above companies
and has companies and representatives throughout the world.

Palgrave® and Macmillan® are registered trademarks in the United States,
the United Kingdom, Europe and other countries.

ISBN 978-1-403-90227-6 paperback

This book is printed on paper suitable for recycling and made from fully
managed and sustained forest sources. Logging, pulping and manufacturing
processes are expected to conform to the environmental regulations of the
country of origin.

A catalogue record for this book is available from the British Library.

Printed and bound in Great Britain by
CPI Antony Rowe, Chippenham and Eastbourne

To past, present and future students of the person-centred approach

Contents

List of Figures and Box

Figures

Box

Acknowledgements

We would like to acknowledge Alison Caunt, formerly of Palgrave Macmillan, who first approached us about writing, and was enthusiastic about this project. Our thanks go to Phil Barnet for his correspondence (which informs sections of Chapter 7); to the anonymous reviewers for their rigorous and helpful comments; and to our own expert readers: Paul Lewin, whom we thank particularly for his advice on and contribution to Chapter 16, Tracey Taylor and Nick Weiss. We owe a special debt to John K. Wood for the generosity, candour and speed of his responses to earlier drafts of the book. In the later stages of production Brian Morrison's thorough and precise copy-editing was immeasurably helpful. His work has clarified and tightened the final text. We also thank Linda Adams, President of Gordon Training International (website: www.gordontraining.com), for granting permission to reproduce Thomas Gordon's credo (Box 9.1 in Chapter 9).

Any writing project demands the love, tolerance, support and encouragement of family and friends. We have received all these in abundance. We want to thank specifically a number of people who offered practical and emotional sustenance to us, severally and collectively: Annette Ansell, William Daniel Braham, Miriam Brown, Felipe Ferrera-Albertos, Pam Geggus, Edwin William Keemar, Anisha Mehta, Robert Powe, Clare Raido, Paul Tudor, and David Webb. Finally we wish to acknowledge our teachers and our students for their enduring generosity and wisdom.

Introduction

If you see this book in a bookshop or on a friend's bookshelf, you may well ask yourself: 'Why another book on the person-centred approach?' and 'Why an introductory book?' These are interesting questions and, given the personal and ecological costs of producing books, important ones to consider and address.

Why another book on the person-centred approach?

The short answer to this question is that this isn't *another* book on the person-centred approach! There are many texts that cover with depth and clarity the legacy of Carl Rogers (1902–87) in the fields of psychology, psychotherapy and counselling. In the past 15 years particularly, there has been a renaissance of interest in his contribution to these fields and, more broadly, to the *approach*. This is reflected in:

- Publications by Combs (1989), McIlduff and Coghlan (1991b), Teich (1992), McIlduff and Coghlan (1993b), Schmid and Wascher (1994), Merry (1995), Du Toit, Grobler and Schenck (1997/1998), Barrett-Lennard (1998), Heron (1998), Hirayama (1998), Merry (1999a, 1999b), Stillwell (2000), Tudor and Merry (2002), Barrett-Lennard (2003) and Tudor and Worrall (2004, in press).
- Books specifically about Rogers, the man and his ideas: De Carvalho (1991), Thorne (1992, 2003 (Second edition)), Suhd (1995), Cohen (1997), N. Rogers (2002) and Rogers and Russell (2003).
- The publication of collections of papers by Rogers: Kirschenbaum and Henderson (1990a,b), and of transcripts of some of his clinical and demonstration work, together with commentaries: Farber,

Brink and Raskin (1996); and by some of the most experienced writers and practitioners in the field: Bozarth (1998), Patterson (2000), Natiello (2001c), Shlien (2003) and Raskin (2004, in press).

- Publications specifically concerning the field of counselling and psychotherapy: Mearns and Thorne (1988, 1999 (Second edition)), Fusek (1991), Thorne (1991), Duncan, Solovey and Rusk (1992), Brazier (1993), Merry and Lusty (1993), Mearns (1994), Prouty (1994), Boy and Pine (1995), Graham *et al.* (1995), Esser, Pabst and Speierer (1996), Gendlin (1996), Mearns (1997), Rennie (1998), Thorne (1998a,b), Boy and Pine (1999), Morton (1999), O'Leary (1999), Hughes and Buchanan (2000), Pörtner (2000), Mearns and Thorne (2000), Gaylin (2001), Prouty, Van Werde and Pörtner (2002), Thorne (2002), Worsley (2002), Keys (2003), Sommerbeck (2003), Tolan (2003), Wilkins (2003) and Tudor and Worrall (2004, in preparation).
- The publication of collections of papers from person-centred and experiential conferences: Lietaer, Rombauts and Van Balen (1990), Hutterer *et al.* (1996), Marques-Teixeira and Antones (2000) and Watson, Goldman and Warner (2002).
- The publication of themed collections of papers edited by Thorne and Lambers (1998), Fairhurst (1999), Lago and MacMillan (1999), Merry (2000b), Bozarth and Wilkins (2001), Haugh and Merry (2001), Wyatt (2001), Cain (2002) and Wyatt and Sanders (2002).
- A collection of person-centred literature in the International Archives of the Person-Centered Approach at the Universidad Iberoamericana in Mexico (website: www.aiep.bib.uia.mx/aiep); as well as other comprehensive collections available online at www.pce-world.org (developed by Germain Lietaer) and www.pca-online.net (by Peter Schmid).[1]
- The formation of the Network of European Associations for Person-Centered and Experiential Psychotherapy and Counseling (website: www.pce-europe.org); and a new World Association for Person-Centered and Experiential Psychotherapy and Counseling (website: www.pce-world.org), and its journal *Person-Centered and Experiential Psychotherapy.*

Whilst there is a wealth of literature on the various applications and influences of the person-centred approach, no one book has, to date, introduced

---

[1] We are aware that we have cited English language publications and that there is a significant literature in others languages (Dutch, German, Japanese, Portuguese and Spanish) for further details of which see Peter Schmid's website: www.pca-online.net.

the person-centred approach as an *approach* to life both in and beyond *therapy*, which is a generic term we use throughout to include psychotherapy, counselling and counselling psychology. This book offers such an introduction to the philosophy, principles, theory and key concepts of the approach. We look at person-centred approaches to human development, personality and sexuality; relationships, parenting and family life; education and learning; citizenship and the personal, local and global issues of justice, peace and conflict; the wider social systems of couples, groups, communities and organisations; and the environment. We also present or re-present a person-centred approach to therapy. The person-centred approach has also been extensively researched and indeed has made a contribution to ideas about research (see Rogers, 1985; Barrineau and Bozarth, 1989; Moustakas, 1990). Barrett-Lennard's (1998) excellent book also provides references to and summaries of other pertinent research studies in many of the fields of application which we consider in this book. We do not claim to be experts in all these areas, and there are many aspects of life which we do not explore here. We do claim a passion for the approach and for the applicability of its principles to all aspects of life.

Two principal concerns inform our writing:

1 That the person-centred approach is often misrepresented and misunderstood, even by its proponents. In this book, we want to represent the approach accurately and thoroughly. Despite popular and usually uninformed opinion, the approach is rigorous, robust and relevant to modern and postmodern life.
2 That, conversely, person-centred practitioners can be too precious about the purity of the approach. Debates about whether something – or someone – is or is not person-centred are intellectually and clinically sterile, and leave person-centred practitioners defensive, in a ghetto of their own making.

Accordingly, we assume, and argue, the following:

   That the person-centred approach offers a comprehensive, coherent and holistic *approach* to human life and concerns.[2]

---

[2] In this book we focus on the human organism and human life. We are also aware of the potential of applying the approach to relationships with other forms of life such as animals (see Birch, in preparation).

▪ That we live in a complex and diverse world. Philosophically, professionally and personally we welcome the challenges that come with complexity and even chaos. Whilst holding the integrity of the approach, we also acknowledge the existence and relevance of other philosophies, theories and practices.

▪ That we need to be thoroughly familiar with the history and roots of the approach in order to deepen our understanding of it; and that we need to compare it with other approaches in order to widen and sharpen our appreciation and understanding of it. Throughout the book we have referred to literature within and beyond the approach in order to locate it within, alongside, and sometimes apart from other theories and theorists.

Why an introductory book?

The short answer to this question is that, given its scope, this book can be only an introduction! This said, at the same time as introducing the person-centred approach, we are also giving an overview of its scope and application. Given limitations of time, deadlines, word counts, cover price, and so on, we have wanted to balance our wish to be comprehensive with the need to be accurate and readable. Ultimately only you can assess our success.

As practitioners, trainers and writers who identify with the person-centred approach, we have a strong motivation to ensure its 'fair representation', especially as it is often misconceived and misrepresented. For examples of this, and responses, see Barrett-Lennard (1983), Tudor and Merry (2002) and Wilkins (2003). Some articles are positively hostile and, more insidiously, many are inaccurate, even in the main journal of the approach. We are aware that no one has the monopoly on truth or representation, and that, within the person-centred approach, different traditions or tribes emphasise different concepts, theories and practice (see Chapter 2). Nevertheless, it seems important to us to have a book which acts as both an introduction and an overview to the approach, and which is committed to philosophical consistency, historical accuracy, and theoretical rigour.

This said, we do not want to reify or concretise person-centred theory, precisely because this would be antithetical to its philosophy. In the principal presentation of his theory Rogers (1959) hopes that we will see his work as 'a fallible, changing attempt to construct a network of gossamer threads which will contain the solid facts' (p. 191). He goes on to say that if we can do this, then theory will 'serve, as it should, as a stimulus to further creative thinking' (*ibid.*, p. 191). Rogers' emphasis on creativity and fluidity parallels his belief in the constant movement of organisms and in the quest of human organisms for more complex stimuli and understanding. It is for each of us to find our own way to be with the ideas and principles and not simply to mimic his way of being. Echoing Jung, Rogers is reported to have said that he was glad that he didn't have to be Rogerian! The broader point is that none of us has to be 'Rogerian'. Our task is to become fully ourselves. In an interview with Rogers, Frick (1971) elicits this point:

> **Frick:** You would like to wipe away the slate of theory and encourage a fresh look?
> **Rogers:** That's right and then the student would have to start to figure out, 'Well, what do I think makes sense out of this?' even though his theories were crude and incomplete and so on. He would get a great deal from the experience. (p. 100)

Thus, each generation needs its own introduction, reconstructing the gossamer threads of theory, reviewing and renewing the approach, especially in a changing world. Rogers wrote his key works between 1951 and 1980, between a quarter and a half a century ago. Inevitably much of it has dated and needs, literally, updating, particularly in the context of changing ideas and understandings of relationships, and in the light of new discoveries and developments in a variety of disciplines. It is a tribute to Rogers that, after more than 60 years of the person-centred approach, people still find his work refreshing and relevant. In many ways he provided the threads, the theory and, perhaps most importantly, the philosophy of an *approach* to life.

The readership

We anticipate that this book will be of interest to people across a broad spectrum:

- If you are unfamiliar with the approach, this book may act as an introduction, a guide and a reference for ideas: in all, an overview of the applicability of the person-centred approach to a number of areas and arenas.
- If you are already familiar with the approach, or a version of it, we hope this book will interest, stimulate and challenge you. We hope you will read freely, subjectively and with a willingness to see something new in

the ideas. We have written it so as to offer you opportunities:

To increase, develop and reassess your *knowledge* and *comprehension* of the approach;
To widen the fields of its *application*, especially beyond therapy;
To encourage both the *analysis* and *synthesis* of ideas; and, ultimately,
To stimulate your ability to reflect on the philosophy and theory of your practice, whether as a therapist, supervisor, student, teacher, facilitator, consultant or activist, and to *evaluate* both what you know and do as well as the approach itself.

In this we are explicitly drawing on and aiming to meet Bloom *et al.*'s (1956) taxonomy of educational objectives. Some educationalists may argue that such a taxonomy (as above) has all but withered away in the light of modern concerns with learning outcomes, quality assurance and customer satisfaction. However, we think that it is precisely the ability to analyse, synthesise and evaluate ideas, based on comprehension and knowledge of a given field and its applications, that marks a reflective, critical and independent thinker and practitioner.

If you are seeking to train or develop, as a psychotherapist or counsellor, as a teacher or educator, groupworker or organisational consultant, as a practitioner in health and related professions, or if you are involved in conflict resolution, mediation or the peace movement, this book may help orient you towards an appropriate and satisfying training course or stimulate your participation in your current training.

The process and structure of the book

Collectively and individually the person-centred approach is our passion and inspiration. As a group of writers we have a common denominator in our lives: Temenos, an independent psychotherapy and counselling training organisation located in Sheffield, England. Temenos means 'a piece of land, marked off from common uses'; for more about the history and philosophy of Temenos the organisation see Embleton Tudor and Tudor (1999), Tudor and Embleton Tudor (1999) and Horsfield (1999) and the website www.temenos.ac.uk. As a training organisation and as a business we strive to embody the person-centred approach in all our activities and endeavours. Our training introduces students to the *approach* (in a first year) before they specialise in clinical, organisational or educational applications, all of which routes lead to graduate and postgraduate diploma qualifications.

As a group of writers we comprise a graduate, directors/partners, tutors and facilitators of Temenos. We came together as equals in this writing venture, reflecting a key principle we hold dear: to share power and to flatten hierarchies. Some of us are more experienced as writers than others. This has served as an advantage and a treasured learning experience for all of us. The book grew from its inception as a concept through to its conception, since when it has (almost) taken on a life of its own: as an organism tending to actualise, flowing and developing as new chapters have emerged from discussion and writing. As the idea gestated it became clear that we could visualise a final text (albeit that this changed!) about which we would feel passionate: a text which would place the approach in its historical context, and which would provide a thorough and rigorous introduction or re-presentation to the subject. The book, eventually, was born!

During the months that we have been writing it, our relationship with the emerging book had been filled with excitement and fear, joy and despair, anguish and satisfaction. The group of co-authors have changed during the process. The original group formed and then re-formed as one dropped out, another came and went and, in the final stages, one more withdrew, all for valid and pressing reasons. To those who were involved and left, thank you for your contribution to the life and energy of this book, for your interest and support, and for ideas, which have had an influence on the final version. Arranging meetings with seven, six and even five people has proved a logistical nightmare and our group time has been limited. The process has brought with it experiences of intimacy, as we revealed our writing to one another, and a sense of togetherness which feels greater than the amount of actual time we spent all together. This is a genuinely co-authored book. Although clearly one or two of us have, at any one time, initiated a phrase, a paragraph, a section or a chapter, we have all contributed to the whole and 'stand by', if not entirely agree with, every word. Inevitably the style of writing changes, and whilst we have edited it thoroughly, we have not wanted to smooth out differences of style. Occasionally, one of us individually has written a particular passage or section, and where it has made sense to do so we have noted this. We vary the use of personal pronouns.

The structure of the book also developed and emerged over the course of its writing, changing as the result of feedback and further consideration. In many ways it is difficult to represent in a linear book an approach which values fluidity, and in which the individual cannot be understood outside of the context of their environment. Living with the inevitable limitations of book form, we begin in Part 1 by discussing first principles. In Chapter 2 we give an overview of the philosophical values which underpin the approach, and a brief history of the approach, as well as its context, theoretical scope, and key concepts. We follow this with two chapters on therapy, as that's where the origins of the person-centred approach lie. In the first we present a brief history of the person-centred approach to therapy; its theory of therapy, including the conditions, processes and outcomes of therapy; the implications of other theoretical perspectives for the approach; and some comments about the context of therapy. In Chapter 4 we discuss the person of the therapist, including their education, training, personal development, personal therapy, and supervision. We look also at some key issues in training and practice, and at the context and organisation of therapy. Although we all live and work in the United Kingdom, we think that the discussions in this chapter have a wider relevance and application.

In Part II we focus on the person at the centre of the approach. In Chapter 5 we explore the emerging person. Person-centred therapists and theorists have largely ignored the areas of infant and child development and we are pleased to begin to fill this gap in the literature. We continue this exploration of continuing human needs in Chapter 6 and give an overview of person-centred personality theory. The person or organism cannot be understood (let alone analysed) outside of her environment. In Chapter 7 we explore the person in context and develop the theme, which runs throughout the book, of the necessity for us as human beings both to differentiate *and* to integrate experiences.

Having established the inevitable and necessary interplay between individual organism and environment, we discuss in Part III a number of implications and areas of the approach. In Chapter 8 we present the contribution Rogers and others have made to our understanding of personal relationships and, in Chapter 9, focus on the relationship between parent and child. In Chapter 10 we consider person-centred thinking about education, schools, schooling and life-long learning. Rogers' work has had a profound impact on education, especially in the understanding and theory of education and learning based on relationship, a perspective which appears somewhat under attack in an age of 'standards' and tests. We are particularly critical of what we see as 'schooling', as distinct from education, in many spheres, and of unnecessary regulation and testing in education and training. As educators ourselves we are supportive of students and teachers and, at the end of this chapter, we provide some supportive suggestions for teachers. In the last chapter in this part (Chapter 11) we link Rogers' ideas about the 'emerging person' to interest in and concern about citizenship, and follow this with two discussions about justice and restorative justice, and about peace in the context of Rogers' work on conflict resolution, discussions which are all too topical today.

In Part IV we move beyond the individual person and individual therapy to apply the approach to systems. We begin in Chapter 12 with the couple or dyad and move through group (Chapter 13), community (Chapter 14) and organisation (Chapter 15) to the wider social and natural environment itself (Chapter 16). In each chapter in this part of the book we give a brief overview of the person-centred approach to the particular system; consider the implications for the system of the approach, and vice versa; and include a 'case study' of some work with the system from a person-centred perspective. Some discussions in this part of the book are less well developed than others, notably (for us) on the environment. In part, this is because the application of person-centred principles to this subject is relatively unformed and new. Rather than not tackle it at all, we prefer to acknowledge this and, we hope, to provide some stimulus for further, creative thinking. We conclude each chapter in the book with a summary of points made in the chapter.

We have taken a number of chapter headings from the title of Rogers' own works. Whilst this honours our inspiration and our roots, we move within each chapter beyond the writings of Rogers and his contemporaries in the hope of making this a book relevant to our contemporary world. Our interest in the history of ideas is reflected in the fact that, when we refer in the text to key figures in the development of ideas, we have followed the first reference to them with their dates, such as Carl Rogers (1902–1987). We hope this will be of interest to you and help you locate the chronology of people, their ideas and influences in this significant and exciting development of psychology in social context.

First Principles

In the first part of this book we consider the fundamental principles of the person-centred approach. We begin with a chapter on key principles and follow this with a review of the philosophical roots of the approach. Rogers based the broadening and all subsequent applications of the person-centred approach, beginning with the approach to therapy, on these key principles. The following two chapters in this part reflect this and address the person in therapy and the person of the therapist.

First Principles

The person-centred approach is, literally, an approach to the person. Wood (1996) puts it well:

> ... it is neither a psychotherapy nor a psychology. It is not a school ... itself, it is not a movement ... it is not a philosophy. Nor is it any number of other things frequently imagined. It is merely, as its name implies, an approach, nothing more, nothing less. It is a psychological posture, if you like, from which thought or action may arise and experience be organized. It is a 'way of being'. (pp. 168–9)

Rogers first wrote about the 'person-centred approach' to therapy in 1977 (Rogers, 1978b). It is the current term used in preference to 'client-centred therapy' and, before that, 'non-directive therapy' and 'relationship therapy'. These terms represent the historical development of the approach, for further accounts of which see Zimring and Raskin (1992), Wood (1996), Barrett-Lennard (1998) and Tudor and Merry (2002). The term 'person-centred approach' is an inclusive one in that it describes any formal, informal or professional work which accords with the principles of the approach.

Sanders (2000) identifies three 'primary principles' of the approach:

- The primacy of the actualising tendency.
- The necessity and sufficiency of six therapeutic conditions.
- The primacy of the non directive attitude, at least in terms of the content of the helping situation.

We will explore these ideas in more detail later in this chapter. Sanders (2000) distinguishes these three principles from what he views as secondary principles such as autonomy, equality and holism. Two further ideas are central to the person-centred approach. One is fluidity. In a paper on the process of psychotherapy Rogers (1953/1967a) acknowledges that he values fluidity as a desirable state of being. This is characterised by: living and accepting our feelings, experiencing things with immediacy, and having a free-flowing internal communication with ourselves and similar external communication with others. The second is creativity. Rogers (1954/1967c) discusses the importance of creativity, and sees that it is based on three 'inner conditions' of openness to experience, an internal locus, or place, of evaluation, and an ability to toy or play with elements and concepts. He argues that there is a social need for creativity, that it depends on a nurturing environment (Rogers, 1975/1980) and that it is one of the outcomes of therapy (Rogers, 1959). Others within the approach have taken up these ideas, and especially his daughter in her work on creative and expressive therapy (N. Rogers, 1993).

The philosophical values of the person-centred approach: roots and affinities

Before we go any further, we want to look at the philosophical roots of the person-centred approach, and then at its affinities with some contemporaneous philosophies. We do this for a number of reasons. Rogers was interested in exploring philosophical values, and in articulating the philosophical bases of person-centred practice. 'In these days', he said 'most psychologists regard it as an insult if they are accused of thinking philosophical thoughts. I do not share this reaction. I cannot help but puzzle over the meaning of what I observe' (1960/1967, p. 163). He also took the view that it wasn't possible to divorce values from practice, in the sense that whatever we do necessarily shows something of what we believe.

The person-centred approach did not spring, Athene-like, perfectly formed and fully armed from the head of a God. Looking back over his life in a paper first presented at a conference in 1973, Rogers says that he learned primarily from clients and group participants, then from younger colleagues, and then, 'much farther down the scale', from his reading of other people's works. He goes on to say that although he did not gain his ideas from what others wrote, he occasionally found that other writers confirmed him in what he had been thinking tentatively, and 'lured' him to go further (Rogers, 1974/1980). In this chapter we want to look briefly at some of those other writers, schools and philosophies whose ideas informed, confirmed or encouraged Rogers' own thinking. We start by looking at Christianity, which is one of the world-views into which Rogers was born, and the ground in which the approach has its roots. We then look briefly at existentialism and phenomenology, two of the major schools of philosophy with which Rogers identified. We finish by looking at the relationship between the values that underpin the approach, and the personal values of individual practitioners.

Christianity

We think it's important to begin with Christianity simply because it was, from an early age and for many years, important to Rogers. He was born into a Christian family and grew up steeped in Christian thinking, practice and ethics. His father came from Congregational stock, and his mother from Baptist. The family prayed together daily and went to church on Sundays. Kirschenbaum (1979) tells us that Rogers learned to read early, and that one of the first things he read and re-read was a book of stories from the Bible. He was a member of a Christian delegation to China in 1922, and began training for the Christian ministry at Union Theological Seminary, New York, in 1924.

By 1926 Rogers had left Union Seminary, abandoned his plans to train for the ministry, and moved across the road to Teachers College, part of Columbia University, where he studied psychology and education. Kirschenbaum (1979) and Cohen (1997) agree that one of the events that precipitated Rogers' move away from Union and away from the Church was a series of unstructured and unfacilitated classes in which Rogers and his fellow students had the space to think freely about the religious and philosophical questions that vexed them. Having thought freely, Rogers chose a different career. From early in his life, then, it's clear that Rogers valued freedom of thought, that he thought deeply about moral and philosophical values, and that he acted consistently with what he discovered he believed, even if such action caused conflict with those around him.

Rogers' life's work stands in curious relationship to this early faith. Christianity, for instance, posits an external God who is the source of authority, forgiveness and hope. Men and women are born tainted with the original sin of Adam and Eve, who disobeyed God and were banished from the Garden of Eden. Most versions of Christianity seek to regulate behaviour through a more or less codified series of commandments and strictures. Rogers, on the other hand, came to see the individual as her own best authority. He saw men and women as born healthy and creative, and he believed that under appropriate conditions their behaviour would be naturally constructive and social, and therefore not in need of regulation, direction or punishment from the outside.

One expression of Rogers' earlier faith surfaced again towards the end of his life, when he became interested in mystical spirituality and 'all types of paranormal phenomena' (Rogers, 1980b, p. 92). 'Interested' may be too strong a word, and 'spirituality' might not be accurate either. However, having been committed to a spiritual discipline until his early twenties, and then resolutely secular for most of his adult life, Rogers began late in life to allow again the possibility of realms of experience beyond the immediately knowable. In the months immediately before and after the death of his wife, Helen, in March 1979 he had experiences which left him 'more open to the possibility of the continuation of the individual human spirit' (*ibid.*, p. 91). Thorne in particular (1991, 1998) has explored the relationships between person-centred practice and the mystical or transpersonal spirituality of the Anglican tradition in Christianity.

Another strand of the Christianity Rogers grew up in figures significantly and consistently in his thinking, even after he'd moved away from his faith in Christ. His parents lived by and imbued in their children a committed Protestant work ethic. Kirschenbaum (1979, p. 4) reports that Rogers had a sign on his dresser 'in large print, reading, DO IT NOW!'. He was throughout his life an active and pragmatic idealist, concerned not just to write or teach or theorise, but also to make things happen in the world. He was active in the politics of academic psychology, and concerned about the plight of soldiers returning from service in the Second World War. Later in his life he visited Russia, South Africa and Northern Ireland and worked with local groups to seek peaceful resolution of bitter and long-standing conflicts. In these and other ways he was always more than an academic, and more than a theorist.

Rogers saw that there were, broadly, two possible ways of thinking about and responding to life, experience and relationships: objective and mechanistic, on the one hand, or subjective and humanistic, on the other. The first of these, the objective, is characterised by a belief in fact, reality and causality; the second, the subjective, by a belief in personal knowing, personal meaning and organic, rather than strictly causal, relationships. Rogers prized personal, inner meaning rather than fact. He was interested in each individual's unique ways of perceiving and making sense of her world. He saw psychological processes as organic rather than mechanical, was skeptical about the notion that there was one single truth or reality, and questioned the prevailing wisdom that psychological distresses had easily identifiable causes and cures. All of these characteristics show Rogers as a subjective, humanistic thinker.[1]

Within the broad sweep of subjective, humanistic thinking, Rogers aligned himself explicitly with two named philosophical strands: existentialism and phenomenology. He contributed to edited volumes on existentialism (May, 1961) and phenomenology (Wann, 1964). We want to introduce each of these strands briefly here.

Existentialism

Existentialism has a difficult reputation. Warnock (1967) abandons the attempt to define it, saying that short definitions either 'do not make sense' or 'apply to only part of the field' (p. 1). Shand (1994) agrees: 'It is difficult to give any general characterization of existentialism' (p. 246). For our purposes, all we need do is unpack the existentialist belief that *existence precedes essence*. This phrase suggests that we must account for and accept the *fact* of our existence, the fact *that* we exist, before we can define, describe or discuss *who* or *what* we are or may become. Having accepted the fact of our existence, together with its limitations, we are then free to decide who we are by choosing how we behave, and by taking responsibility for our actions. Existentialism prizes these values: freedom, choice and responsibility, and sums them up as authenticity, which is also a word Rogers uses occasionally as a synonym for congruence.

'*I am not*', said Rogers (1955/1967) '*a student of existential philosophy*' (p. 199). Be that as it may, Kirschenbaum (1979, p. 29) suggests that even by the early 1920s Rogers was developing 'an "existential" slant in religion and morality' characterised by a belief 'that good works were more important than ritual or doctrine' and by a need and willingness 'to take responsibility for one's actions'. Rogers was later influenced by his reading of Søren Kierkegaard (1813–55), the first modern existentialist. He took one of Kierkegaard's phrases – to be that self which one truly is – as the title of a lecture which became Chapter 8 of *On Becoming A Person*. In 1957, at about the same time as he was reading Kierkegaard, Rogers had a public

[1] We're calling Rogers a humanistic thinker to indicate that he was concerned primarily with the human rather than with the mechanical, on the one hand, or the divine, on the other. We recognise that humanism is a philosophy in its own right, and we're not intending to locate Rogers there.

dialogue with the existential theologian Martin Buber (1878–1965), and began to use Buber's phrase 'I-Thou' to characterise the kind of relationship he aspired to in his work as a therapist (see Kirschenbaum and Henderson, 1990a; Anderson and Cissna, 1997). He followed this in 1965 with a similar dialogue with another existential theologian, Paul Tillich (1886–1965) (see Kirschenbaum and Henderson, 1990a).

As well as the phrases he appropriated from Kierkegaard and Buber, existential ideas, or ideas that are consonant with existentialism, run through Rogers' work. One of the characteristics Rogers (1958/1967) sees in a mature and fully functioning person is 'a sense of self-responsibility' for his problems (p. 157). Elsewhere (Rogers, 1961), he says that this person becomes autonomous, 'able to be what he is and to choose his course' (p. 88). These are descriptions that an existentialist would recognise, and ends that an existentialist would endorse.

Phenomenology

Phenomenology stems from the work of Edmund Husserl (1859–1938), Martin Heidegger (1889–1976) and Maurice Merleau-Ponty (1907–61). It studies the processes by which we perceive and make sense of the world around us. It suggests that 'reality' is not fixed, out there and objective, but that it depends to a large extent on our perception of it, which is in turn informed by whatever biases, prejudices and perceptual filters we bring to it. All of this endorses a commitment to the primacy of subjective experience, and finds warm welcome and obvious parallels in Rogers' work. The first three of the nineteen propositions, for instance (Rogers, 1951), describe an absolutely phenomenological approach to life, even if they don't mention phenomenology by name once. 'I do not react to some absolute reality', he says (p. 484), 'but to my perception of this reality. It is this perception which for me is reality.' We may also describe empathic understanding as simply, or not so simply, a process of attending phenomenologically to the phenomenological world of another.

Out of phenomenological thinking comes the phenomenological method, which consists of three steps, or rules, intended to help us approach each new experience as openly as possible. This openness to all that an experience may contain allows the meaning or significance of each new experience to emerge from within rather than to come clouded or already shaped by whatever sense we've made of prior experiences.

The first step is to *bracket* everything we think we know. We may have more or less fluently articulated beliefs about life or people in general: life's hard and then you die; you can't teach an old dog new tricks; depressed people don't think well; all men are bastards. We may have formed beliefs about ourselves, or about particular other people in our lives: nothing good ever happens to me; he doesn't like me; I've nothing to offer her; he never works a full day. This first step challenges us to put these beliefs to one side, and to recognise that they're out of date. Even if we have grounds for holding them dear, and even if they turn out to be accurate again this time, they still impede our experiencing of this moment now, and limit what we might learn.

The second step asks that we *describe* our experience rather than judge, evaluate, assess, analyse or interpret it. The line between description and the rest is a fine one. If we see someone crying, for instance, our description of that would be simply to say that we saw his tears. If we were to say that he were sad or upset, we'd be moving away from simple phenomenological description of what we were seeing, to a more or less accurate inference of his emotional process. The discipline of description challenges us to stay close to what we experience through our senses, and to resist any further elaborations, abstractions or inferences. In this way, we can find for ourselves, and allow others to find for themselves, the precisely accurate word to describe what we or they are experiencing.

The third step is to *equalise* what we notice, or to keep the details of what we notice of equal value in their potential significance. Another way of saying this is that it asks us to resist putting any quick or easy hierarchy on what we notice. This step calls us to approach any experience willing for any one aspect or element of it to be as significant to us as any one other. The tone of someone's voice may be as important as the content of what she says. The look in someone's eye may be as significant as his clenched fist or tapping foot. We may have as much to learn from a nagging shoulder pain as from anything else we're thinking, feeling or hearing.

Taken together, these three steps have obvious relevance for person-centred practice. They encourage an open, non-judgemental, or pre-judgemental, stance towards what we experience. They invite an attitude of open-minded enquiry that is ideally conducive to empathic understanding. They ask us to let meanings emerge, and in that they remind us to stay humble about the limits and relevance of our own expertise.

One final point is that Rogers describes the fully functioning person, the person who emerges from a long-enough experience of effective therapy, as living phenomenologically. He suggests that one of the directions taken by such clients (1960/1967) is 'toward living in an open, friendly, close relationship to his own experience' (p. 175). Phenomenological principles, therefore, characterise both person-centred practice and the person who emerges from an experience of person-centred therapy, facilitation or learning.

We're not saying in any of this that Rogers was an existentialist or a phenomenologist. We're saying simply that he recognised existential and phenomenological trends in his own work, that he felt an affinity with those ways of thinking, and that his encounters with some of the thinkers who did call themselves existentialists or phenomenologists challenged him, confirmed him and encouraged him to develop his ideas further.

Personal philosophy

We've argued so far in this chapter that the person-centred approach is informed by philosophical values, and that those values are akin to the values found in phenomenological and existential thinkers. While the person-centred approach is neither exclusively nor completely phenomenological or existential, it shares some of the assumptions and stances of both. We now want to look at some of the implications of this for practitioners aspiring to work in a person-centred way.

Rogers argues that effective practitioners show a high level of congruence or consistency between what they experience, what they symbolise in awareness and what they communicate. We want to extend this idea, and to suggest that the personal values and beliefs of individual practitioners need, if they're to practice effectively, to be congruent with the philosophical values of the approach in which they practice. Another way of saying this, and perhaps a more provocative way, is that the higher the level of congruence between an individual practitioner's personal values and the values that underpin the approach to which she subscribes, the more effective a practitioner she will be. We suggest that this is true whatever the approach. Congruence is desirable internally and externally.

Given this, we think that practitioners in any field of work who want to practice in a person-centred way need to explore whether and how their own personal views and beliefs fit with phenomenological and existential principles. We're not saying that person-centred practitioners should necessarily share the creed that Mearns and Thorne offer (1988). The approach, after all, is not about signing up to any one-size-fits-all manifesto. We think it's important, though, to acknowledge that a person will struggle to work with integrity in a person-centred way to the degree that there is dissonance between the values he holds and the values that underpin the approach. We look at some of the implications of this for the training of therapists in Chapter 4.

A brief history of the approach

In their review of the history of the person-centred approach, Zimring and Raskin (1992) divide the first 50 years into four major periods:

- The first period begins in December, 1940 with Rogers' talk at the University of Minnesota on 'Some Newer Concepts of Psychotherapy', which was subsequently published in Rogers (1942). This first period is characterised by the development of two aspects of the therapist's role: that of responding to feelings, as distinct from content; and the acceptance, recognition and clarification of positive, negative and ambivalent feelings.
- The second decade begins in the 1950s with the publication of *Client-Centered Therapy* (Rogers, 1951). In this decade Rogers outlined the framework and structure of the client-centred approach (Rogers, 1959), his hypothesis for therapy and therapeutic change and, specifically, the necessary and sufficient conditions of personality change (Rogers, 1957, 1959).
- The third period of the 1960s is marked by the publication of *On Becoming a Person* (Rogers, 1961/1967b), the title of which conveys the direction of Rogers' interest and thinking with its emphasis on experience and experiencing, being and becoming. Rogers' interest in the concept of congruence may also be traced back to this period.
- The fourth decade is characterised by Rogers' increasing interest in the applications of the principles of client-centred therapy to other areas of life such as education (Rogers, 1969, 1983), groups (1970/1973), and conflict resolution. The phrase 'person-centred approach' becomes more widely used during this time. We see this fourth phase as encompassing the two decades of the 1970s and 80s up to Rogers' death in 1987.

To this history we add a fifth phase, beginning with Rogers' death, and characterised by:

- A decline in the influence of the approach in the USA and its growth in Europe, South America and Japan.
- The establishment in Britain and elsewhere of a number of person-centred training courses.
- The emergence of a new generation of practitioners and writers influenced by Rogers, though not necessarily having had direct contact with him, and
- A reconsideration and re-presentation of person-centred theory and practice and its relationship with other therapeutic traditions.

Context

The person-centred approach to therapy is generally viewed as part of the 'third force' or humanistic therapy tradition. The first two 'forces' are:

- The psychodynamic tradition, represented by the work of Sigmund Freud (1856–1939), Carl Jung (1887–1961) and Melanie Klein (1882–1960), and their eponymous schools of psychoanalysis.
- The behavioural tradition, based originally on the work of behaviourists I. P. Pavlov (1849–1936), John Watson (1878–1958) and B. F. Skinner (1904–90), and now represented by a number of schools of and approaches to therapy such as Behaviour Therapy, Personal Construct Therapy, Cognitive Therapy, Cognitive Analytic Therapy, Cognitive Behavioural Therapy and Rational Emotive Behaviour Therapy.

'Third force psychology' was a term coined by Abraham Maslow (1908–70) to describe a psychology which *builds* on these two earlier traditions, and emphasises especially the creative, constructive, aesthetic and aspirational qualities of human nature and human beings. As such it influenced the personal growth movement of the 1960s and informed the development of a number of therapies such as neo-Reichian body therapies, Gestalt Therapy, Psychodrama, Transactional Analysis and Psychosynthesis. Despite differences in theory and practice between these 'schools', these therapies, and their therapists, share a number of core beliefs and values:

- Regarding human nature: that the individual is unique, is in relationship with others and the environment, embodies basic 'OK-ness' and is motivated towards actualisation; that the person is more than the sum of her parts and is, at core, an integrated and self-regulating whole; and that dis-ease and dysfunction arise as a result of being out of balance.
- Regarding the aims of growth and therapy: that the aims of growth, supported by therapy, are: awareness of self, others and the environment; the actualisation of our inherent and developing capacities to a state of wholeness, completeness and integration; a move towards authentic behaviour; and a fuller acceptance of self and others.
- Regarding the nature of the therapeutic relationship: that the therapeutic relationship is the principal vehicle of change, a perspective informed by Rogers' early work and a major contribution of the person-centred approach to humanistic thinking; and that, therefore, and in order to be effective, the therapist needs to embody awareness and genuineness and

to be open, acceptant, respectful, valuing and empathic of the client, qualities which are also the basis for the therapist's ability to be challenging and even confrontational.

In the last 20 years there has been an increasing interest in the spiritual aspect of psychotherapy and counselling. This has led some to refer to this as a 'fourth force' of psychology. Menahem, for instance, (1996) comments on one of Rogers' cases from this perspective. Contemporaneously the concept of integrative therapy has emerged as a claimant for the title of fourth force, a claim which is critiqued in Tudor and Worrall (2004, in preparation). In a number of ways the person-centred approach to *therapy* developed out of disagreements with elements of psychodynamic and behavioural psychology, specifically as regards the actualising tendency, the attitude of non-directivity, and diagnosis. However, although the person-centred approach to therapy is almost universally viewed as located within, and even as synonymous with, the humanistic tradition, it is in some respects as different from some other humanistic therapies as it is from the other forces: 'the governing feature of person-centred therapy (PCT) is not its "humanistic" orientation but its forsaking of mystique and other "powerful" behaviours of therapists. In this regard many humanistic therapies are as different from PCT as psychoanalysis' (Mearns and Thorne, 2000, p. 27). Whilst we find the taxonomy of psychological 'forces' of historical interest, we think that comparing theories is a more complex process than simply locating an approach to therapy within a bigger 'force' or tradition. In our view, the more rigorous, coherent and, ultimately, satisfying way to compare theory and practice is to explore and understand the philosophical principles which underpin an approach or 'school' of therapy, and the ensuing assumptions which inform its methodology. In this book we are concerned to locate the person-centred approach and then to compare it, on the basis of these underlying assumptions, with other approaches in the fields of child development, parenting, education, therapy, group work, industrial relations, community building and conflict resolution.

Theoretical scope

The person-centred approach offers a relatively comprehensive theoretical account of life, experience and relationships. Rogers wrote extensively over five decades, and he places at the centre of his major theoretical statement (1959) a theory of therapy, which comprises views about the nature of the human organism, which we discuss later in this chapter; and about the conditions, process and outcomes of therapy, which we explore further in the next chapter. He also presents a theory of personality; a theory of the 'fully functioning person'; and a theory of interpersonal relationships. Finally, he discusses the theoretical implications for a number of human activities including family life; education and learning; groups, group leadership and group conflict. There is now also an extensive literature which encompasses over 60 years of person-centred practice, research, writing and theoretical development.

As with many other approaches to psychology, psychotherapy and counselling, the person-centred approach encompasses a number of traditions, especially the experiential, with which it is often linked. Lietaer (1990) suggests that the termination of the Wisconsin project, in which Rogers and colleagues (Rogers *et al.*, 1967) researched the use and efficacy of client-centred psychotherapy with people diagnosed with schizophrenia, was a crucial moment in the history of the approach, subsequent to which we may trace four discernible 'factions' or schools within or associated with the approach:

- A group around Rogers, who was then based in the Center for the Studies of the Person, La Jolla, California. This group continued to develop the philosophy and practice of the approach in ways which were consistent with Rogers' original formulations of it.
- A group around Eugene Gendlin (b. 1926) who developed focusing and experiential therapy in the European tradition of existential and phenomenological philosophy. This is represented in the more recent work of Rennie (1998) and Worsley (2002). A further development of this tradition is 'pre-therapy', for details of which see Prouty (1976, 1990, 1994) and Van Werde (1994, 1998, 2002).
- A group around Charles Truax and Robert Carkhuff who proposed and developed an eclectic model of the helping relationship (Truax and Carkhuff, 1967) and a 'skills based approach' to counselling, perhaps developed most notably by Egan (1997).
- A group around David Wexler (b. 1946) and Laura Rice (b. 1920) who chose cognitive learning psychology as a theoretical framework for their development of the approach (Wexler and Rice, 1974).

Such developments are controversial, welcomed by some and disputed and despaired of by others. For Raskin (1987) 'each of the neo-Rogerian methods takes something away from the thorough-going belief in the self-directive capacities that is so central to client-centered philosophy' (p. 460).

Others welcome the growth of the 'family' of person-centred and existential psychotherapies and the inevitable tensions inherent in such a large family. This family, and its tensions, now has a voice in *Person-Centered and Experiential Psychotherapies*, a new journal which, according to its editors, 'seeks to provide a forum for exploring these tensions and commonalities and for a dialogue among the positions, presenting the developments within the paradigm to the wider world of therapy practice, accreditation, and academia' (Elliot, Mearns and Schmid, 2002, p. 1).

Key concepts

We said earlier that we would introduce some of the key concepts of the approach, and that's what we're about to do now.

The organism

Writing in the early 1950s, Rogers (1953/1967) says that 'the inner core of man's personality is the organism itself, which is essentially both self-preserving and social' (p. 92). This single sentence sums up beautifully one of the ideas at the heart of the person-centred approach: the idea of the organism. Rogers takes the idea of the organism so much for granted that when he defines (1959) the key theoretical concepts or constructs of the person-centred approach, he doesn't even bother to define the organism, although it turns up in the first sentence of the first definition. Our suspicion is that he saw no need to define it. Generally, he was a careful writer, and he was defining the key theoretical concepts or 'constructs' (p. 194) of the approach. If he didn't define the organism, we suspect it was because he saw it as a given, as something he didn't need to define, rather than as something intangible that he and his colleagues had conceived or construed.

The organism often stands as a synonym for the individual human being, and when Rogers uses the term, he intends to signify especially the visceral, sensory, bodily, instinctual, unselfconscious aspects of the human being, rather than the more reflective, considered and self-conscious aspects. For these latter aspects, Rogers uses the word 'self'. The self, as Rogers understands and describes it, takes shape when the organism can say: this is me, this is who I am, this is what I'm like, a process which is clearly observable over the first two years of an infant's life. It is the product of an organism's capacity to reflect on its own experience of itself, and to look at itself as if from outside. For reasons that aren't exactly clear to us, the person-centred approach, and humanistic thinking generally, seems more interested in the idea of the self than it is in the idea of the organism. Person-centred thinkers and practitioners have elaborated ideas about the self more fully than they have ideas about the organism, and the self has also been a more fashionable idea both within and outside the person-centred approach. More recently, and within the person-centred approach, Mearns (1997) has taken to writing about 'the Self'. Rogers (1953/1967a), however argued that 'one of the fundamental directions taken by the process of therapy is the free experiencing of the actual sensory and visceral reactions of *the organism* without too much of an attempt to relate these experiences to the self' (p. 80, our emphasis). Seen like this, the process of successful therapy means a return to the visceral and unselfconscious life of the organism, and a move away from the self. For this reason we find the popular term 'organismic self' particularly clumsy, unhelpful and confusing. It conflates into one term two ideas that Rogers went to some pains to describe separately.

If we return to the quotation at the beginning of this subsection, we see that Rogers described the organism as 'self-preserving and social'. It's worth looking briefly at each of these terms. The organism is 'self-preserving' in the simple sense that it does whatever it can to stay alive. The choices it makes will be in the direction of continuing life. The organism is 'social' in the sense that it chooses to live with and among other organisms. The choices it makes will take others into account.

The actualising tendency

Rogers (1951) asserts that the organism has one basic tendency and striving: 'to actualise, maintain, and enhance the experiencing organism' (p. 487). This introduces a second key concept in person-centred thinking: the actualising tendency. We cannot think about the organism without reference to this actualising tendency. One is not viable without the other and any theoretical separation of the two runs the risk of losing a coherent understanding of the person-centred approach. The significance of this idea to person-centred thinking becomes clearer if we read a passage first published in 1954, where Rogers (1954/1967a) says that the organism's tendency to actualise is both 'the mainspring of life' and, 'in the last analysis, the tendency upon which all psychotherapy depends' (p. 35). This could hardly be clearer. Both the continuing life of the organism, and the endeavour of psychotherapy, depend on the organism's innate tendency to actualise. This will have profound implications for the way Rogers sees the role of any therapist or facilitator, and we'll explore those later.

The actualising tendency is a difficult notion to talk about. It has a precursor in Aristotle (384–322 BCE), who suggests that every natural thing 'contains within itself a source of change and of stability' (1996, p. 33). He contrasts 'every natural thing' with 'a bed or a cloak', neither of which has any 'intrinsic impulse for change' (*ibid.*, p. 33). This phrase, an 'intrinsic impulse for change', both describes and prefigures what we're talking about here. Many other philosophers and therapists have talked about this force of Nature. Eric Berne (1910–70) the founder of transactional analysis, cites Zeno the Semite as having thought much about this force as *physis* in connection with the growth and development of living things (1947/1971). Edwards (1967) sees *physis* reflected in the works of both the Stoics and the Epicureans. Clarkson (1992) quotes Heraclitus and Aristotle on the subject. Berne (1947/1971) describes *physis* as 'the force of Nature, which eternally strives to make things grow and to make growing things more perfect' (p. 98). More recently, and more poetically, the actualising tendency is Dylan Thomas' (1952) 'force that through the green fuse drives the flower' (p. 8).

It's worth remembering that if we talk about the actualising tendency, or, worse still, the Actualising Tendency, or AT, we risk reifying it, conceptualising it as something solid and separate from the organism, as if it exists on its own. We think it is helpful rather to think and talk about 'the organism's tendency to actualise'. This reminds us that we're talking about an aspect of an organism's nature, rather than an entity within it. We would go further, and agree with Keen (1983) that it is even more helpful to use verbs rather than nouns: 'no noun can capture the pulsing commonwealth of cells that make up any living thing. We exist as verbs, always in process' (p. 199). So, putting a verb at the centre of the idea we are describing, we prefer to say that 'the organism tends to actualise'. One advantage of putting it this way is that it locates the tendency in the organism and captures the idea that the organism is continuously in motion. We'll come back to this idea shortly.

When Rogers talks about the organism's tendency to actualise he means to convey the idea that it is in our nature to grow. A plant, he says, doesn't need to be made to grow. Given the right conditions, it will grow. It can't not. The conditions don't make the plant grow. They are simply the conditions most conducive to the plant's innate tendency to become the most of itself that it can become. As with plants, so with people. Given the right conditions, people too will thrive, and become the best and the most that they can become.

Rogers viewed the organism's tendency to actualise as its basic property. Drawing on Rogers, Barrett-Lennard (1998) suggests that it has five further properties.

1 *The organism behaves as an organised whole, responding to its own, moving perceptual field*

This proposition contains three distinct ideas: one, that an organism's reality is what it perceives; two, that this field changes; and three, that an organism responds to this reality as an organised whole. What does all of this mean? One of us likes custard, and one of us does not. For each of us, our perception is our reality. It's no good saying: 'Why dislike it? It's only custard.' As it is, the custard is just custard and does not change. Each of us makes of the same custard a different reality, and behaves accordingly. This is why empathic understanding of another person's reality is of such importance to the person-centred approach. If we take seriously the idea that a person's perception is his reality, it is obviously nonsense for a therapist to argue with a client's perception of his mother or his partner simply because the therapist sees their behaviour differently: 'the best vantage point for understanding behavior is from the internal frame of reference of the individual himself' (Rogers, 1951, p. 494).

The second aspect of this proposition is that a person's perceptual field is moving. Our 'perceptual field' is simply all that we may perceive, the sum of inner and outer events that we may potentially notice. This aspect of Barrett-Lennard's proposition carries the simple idea that the world around us and within us moves and changes continuously. What there is for us to be aware of, therefore, changes continuously too.

The third aspect of this proposition is that the organism's response to changes in its world is both whole and organised. Taking our earlier example, our 'need' to eat custard (or not) is a whole-body response, embodied in every cell of our being. We see this most clearly in children when they respond to something with wholehearted joy or sadness, anger or fear. The behaviour of the organism is organised around the urge to satisfy our needs as we perceive them. This principle organises our behaviour. Rogers (1951) puts it this way: 'behavior is basically the goal-directed attempt of the organism to satisfy its needs as experienced, in the field as perceived' (p. 491). This proposition helps the practitioner to hold another in unconditional positive regard: if we can see and understand someone's behaviour always as their best attempt to reach for what they think they need in the world as they see it, then we do not need to condemn, praise, judge or evaluate it in any way.

2 *The human organism interacts with perceived 'outer' and 'inner' reality in the service of the actualising tendency*

We interact with our perception of the reality outside, and with our perception of inner needs and sensations, with one purpose: to maintain and enhance the organism. As Rogers (1951) puts it: 'rather than many needs and motives, it seems entirely possible that all organic and psychological needs may be described as partial aspects of this one fundamental need' (pp. 487–8). Outer reality refers to the environmental reality or context in which we live, love and work: enough to eat and a warm enough house, loving, stimulating, neglectful or abusive parents, kind or inconsiderate neighbours, supportive or critical friends, a happy or unduly stressful workplace. Our inner reality consists of whatever we may experience viscerally and emotionally; whatever sense we make of what we experience; and whatever view or concept we have of ourselves: good or 'good enough', kind, harassed, stupid or oppressed.

As we discuss in Chapter 9, at best, our outer reality, initially provided by our primary carers, will be geared towards meeting our organismic needs for nourishment, security, acceptance, understanding and love, given and received. If, however, our organismic interaction with our environment is frustrated in some way, we learn to adapt. Imagine a child who is hungry, and who reaches for an apple to eat. Her father slaps her and says: 'You can't have that. You've just eaten. You can't be hungry. Wait for your tea.' This child may learn a number of things from this experience:

- That access to food is mediated.
- That her needs are or have to be evaluated by an external other.
- That expressing a need meets with physical abuse.
- That she has to be satisfied with what she has (just) been given.
- That her own evaluation of her needs, i.e. (still) being hungry, is untrustworthy or 'wrong'.
- That she has to delay satisfaction or gratification of her needs.

The perception she has, and the sense she makes, of this interaction are crucial for development and learning. She may hold out for getting her hunger satisfied and take any consequent abuse; she may deny her awareness, initially of being hungry and, perhaps more generally, of knowing what she needs; or she may distort certain perceptions of herself and begin to believe that she is greedy, ungrateful or 'too much' for her parents. This vignette illustrates a common, everyday occurrence that, potentially, gives rise to all kinds of harmful processes in later life: eating disorders, passivity, compliance and anti-social behaviour. It shows too how people come to have problems knowing what they want and who they are, a concept which forms the basis of Rogers' (1951) theory of personality.

3 *The organism develops an organismic valuing process*
   Through healthy and supported development (see point 2 above and Chapter 9) we learn to value experience, moment by moment, according to whether it satisfies an organismic need. This moment-by-moment evaluation is continuous and life-long. The more often I evaluate experience against my organismic criteria, which are whether or not an experience satisfies my organismic needs and maintains or enhances the organism that I am, the more likely I am to continue to do that. The reverse is also true: the less often I value my experience according to my organismic criteria, the more likely I am to seek the evaluation of others.

   This concept of valuing our own experience lies at the heart of the person-centred approach and is at odds with much of the way of the world. The metaphor and influence of the external 'gold standard' is pervasive, and increasingly so in the fields of education, which we look at in Chapter 10, and in the training of therapists, where most courses sit more or less (un)comfortably with external validation, and most counsellors and psychotherapists seek external accreditation and/or registration. For more on this, see Chapter 4.

4 *Differentiation is an important effect of the actualising tendency*
   Following Rogers, Barrett-Lennard is referring here to the process by which the organism becomes conscious of its own difference from the material world and from others around it. In other words, the organism gradually becomes aware of self, aware of others, and aware of the differences and relationships between self and others.

5 *The organism is always in motion*
   Given that we are interacting with ourselves, others and the world around us in order to maintain and enhance the organism that we are, we may describe the human organism as in continuous motion. This is true physically and psychologically, in awareness and, with organic processes such as the regulation of heart beat and body heat, out of awareness. Breathing, walking, dreaming, loving, hurting, healing, ageing and understanding are all ways in which the organism is in motion.

We have two aims in putting the organism at the beginning of this book. The first is that we want to honour the central significance that Rogers gave it in his thinking. The second is to reclaim the person-centred approach as an organismic approach, rather than an approach based on and built around the concept of self. Tudor and Worrall (2004, in preparation) discuss further some of the implications of this for the theory and practice of psychotherapy.

We want to finish this discussion of organism and self with a note about the difference between actualisation and self-actualisation. Just as Rogers (1959) defines organism and self as separate concepts, so he defines actualisation and self-actualisation as distinctly separate and related processes. Over the years, other humanistic writers have used the term self-actualisation where Rogers would use the term actualisation, and this has led to confusion both within the person-centred approach, where some people miss or misunderstand the distinction Rogers made, and between person-centred practitioners and others, where the same term has different meanings depending on who's using it. Even Seeman (1988), an explicitly person-centred writer and theorist, uses one term to mean the other in the title of a paper published in the *Person-Centered Review*, 'Self-actualization: A reformulation'. To clarify: Rogers (1959) defines the actualising tendency as 'the inherent tendency of *the organism* to develop all its capacities in ways which serve to maintain or enhance the organism' (p. 196, our emphasis). Not surprisingly, self-actualisation is 'the actualization of that portion of the experience of the organism which is symbolized in the self' (p. 196). The corollaries of this are that actualisation is an organismic and trustworthy process, and that self-actualisation is both necessary and trustworthy to the degree that the organism and self are congruent. The more organism and self-concept are incongruent, the greater will be the tension between the pull of organismic actualising and the pull of self-actualisation, and the less bearable the distress.

The necessary and sufficient conditions

It follows from the description of the organism and its innate tendency to actualise that the task of any helper is simply to provide whatever conditions best facilitate that tendency. On the basis of his observations about his work Rogers (1957, 1959) suggests that there are six conditions that are both necessary and sufficient for the organism to actualise. We will discuss them in detail in the following chapter, and for now all we want to do is list them.

1   The first condition is that two people must be in some minimal relationship or 'contact' (Rogers, 1959, p. 213).
2   The second is that one person, the person receiving help, must be aware at some level of some anxiety or concern or discrepancy in his life.
3   The third condition is that the person proposing to help must be relatively whole or integrated for the time that he is in the relationship. Rogers uses the word 'congruence' (1959, p. 213) to describe this.

4   The fourth condition is that the person proposing to help must work towards understanding the other as if he were seeing things through the other's eyes. Rogers describes this particular kind of understanding as 'empathic understanding' (1959, p. 213).
5   The fifth condition is that the person proposing to help accepts the other and the other's perceptions without judgement, condition or evaluation. He offers the other what Rogers calls 'unconditional positive regard' (1959, p. 213).
6   The sixth and final condition is that the person receiving help should perceive, to a minimal degree, the other's empathic understanding and unconditional positive regard.

The process of growth or change, suggests Rogers, 'often commences with only these minimal conditions' and 'never commences without these conditions being met' (1959, p. 213).

Non-directive practice

What are the implications of any or all of this for practice? We could sum up all that we've said so far about the nature of the organism and the qualities of its tendency to actualise in one simple assumption: that the organism is trustworthy and does not need to be controlled or directed from the outside. This leads in person-centred thinking to the principle of non-directive practice: a decisive and radical commitment to trust the capacity of the individual organism to make its own decisions and to take its own directions. Essentially, being non-directive describes the attitude, rather than the behaviour, of the person-centred practitioner and, thereby, distinguishes the person-centred approach from more analytic and directive approaches to therapy. Merry (1999a) refers to it as describing:

> a general non-authoritarian attitude maintained by a counsellor whose intention is empathically to understand a client's subjective experience. It refers also to the theory that the actualising tendency can be fostered in a relationship of particular qualities, and that whilst the general direction of that tendency is regarded as constructive and creative, its particular characteristics in any one person cannot be predicted, and should not be controlled or directed. (pp. 75–6)

The non-directive principle is, clearly, a counsel of perfection. Patterson (1993/2000) has suggested 'that anything we do, in or out of counseling, has some influence on others' (p. 67) and Lietaer (1998) says that 'it makes little sense to wonder whether a therapist is directive or not. It only makes sense to see in what way he or she is directive or task-oriented' (p. 63). Notwithstanding the truth of those two statements, person-centred practice depends on the non-directive attitude of the practitioner, on her willingness for her clients to find and take their own directions, whatever she herself would do, and whatever she thinks they should do. Rogers (1954/1967b) suggests that the more personally secure the therapist, the more likely it is that she will be able to afford her clients this level of freedom. Writing about his relationship with a client, he asks:

> Am I secure enough within myself to permit him his separateness? Can I permit him to be what he is – honest or deceitful, infantile or adult, despairing or over-confident? Can I give him the freedom to be? Or do I feel that he should follow my advice, or remain somewhat dependent on me, or mold himself after me? (pp. 52–3)

The nature of non-directive practice and its implications are the subject of much debate within the approach. See, for instance, Snyder (1945), whose investigation into non-directive psychotherapy influenced Rogers' own thinking; Raskin (1948) on the development of non-directive therapy; Cain (1989c) on the paradox of non-directiveness; Grant (1990) on different conceptions of non-directiveness; and Patterson (2000a) for a review of recent discussions.

Having explored the philosophical values of person-centred practice, and looked at its first principles, we want to look in the next chapter more specifically at person-centred approaches to therapy.

SUMMARY

- The person-centred approach is simply an approach to thinking about and relating to the person.
- Rogers was brought up Christian, and identified himself subsequently with the phenomenological and the existential schools of philosophy.

SUMMARY (cont'd)

- The personal philosophy of the practitioner is significant in her work, as is the relationship between her personal philosophy and the philosophical values of person-centred practice.
- One history of the development of psychology sees analytical schools constituting a first force of psychology, behavioural schools constituting a second force, and humanistic schools constituting a third force. The person-centred approach is generally located within the third force.
- Three key concepts underpin the theory of the person-centred approach: the nature of the organism and its tendency to actualise; the six necessary and sufficient conditions of growth and change; and the non-directive attitude of the practitioner.

The Person
in Therapy

3

In this chapter we look first at a history of the person-centred approach to therapy. We then explore Rogers' theory of therapy, and, at the end of this chapter, take a person-centred view of some of the popular and prevailing ideas from psychoanalysis.

A brief history of the person-centred approach to therapy

The person-centred approach to therapy differs from the prevailing orthodoxies of the 1940s and 1950s in many ways. Perhaps the most significant and useful difference – significant in that it distinguishes the person-centred approach from *all* of the other orthodoxies, and useful in that it highlights a central and defining feature of the approach – is the emphasis it gives to the relationship between therapist and client. The medical model worked through surgical or pharmaceutical intervention; analytical models involved the development, maintenance and explication of transferential relationships; behavioural models worked with stimulus and response only, and didn't originally see much need to attend to the relationship between stimulus and response or between therapist and client. For Rogers (1939), the present-centered relationship between therapist and client *is* the therapy. The relationship, he says, 'deals entirely with present situations' and 'primarily' with 'those feelings which center on the worker' (p. 343). He might even have called the approach 'relationship therapy', and in this he acknowledges the influence of Otto Rank (1884–1939):

> Relationship therapy is a point of view stemming originally from the thinking of Otto Rank, modified and expressed by different workers. The concepts

underlying this book are much influenced by the Rankian group. (Rogers, 1942, p. 439)

Rank was a locksmith, self-educated, and the first of Freud's disciples to write a psychoanalytic book, *Künst und Künstler* [Art and the Artist] (1907). He broke with Freud in 1926, moved to Paris and then, in 1930, settled in America. Though largely unacknowledged, Rank is now seen as a forerunner of ego psychology, object relations theory, interpersonal psychology and Rogers' client-centred therapy, and there is a resurgence of interest in his work (see Menaker, 1996).

The most significant of the 'different workers' to whom Rogers refers was Jessie Taft. Taft was a clinical psychologist who worked especially with children. Rank was her analyst for a time, and she and Rank taught together at the University of Pennsylvania School of Social Work. She later translated some of Rank's works into English and wrote his biography. In 1970 Rogers described her book, *The Dynamics of Therapy in a Controlled Relationship* (Taft, 1933), as 'a small masterpiece of writing and thinking' (Rogers and Hart, 1970, p. 515).

Rogers' ideas about the nature of the relationship developed over time. Originally, he saw the therapist's role in the relationship almost in terms of the Freudian analyst, offering a blank screen on to which clients can project their feelings and fantasies:

> ... the client finds in the counselor a genuine alter ego in an operational and technical sense – a self which has temporarily divested itself (so far as possible) of its own selfhood, except for the one quality of endeavoring to understand. (Rogers, 1951, p. 40)

He gradually came to endorse a relationship in which he was more fully and more spontaneously present, 'even when the attitudes I feel are not attitudes with which I am pleased, or attitudes which seem conducive to a good relationship' (Rogers, 1954/1967a, p. 33).

A theory of therapy

Whatever other relationships he explored, Rogers remained consistently interested in the therapeutic relationship. He grew the theory of the approach out of his experience as a therapist, and locates the theory of therapy at the heart of person-centred thinking. The other areas which have embraced person-centred thinking are extrapolations from this central and starting point: the therapeutic relationship.

In all of his writings about this relationship, Rogers asks four questions:

1   How does psychological malaise develop in an organism in the first place?
2   What are the optimal conditions for the growth of the human organism?
3   What is the process by which therapeutic change happens?
4   What are the characteristics of the organism at the height of its potential?

We consider the first question in Chapter 6. The next three questions give us a way in to thinking about the conditions, process and outcomes of therapy and a structure to this part of the chapter.

What are the optimal conditions for growth?

Perhaps the first thing to notice is the question itself. Rogers does not ask what a therapist needs to do to a client in order to facilitate change. He asks what qualities of relationship a therapist might usefully offer in order to foster a client's own capacity to grow. The question implies a process that is seminal rather than mechanical, agricultural rather than industrial; and it is a question that is possible only if we assume a tendency to actualise: an innate and robust tendency towards growth. As we have seen, person-centred approaches to therapy are based on this assumption that every human being carries internally 'the capacity and the tendency, latent if not evident, to move forward toward maturity' (Rogers, 1954/1967a, p. 35). Rogers describes this tendency to actualise as 'the mainspring of life' and says that it 'is, in the last analysis, the tendency upon which all psychotherapy depends' (*ibid.*, p. 35). In a subsequent paper Rogers (1963) returns to this theme:

> ... the most impressive fact about the individual human being seems to be his [*sic*] directional tendency toward wholeness, toward actualization of his potentialities. I have not found psychotherapy effective when I have tried to create in another individual something which is not there, but I have found that if I can provide the conditions which make for growth, then this positive directional tendency brings about constructive results. (p. 4)

We are concerned here with these 'conditions which make for growth'. We have begun this discussion of those conditions with a reminder of the tendency to actualise because they are predicated on its existence and make sense only if we accept it as a functional concept.

Having framed the question in this way, and abstracting from his own clinical experience and 'pertinent research', Rogers describes six conditions which he saw as both necessary and sufficient for therapeutic growth. The conditions are necessary, in that each needs to be met; and they are sufficient, in that no other conditions seem necessary. These conditions describe the qualities relevant for therapists or helpers in any situation where they expect or intend constructive personality change.

Rogers (1959) writes as follows:

For therapy to occur it is necessary that these conditions exist.

1   That two persons are in *contact*.
2   That the first person, whom we shall term the client, is in a state of *incongruence*, being *vulnerable* or *anxious*.
3   That the second person, whom we shall term the therapist, is *congruent* in the *relationship*.
4   That the therapist is *experiencing unconditional positive regard* toward the client.
5   That the therapist is *experiencing* an *empathic* understanding of the client's *internal frame of reference*.
6   That the client *perceives*, at least to a minimal degree, conditions 4 and 5, the *unconditional positive regard* of the therapist for him, and the *empathic* understanding of the therapist. (p. 213)

Of the six conditions, congruence, unconditional positive regard and empathic understanding, the three conditions which the counsellor alone brings to the relationship, have come to be identified as the 'core conditions'. This term seems to have been coined by Carkhuff (1969a,b) who used it to identify, from different orientations to therapy, 'core, facilitative and action-oriented conditions' by which the helper facilitated change in the client. In addition to empathic understanding, respect and genuineness, the conditions Carkhuff identified included: specificity in emphasising emotional experiencing, concreteness in problem-solving, the ability to confront and the ability to interpret the helping relationship. Many trainers, practitioners and theorists focus, to our eyes, excessively or even exclusively, on these three conditions. In both editions of *Person-Centred Counselling In Action*, for instance, Mearns and Thorne (1988, 1999) devote a chapter to each of these core conditions. In *Person-Centred Therapy Today* (Mearns and Thorne, 2000) they remind us that the core conditions were originally 'accompanied by three others' (p. 88) but do not say much more about them. They do however acknowledge that they may themselves 'have colluded with the tendency to separate them out in a devitalizing way by affording each condition a separate chapter' (p. 86). More recently, a series of books which aims to address Rogers' therapeutic conditions, affords one volume to each of the core conditions, respectively: congruence (Wyatt, 2001), unconditional positive regard (Bozarth and Wilkins, 2001), and empathy (Haugh and Merry, 2001), conflates two of the other conditions into one volume (Sanders and Wyatt, 2002) and does not address the remaining condition, client incongruence, explicitly at all. We think this is a problem. Rogers described *six* conditions and grew his theory around them. Ongoing practice and research may suggest that there are five or seven or fewer or more necessary and sufficient conditions, or that the conditions are individually necessary or sufficient to different degrees in different contexts. However, simply to ignore or demote three of the conditions in favour of three others, without any explicit or rigorous rationale for doing so, is unhelpful. It compromises the theoretical integrity of the approach as Rogers developed it and left it; it leads to a skewed and partial view of the person-centred approach; and it hinders coherent thinking about and development of person-centred practice.

Here we briefly introduce all six necessary and sufficient conditions:

1 *That two persons are in* contact
   Our experience is that students and beginning therapists often find this notion of psychological contact confusing, and imagine that it means something more complicated than it does. Rogers (1959) calls psychological contact 'the *least* or minimum experience which could be called a relationship' (p. 207). He suggests simply that a minimal relationship must exist, a relationship in which each person 'makes a perceived or subceived difference in the experiential field of the other' (*ibid.*, p. 207), and that this 'minimal relationship' is sufficient for therapeutic work to begin. Although the language is arcane, the meaning is clear. Client and therapist need to be simultaneously aware of each other before anything therapeutic can begin to happen. So, two people, awake, and in the same room, are in psychological contact. Two people talking on the phone are in psychological contact. Rogers does not rule out the possibility of psychological contact even when one person is in a psychotic state. The contact Rogers is describing is not about feeling close to each other, or even about recognising each other as human beings. He does not call it emotional contact or affective contact. It is simply about mutual awareness of each other's presence. All that Rogers is doing is

naming explicitly an element of the therapeutic frame which many writers take for granted.

As Rogers describes it, psychological contact is a digital or binary phenomenon. Two people are either in psychological contact, or they are not. It is not a matter of degree. He says explicitly that the other five conditions 'exist on continua', thereby implying that this one does not (Rogers, 1959, p. 215). More recently, Mearns has argued that there are degrees of psychological contact. Some of us think he is mistaken. We agree that there are degrees of empathic understanding, of mutual warmth, of feelings of closeness. However, all that Rogers (1959) intends to define here is, in his own words, a 'simple contact between two persons' (p. 207).

2   *That the first person, whom we shall term the client, is in a state of* incongruence, *being* vulnerable *or* anxious

For therapy to be effective, Rogers (1959) argues that the client must be experiencing some discrepancy or incongruence between 'the self as perceived, and the actual experience of the organism' (p. 203). So, a person is incongruent if he or she experiences something at odds with his or her picture of self. This at-odds-ness exacts a psychological cost. In order to maintain the integrity of her self-concept, a person will deny or distort any experience that is inconsistent with it. The greater the discrepancy between self-concept and experience, the greater the likelihood of unhappiness or distress. One implication of client incongruence being one of the necessary and sufficient conditions is that the client, the person coming to see a therapist, needs to bring some self-identified sense of something awry. He need not have articulated this very clearly, but does need to have recognised something wrong, however dimly. In many ways this definition of client incongruence implies a statement about the client's level of motivation: therapeutic change is more likely if he comes with some awareness of something not right in his life, and unlikely if he comes unwillingly for therapy having been 'sent' by a third party. One of us (MW) spent many years working with men and women sent by the courts as an alternative to prison sentences, and can testify to the strains of working with clients who had not chosen voluntarily to be worked with, and who did not identify for themselves anything they wanted to change. On a similar point, Thorne (1991) writes as follows:

> ... clients who perhaps have most to gain from person-centred therapy are those who are strongly motivated to face painful feelings and who are

deeply committed to change. They are prepared to take emotional risks and they want to trust even if they are fearful of intimacy. (p. 31)

This is equally true of clients considering any form of counselling or psychotherapy. Client incongruence, which Rogers (1957) describes as 'a basic construct in the theory we have been developing' (p. 96), is one way of conceptualising that state of affairs in a client's experiencing of life that precipitates his initial call to a therapist. Although the language may be particular to the person-centred approach, the idea of some discrepancy or anxiety is widely held. Different theoretical orientations use different language: Freudian psychoanalytic theory talks about the primary defence; Reich (1933/1961) thinks about 'character structure'; Horney (1939) calls it 'basic anxiety'; in gestalt therapy, Perls, Hefferline and Goodman (1951/1973) see it in terms of 'interruptions to contact'; writing about group analysis, Bion (1961) talks about 'basic assumptions'; and in primal therapy Janov (1973) identifies the 'primal scene'. Whilst these terms are not correlates, they articulate, from different theoretical perspectives, an understanding of the key issue or issues that may underlie a person's presenting problem.

Finally, we want to say something about what incongruence is not. Despite what some counsellors might say, a client who laughs or smiles and cries while telling a story the counsellor finds upsetting or frightening is not necessarily incongruent. Client incongruence is much more than a momentary inconsistency of one part of a client's expression (or experience) with another. We agree with Brazier (1995) who argues that 'what is consistent and what is inconsistent is more a function of the depth of perception of the observer than a description of the actual state of the person in question' (p. 221). This client's laughter and tears may both be authentic expressions of some aspect of his experiencing. The fact that they seem to be inconsistent one with the other does not necessarily imply incongruence.

3 *That the second person, whom we shall term the therapist, is* congruent *in the* relationship
From his clinical experience Rogers infers that effective therapy is more likely if the therapist is 'congruent'. The word is an unusual one, and means, according to Rogers (1959) 'that the therapist's symbolization of his own experience in the relationship must be accurate' (p. 214). In simple terms, this means that the therapist must be able to put accurate words to his experience of being in the relationship with his client. He

need not say these words to his client, but must at least be able to say them to himself.

As we've seen, Rogers was writing at a time when the prevailing models of help for a person in distress were medical, psychoanalytical or behavioural. All of these, to some extent, emphasised the therapist's role and function rather than her person, and all, to some extent, treated the person in distress as a mechanism to be fixed or cured. Here, Rogers was essaying something radically different. His recognition that the person of the therapist was a significant part of the therapeutic relationship is one expression of this. It is also, historically and contextually, a contentious move away from the therapist as expert or blank screen. Times have changed, and this idea is less contentious now than it was in the middle of the 1950s. The idea that therapists should behave authentically, and that this is therapeutically helpful, appears in many traditions. In a recent paper, Haugh (1998) explores some of the complexities of congruence, and shows how the notion has parallels in Jungian work, transactional analysis and gestalt therapy. Dryden (1990), writing as a rational-emotive therapist, also argues for a high level of therapist openness or transparency: 'rational-emotive counselors strive to be as open as therapeutically desirable and do not refrain from giving highly personal information about themselves should their client ask for it' (p. 17). The requirement for therapists to be whole and integrated is often linked to the requirement that counsellors or psychotherapists themselves experience their own counselling, psychotherapy or personal development work both during their training and as a part of their ongoing professional development. We will look at this in more detail in the next chapter.

Some writers see congruence as having two elements: Lietaer (1993) distinguishes between inner genuineness and outer genuineness (or transparency); and Brazier (1993) makes a similar distinction between implicit congruence (to do with internal self-awareness) and explicit congruence (to do with communication). Elsewhere, drawing on Rogers (1961/1967d), two of us have distinguished four features or elements of congruence: self-awareness, self-awareness in action, communication and appropriateness (Tudor and Worrall, 1994). Significantly, Rogers does not find that a therapist has to communicate their internal awareness to a client in order for therapy to be effective. Congruence is, therefore, neither the same as nor an excuse for self-disclosure. Writing about the relationship between congruence and counter-transference, Wilkins (1997) captures the essence of congruence well: 'what is important is that I am open to my experience, whatever it is. This experience need not be communicated directly to my client although I believe that any denial of it to myself or to others is recognised and is counter-therapeutic' (p. 41). One implication of this is that a client may not notice when his therapist is congruent, but will almost certainly notice when she is not.

4   *That the therapist is* experiencing unconditional positive regard *towards the client*
     Bozarth (1996) has argued that, of the six conditions, it is unconditional positive regard which is the 'primary change agent' (p. 48). More specifically, it is the client's experiencing of this, of the counsellor's unconditional acceptance of all that he or she is at any moment, that is therapeutically effective. Given what we have already said about the counsellor's integrity or congruence, it follows that the effective counsellor will be experiencing, rather than merely demonstrating, an unconditional acceptance of her client. This, of course, makes it clear that we are not talking about liking. We cannot force affection for our clients, although, if we were unscrupulous, we could probably pretend it. We can, though, however we feel about them, choose to see them as competent to direct their own life, and behave towards them accordingly. From this perspective, unconditional positive regard can be seen as the operational evidence of a counsellor's trust in her client's capacity and tendency to actualise.

5   *That the therapist is* experiencing *an* empathic *understanding of the client's* internal frame of reference
     Empathic understanding describes the counsellor's accurate understanding of the client's awareness and experience, and accurate perception of the client's internal view of and beliefs about their own world. In this, 'accurate' means that the therapist sees things as the client sees them, not as the therapist would see them if she were in the client's place, nor how she thinks the client should see them. It is essentially an attitude, a stance of willingness and openness towards another person, rather than the technique of reflective listening with which it is sometimes confused and equated. It requires the counsellor to understand the client 'as if' they are seeing life through their client's eyes but without losing their own individuality and separateness. It is this that distinguishes empathic understanding from sympathy, and an empathic relationship from a symbiotic or collusive one. When we are responding empathically to clients, we are saying:

     (a)   that we understand what they are thinking, feeling and experiencing, and

(b)   that we understand something of how they come to be thinking, feeling and experiencing those things in that way.

We are not saying that we think they are right, whatever that means, to be thinking what they are thinking, nor are we agreeing with what they are thinking. We are saying simply that we see and accept that this *is*, in this moment, what they are thinking, feeling and experiencing.

Empathic understanding is most often expressed through attentive and reflective listening, where a therapist listens carefully and may reiterate what she has heard and understood of what her client has said. Rogers was influenced here through Taft by the work of Rank who originally taught therapists to 'listen' for feelings through discerning the patterns in what clients say. Expressing empathic understanding is thus much more than summarising or paraphrasing what the client has just said, although these are examples of what may be termed 'empathy skills'. It is often about sitting with clients as they struggle to find and articulate the meaning of what they are experiencing.

The person-centred approach does not hold a monopoly on empathy. The idea appears in the work of Jacob Moreno (1890–1974) and the existential psychoanalyst Karl Jaspers (1883–1965) and, from Heinz Kohut (1913–81) onwards, it is strongly associated with the work of self-psychologists, who talk about 'empathic attunement'. Kahn (1997) writes beautifully about the notion of empathy and uses it as a touchstone with which to explore the relationship between psychoanalysis, self-psychology and the person-centred approach. It is also the subject of a recent volume which is unusual in that it brings together papers from the client-centred, psychodynamic and experiential approaches (Bohart and Greenberg, 1997).

6   *That the client* perceives, *at least to a minimal degree, conditions 4 and 5, the* unconditional positive regard *of the therapist for him, and the* empathic *understanding of the therapist*
The counsellor has some responsibility to communicate her unconditional positive regard and empathic understanding: 'unless some communication of these attitudes has been achieved, then such attitudes do not exist in the relationship as far as the client is concerned' (Rogers, 1957, p. 99). This statement honours the centrality of the client's subjective experience in the therapeutic process, and has various implications for the counsellor. One is that she needs to develop a capacity to communicate her experiencing in ways which do not compromise the

principle that the process should be led by and centred in her client. The second is that she needs to develop an ongoing sensitivity to her client such that she may notice when her client seems to be feeling missed or misunderstood.

Although some of these needs may be met through skills training, skills in a vacuum carry a risk that the counsellor will seem to understand rather than understand, and seem to trust rather than trust. Haugh (1998) has written of the danger 'that the therapist may be encouraged to engage in behaviours and responses that are informed by' their intention to be experienced by the client in a particular way (p. 48). Although it is important that the counsellor develop the capacity to communicate, we argue that it is her experiencing of empathic understanding and unconditional positive regard which is both prior and essential.

Logically, all of this may suggest that this sixth condition is the crucial one, and, indeed, Rogers (1958/1967) refers to it as the 'assumed condition' (p. 130). It does not matter how empathic or unconditional a therapist is, nor how skilled she is in other areas. All that matters is a client's experience. We remember moments when clients have found our responses more empathic, more unconditional, and therefore more helpful than we had either intended or expected. We are not saying that we should neglect the attitudes of congruence, empathic understanding and unconditional acceptance. We are not saying that we should ignore the skills of attentive listening and respectful responding. We are saying that we need to be humble enough to see that for therapeutic purposes these skills are effective only in so far as they appear in the eye of the beholder, the client. We'll look more at the relationship between the therapeutic attitudes and the teaching of skills in the next chapter.

What is the process by which therapeutic change happens?

Ever the scientist, Rogers was interested not only in how to facilitate change, but also in the nature of that change, in how it happened, in what it looked like (from the outside) and in what it felt like (from the inside) while it was happening.

He made a number of attempts to describe the process systematically. In 1942 he identified 12 steps (Rogers, 1942). He devoted the two longest chapters of *Client-Centered Therapy* (Rogers, 1951) to 'The Therapeutic Relationship as Experienced by the Client' and 'The Process of Therapy'.

In 1961 he presented a description of the therapeutic process in seven stages (Rogers, 1958/1967). This model is probably the most widely known and most popular of his attempts to describe the therapeutic process.

Rogers was clear that he meant this seven stage model to be descriptive rather than predictive or diagnostic, and that it arose out of what he called (1958/1967) 'a naturalist's observational, descriptive approach to' the events of therapy (p. 128). He also suggested that the number of stages was arbitrary, and that whether there were 'three stages or fifty, there would still be all the intermediate points' (*ibid.*, p. 131). In our experience, students and practitioners who try to think about their work through the lens of this seven stage model often get lost or confused in the fine distinctions between the different stages. Does this particular behaviour put a client at the end of stage 5 or the beginning of stage 6, for instance? We think that these difficulties point to a flaw in the model.

Rogers (1958/1967) tells us that he wants 'to learn something of the *process* of psychotherapy, or the *process* by which personality change takes place' (p. 126). Although he wants us to see this chapter as a description of that process, and although he's careful to hold that the sequence of the seven stages is not invariant, and that seven is an arbitrary number, what he offers us is, still, in essence, another stage theory. This leaves a tension at the heart of the chapter between the material Rogers is describing and the way he chooses to describe it: he uses a linear, numerical and apparently objective framework to describe a process that is fluid and organic. Phillips (1994), writing over 40 years later, comes to a similar conclusion. 'All modern theory', he says, 'is written in the shade of Heraclitus. But however inclined we are to the idea of process, our language seems to need punctuation' (p. 160).

One significant consequence of this is that the chapter invites therapists to think diagnostically about their client, and to think about their client's progress rather than their process, about their movement from one stage to the next rather than their experiencing of each moment. Neither of these ways of thinking is intrinsically wrong. They are, however, at odds with the phenomenological values which inform person-centred practice.

'Criticism', says Kosko (1994), 'fails without a working alternative' (p. 15). We've been critical of the seven stage model and of the use some people make of it. Our working alternative is this. Rather than getting lost in the minutiae of the particular stages, it seems to us more important and useful to focus on the phenomena that Rogers identified as evidence of movement from one stage to the next. He described seven such indicators, and although we'll list them here, there's no substitute for reading Rogers' own words about them (Rogers, 1958/1967). Given sufficient experience of being received consistently over time, Rogers suggests that people will show:

1   A loosening of feelings.
2   A change in their manner of experiencing.
3   A shift from incongruence to congruence.
4   A change in the manner in which, and the extent to which, they are willing to communicate self.
5   A loosening of their cognitive maps of experience.
6   A change in their relationship to their problems.
7   A change in their manner of relating.

In broad terms Rogers describes a movement from fixity to fluidity, from closed to open, from tight to loose, and from afraid to accepting. It is also significant that Rogers described the process of therapy as changes and developments as the client experiences them. In this sense he was writing, literally, from a client-centred perspective which was challenging and radical, then and now.

The last thing we want to say about this chapter on the process of therapy is that it shows Rogers (1958/1967) condensing his thinking about the six conditions into one condition: 'throughout the discussion which follows, I shall assume that the client experiences himself as being fully *received*' (pp. 130–1).

He suggests that this term implies 'the concept of being understood empathically, and the concept of acceptance' and that 'it is the client's experience of this condition which makes it optimal, not merely the fact of its existence in the therapist' (1958/1967, p. 131). The process of change then, for Rogers, depends absolutely on a client's experience of being understood empathically and accepted.

What are the characteristics of the organism at the height of its potential?

Throughout his work, Rogers explores and describes how human beings seem to respond if they experience the optimal therapeutic conditions. One end point of this process of exploration is to speculate about what a person might look like who had spent enough time experiencing those conditions consistently and at depth. For such a person, Rogers (1959) coins the term 'fully functioning'. He devotes two pages of this paper to a theory of this fully functioning person, and sees it as a summation of trends already implicit in the theories of therapy and of personality. He defines ten characteristics of the fully-functioning person, as follows:

1   He [*sic*] will be *open to his experience*, and exhibit no *defensiveness*;
2   All *experiences* will be available to *awareness*;
3   All *symbolizations* will be as accurate as the experiential data will permit;
4   His *self-structure* will be congruent with his *experience*;
5   His *self-structure* will be a fluid gestalt, and will change as it assimilates new *experience*;
6   He will *experience* himself as the *locus of evaluation*, and his *valuing process* will be a continuing *organismic* one;
7   He will have no *conditions of worth*, and will *experience unconditional positive self-regard*;
8   He will meet each situation with behavior which is a unique and creative adaptation to the newness of that moment;
9   He will find his *organismic valuing* a trustworthy guide as to what he should do; and
10   He will live with others' harmoniously because of the rewarding character of reciprocal *positive regard*. (Rogers, 1959, pp. 234–5)

Clearly, these statements are consistent with a person at stage 7 of the model we looked at above. Some of our critiques of that model are relevant here too. Although it's probable that Rogers intended this description to be no more than that, a description, the language invites aspiration, on the part of therapists for their clients and on the part of therapists and clients for themselves. This has consequences. Therapists who see the fully functioning state as one to strive for, and to push or facilitate their clients towards, risk compromising the principles of non-directiveness and client autonomy. We think it's important to see and to hold that Rogers was thinking theoretically and descriptively here. The fully functioning person is a theoretical possibility only, dependent upon receiving consistent and optimal conditions that are simply not humanly possible. We prefer to think that the organism is always functioning as fully as it possibly can given the conditions within it and around it.

The context of therapy and its boundaries

When we think of therapy we tend to think of two people sitting in a room talking for an hour or 50 minutes each week. Although this is the norm, it carries a number of assumptions. Tudor (1997) challenges the primacy or 'default setting' of individual therapy, and in Chapter 13 we discuss the contribution the person-centred approach has made to our understanding of groups and group process. Although 'sitting in a room talking' is probably the most usual and familiar form of therapy, this activity does not have to be undertaken sitting, or lying down, or in a room; neither does the 'cure' depend only on 'talking'. Some traditions, such as neo-Rechian bodywork and psychodrama, emphasise work with the body and movement. Whilst the therapeutic space is most commonly represented by a bounded and boundaried space, ensuring privacy and confidentiality, four walls are not the only way to create a *temenos*, a therapeutic space set aside. Some therapists, especially those working with young people, may well undertake therapy alongside some other activity, perhaps playing pool or walking alongside them in a park. This has a distinct advantage in that the therapist is not always facing the client. Some of the best therapy occurs when the therapist is literally *alongside* the client, just as some of the most intimate conversations with children take place in a car. With regard to working with children, there is a well-established tradition of play therapy using equipment such as a sandtray and various toys; and Winnicott made the important point that the play *is* the therapy.

Time is another boundary and one which is usually set at 50 minutes per session hour. However, there is nothing therapeutically necessary about this particular time frame, which has its origins in the fact that it's the one Freud was used to as a student and as a lecturer. Many therapists today offer or are willing to negotiate different times such as one hour or 75 minutes, a double session for a client travelling from a distance, or two hours for a group. Much of this depends on the needs and availabilities of individual clients and therapists. Some clients, and others at some points in their therapy, may need more time. Someone who finds it difficult to sustain or integrate their therapy may benefit more from two or three shorter sessions a week than from one longer one. In the psychoanalytic tradition it's not unusual for analyst and patient to meet three or four times a week. Mearns (in Mearns and Dryden, 1990) writes about what he calls 'flexible working' (p. 107) and gives examples of this from his own practice. He suggests that there is nothing sacrosanct about some of the traditional ways of going about therapy, and that as long as we attend carefully to the need to practice ethically, we can experiment legitimately with the traditional norms and evolve flexible and creative ways of being with our clients.

All of the above is based on therapy being offered on an 'outpatient' basis, whether in the public, voluntary or private sector. Therapy also takes place in residential settings such as hospitals, psychiatric hospitals (see Rogers *et al.*, 1967; Prouty, Van Werde and Pörtner, 2002), or therapeutic communities, where 'everything is the treatment' and subject to therapeutic gaze and discussion, principally through group therapy and community meetings. For more on this, see Chapter 14.

Sharing life therapy

Against this background, some therapists offer extended contact to their clients, a way of working which Stamatiadis (1990) refers to as 'sharing life therapy'. She defines this as:

> an intense form of working in which client and therapist, instead of meeting for hour-long sessions – meet, work, and share activities of daily life for a longer period of time, from several hours to several days, while residing in the same surroundings. (p. 288)

Stamatiadis describes her work with two clients which involved talking, touch, regressive therapy, feeding, focusing, art work and dream work, the giving and receiving of gifts, and the therapist cooking and cleaning in the client's home. She discusses structuring the duration of sessions in terms of non-limited sessions, sessions limited by agreement and sessions limited by external constraints. She also describes varying the rhythm of therapeutic contact. The location of the meetings included the therapist's office and home, including time with her family; the client's home; and public places usually associated with some activity. Clearly this is an unusual form of therapy and involves a high level of commitment from the therapist (and her family), and a willingness to risk:

> Great personal risks taken by the therapist and her wide range of behaviour seemed to reach the clients beyond their defenses. Such risk taking was palpable enough to mobilize a force stronger than the immobility created by their deep insecurity, by their fear of change, and by the paradoxical comfort they had found in their tragic but [familiar] suffering. (1990, p. 306)

Sharing life therapy shares some of the principles of therapeutic communities in that 'everything is the treatment'. As Stamatiadis puts it:

> … therapy did not take place in an artificial world, under artificial conditions, or according to routine. [Both clients] were convinced that the basis was a person-to-person relationship in which the professionalism consisted in

making all events and circumstances relevant to the clients' ultimate goal of leading a more satisfactory life. (1990, p. 306)

Inspired by this work, and also drawing on the work of Connect (formerly THAT) Therapeutic Community in Birmingham, England, which is influenced theoretically by transactional analysis, two of the authors (LET and KT) ran an intensive therapy group for three years for clients whose needs were not met by the usual therapeutic hour, nor by available community care services.

Long before this group was conceived, we had been aware of a gap in provision for people who were not in need of psychiatric services, but whose distress and disturbance was serious and disabling. Some of the people we knew had tried in desperation to access psychiatric services but were neither 'mad' nor 'bad' enough to be considered for admission or financial support. One person said: 'If I'd turned up smelly and dirty, and threatened to kill someone, they might have listened to me properly.' Some of the group members held responsible professional positions. Others either felt too disabled by their emotional and psychological suffering to work, or were able to hold a position for short periods only. This had an impact on the fees we charged and, although we did charge for the group meetings and individual therapy sessions, overall we worked for a low fee. Most of our clients would have liked the option of asylum and, in an ideal world, would have been served well by a therapeutic community, residential for some, outpatient for others. In many ways we saw what we were offering as filling a gap in theory and in practice: offering what Prouty (1976, 1994) calls pre-therapy for an 'out-patient' population.

Our clients were men and women aged between 19 and 56 and we limited the number to eight, although most of the time we had six or seven members. Membership was by invitation only. We never advertised this group and, at the start of their group membership all its members were in individual psychotherapy with either one of us. It was important that at least one of us had a strong established therapeutic relationship and an opportunity for a thorough, albeit ongoing, assessment of each person, in terms of the possibility of future behaviour which could violate our privacy or endanger ourselves, our young family or our property.

(cont'd)

We have particular skills and experiences which come from our working backgrounds in the field of mental health and illness. We also knew that we had no exact exemplars to draw on, and that as far as we knew this was a unique venture which we predicted would received equal amounts of enthusiasm and scepticism. Given all of this, and given our commitment to evaluate and research this venture, we decided to conduct a multi-disciplinary assessment. We drew on Rogers' (1958/1967) process conception (seven stages) of psychotherapy, the multi-axial diagnostic criteria of the Diagnostic and Statistical Manual of Mental Disorders (American Psychiatric Association, 1994), and the Minnesota Multiphasic Personality Inventory (MMPI) (Hathaway and McKinley, 1943/1970), which, we subsequently discovered, had also been used by Rogers and his colleagues in their study on schizophrenia (Rogers et al., 1967). We engaged an additional supervisor, a colleague with experience of therapeutic communities and of working successfully with people with psychotic problems, some of whom had been considered by psychiatrists as too disturbed ever to lead 'normal' lives, and who, as a clinical psychologist, also scored the MMPIs. We also had and have psychiatric back-up, a retired consultant psychiatrist to whom we could refer for additional assessment, opinion and support; and we corresponded with Regina Stamatiadis whose original article had inspired our work.

Drawing some inspiration from the therapeutic community tradition, we viewed this as 'sociotherapy' as much as psychotherapy.

Initially the group met fortnightly in our consulting rooms next door to our home. We ran a two hour therapy group, followed by up to two hours social time during which we would eat a meal together. People would arrive in time for a six o'clock start, calling in on the way to drop off their contribution to the evening meal, to which we also contributed. After the group, which we conceived as offering a high level of support together with a high level of confrontation, we would all prepare the meal in our kitchen, eat and clear up together. We ended the evening at 10.00 pm. We celebrated birthdays, with special food and a birthday cake and gifts, and festivals and other occasions of significance to group members. In the spirit of offering high levels of support, and recognising the levels of deprivation and abuse experienced by some of our members, we offered physical contact, including holding, both as a reparative experience during which the person might regress, and as responding to here-and-now, present-centred adult relational needs. In this respect it was important that there were two of us so that, if appropriate, everyone could get these needs met during any one meeting. Although it never happened that we offered something we could not deliver, we were attentive to that as a possibility. Given the beliefs of some people that their needs could never be met, or that they were 'too much', this seemed an especially important consideration. Whilst holding, we continued to interact with other group members and we recognised the need to have the support and witness of another therapist as well as of group members. In addition to this group, all members were in weekly individual therapy and some, and some from time to time, would negotiate further contact such as telephone calls in between groups. In the language of social care, we viewed this as working out and negotiating a 'psychotherapeutic care package' for each client. After about a year of the group, we organised for the group to meet without us for the first hour on alternate meetings (see Wolf, 1949). In addition, group members met and made friendships outside the group which were supportive, sustaining and sustained after the group closed.

We ran the group on this basis for three years. Some clients came and went; a few we worked with for all three years. We presented our initial findings to considerable interest (Embleton Tudor and Tudor, 1997). Overall we had mixed 'success', with some clients finding it too much and others not enough. In terms of MMPI scores, most showed significant improvement.

Psychoanalytic understandings

Having discussed person-centred ideas about the conditions, process outcomes and contexts of therapy, we want to end this chapter with a brief look at some psychoanalytic understandings of the same phenomena. Some person-centred practitioners and others may be surprised to see such discussions in this text. We think it is important to discuss these concepts for a number of reasons:

- Because they're out there;
- Because they're dominant; and
- Because we think differently.

Freud was the first psychoanalyst and coined the term 'psychotherapy' over a hundred years ago. He wrote prolifically and his ideas have had a profound influence on both professional and popular culture. Major filmmakers like Alfred Hitchcock, Woody Allen and Brian de Palma have explicitly referenced his ideas in their work. Lewis, Amini and Lannon (2000) see that his 'conclusions permeate our culture in a multitude of ways', and that 'his assumptions have endured for so many years that they are mistaken for fact' (p. 6). Freud (1922) encouraged this. To take one example, he called transference a 'fact' which he and his colleagues had been 'unwillingly compelled to recognize' (p. 369). He said (1910/1962) that transference 'arises spontaneously in all human relationships' and that it 'is everywhere the true vehicle of therapeutic influence' (p. 83) Psychoanalysis, he said 'does not create it, but merely reveals it to consciousness' (p. 83). Freud, then, described one of the key assumptions of his approach as if it were a fact, and it's been 'out there' as such for a long time. All of this invites the belief that it 'exists' independently as *the* truth about relationships in general and about the therapeutic relationship in particular.

One result of this history is that psychoanalytic language and ideas dominate professional discussion. Psychoanalytic ideas seem both to carry and bestow professional authority. This is enhanced by the fact that the early psychoanalysts located themselves within the medical profession, becoming doctors before they became analysts. Transference and the unconscious can easily become the assumed vocabulary of 'case' discussions, supervision and even disciplinary proceedings. We, however, see these concepts as only one possible description or explanation of human experience and we are critical of colleagues of any theoretical allegiance who present it as the one and only truth. We agree with Brodley (2001, unpaginated) when she says that:

> statements and questions that use psychoanalytic terms as if they refer to a shared reality and a shared way of conceptualising people perpetuate fuzzy clinical thought and stimulate irresponsible work. The casual or unexplicated use of psychoanalytic terms is also a form of intellectual bullying. This is especially the case when the terms are employed by clinicians in higher authority than those to whom they are speaking.

In the history of the psychological therapies, person-centred therapists are relative newcomers. In this context it is understandable that some person-centred practitioners feel defensive and reject or attack anything to do with psychoanalysis. We, however, think that it is naïve simply to hold that transference doesn't happen, and that the unconscious doesn't exist. We also think it's arrogant to ignore the wealth of psychoanalytic literature and research. In a world of many theories, and especially from a perspective that promotes relationships through dialogue, it's also unsustainable to close our collective minds to psychoanalytic ideas. Naïve and arrogant are strong words. Living and working within a culture that is predominantly psycho-dynamic, we see a need both to learn the language of that culture and to develop our own. We think it is crucial that person-centred therapists especially have a working knowledge of psychodynamic concepts, can understand the phenomena they describe, and can talk about them from their own perspective. Such openness does not imply agreement or merger with psychoanalytic views. It is precisely because the person-centred approach takes a clear and different position that we are advocating discus-sion and dialogue. The approach, we think, is robust enough.

Person-centred theory differs from psychoanalytic theory in a number of ways. One way to explore these differences is to look at some of the key concepts of psychoanalytic thinking, and to explore person-centred responses to them. As we do this, we want to remember Jacobs' (1988) assertion that many 'psychodynamic terms can be more fully under-stood and appreciated if they can be seen as much as metaphors as literal statements' (p. 9).

Human nature

Summarising Freud's view that human beings are intrinsically irrational, unsocialised and destructive, critiquing it, and wondering why it had taken him so long to see through it, Rogers (1953/1967a) counters with the assertion 'that the inner core of man's personality is the organism itself, which is essentially both self-preserving and social' (p. 92). This emphasis on the constructive and co-operative aspects of human nature is often and easily characterised as overly optimistic and naïve. More accurately, though, the person-centred approach sees that human beings are in continuous *process*, that they are fluid rather than static and that they are motivated not only by deficiencies, anxieties and fears but also by aspirational needs towards growth, development, enhancement and each other. For further discussion of this, see Merry (1999a).

The unconscious

Describing the unconscious, Freud (1922) uses the image of 'a large ante-room, in which the various mental excitations are crowding upon one another, like individual beings' (p. 249). He completes the picture by describing 'a second, smaller apartment, a sort of reception-room, in which consciousness resides' (p. 249) and, on the threshold between the two rooms, a 'door-keeper, who examines the various mental excitations, censors them, and denies them admittance to the reception-room when he disapproves of them' (p. 249).

Writers within the person-centred tradition have had different responses to this notion. Rogers (1963/1978/1980) seems happy with the idea of conscious awareness as long as he contrasts it with 'nonconscious organismic functioning' (p. 127) rather than with unconscious processes. Coulson (1995) and Conradi (1999) call for person-centred practitioners to reconsider the usefulness of the unconscious as a concept. Ellingham (1995, 1997, 1999) pits the person-centred approach against psychoanalysis and criticises the concept of the unconscious, and that of transference, as 'expressions of an outdated, Newtonian world-view' (1995, p. 289). From a person-centred perspective the core problem with the notion of the unconscious is that it implies that meanings, memories, fantasies and other repressed thoughts *exist* there, independently, and will, under the right conditions or with the right help, move from the ante-room of the unconscious into the reception-room of the conscious. This is at odds with the phenomenological principles that inform person-centred philosophy, principles that suggest that we each *create* or *construe* meaning anew every minute.

Interpretation

According to the *Shorter Oxford English Dictionary* (Onions, 1933/1973), interpretation is 'the action of interpreting; explanation, exposition ... the faculty or power of interpreting ... the way in which a thing ought to be interpreted' (p. 1099). Reber (1985) makes the point that

> the very act of interpretation implies the existence of a conceptual schema or model on the part of the interpreter such that what is being observed and interpreted is assumed to conform logically to the facts and explanations inherent in the model. (p. 370)

These definitions highlight a number of problems:

- That the power lies with the interpreter and with their model.
- That both lie outside the client.
- That the model against which the interpretations are made may lie outside the client's frame of reference.

At best, interpretation is one way of communicating understanding. This has led to some debate within person-centred circles concerning the precise nature of understanding. Suppose a client cries and the therapist refers to his sadness. Is that reflection or interpretation? As we argued in the previous chapter, phenomenological principles would suggest that a simply descriptive response ('I see your tears') is more helpful than the interpretation of them ('I see that you're sad').

Warner (2000) has contributed to this debate in an important paper on 'interventiveness' which she defines as 'the degree to which a therapist brings in material from outside the client's frame of reference and the degree to which this is done from a stance of authority or expertise' (p. 31). Interpretation would be one form of intervention. She identifies a five level framework to describe therapist responses and styles:

- Level 1 – This largely hypothetical level describes the therapist's pure intuitive and non-invasive contact.
- Level 2 – At this level the therapist conveys *only* his understanding of his client's internal frame of reference.
- Level 3 – At this level the therapist may, if a client asks, offer her own thoughts, feelings and experiences into the therapeutic relationship, always in ways which leave the client free to decide what use to make of it.
- Level 4 – At this level the therapist may sometimes decide to offer her own thoughts, feelings and experiences into the therapeutic relationship, from a position of authority or expertise.
- Level 5 – At this level the therapist makes interventions in such a way that the client may be unaware of both the interventions themselves and of the therapist's purpose or motivation in making them.

This framework describes all therapies and forms of helping, and helps define and distinguish the person-centred practitioner from more directive and interpretive therapists. Warner suggests that there is a fundamental dividing line between Levels 3 and 4, between the more client-directed therapies which focus on the nature of the client's process (Levels 1–3), and the more authoritative or directive therapies (Levels 4 and 5) where therapists take more authority to intervene according to their own theoretical orientation or personal preference. She suggests that clients benefit from all manner of therapies, and that what confuses them is when therapists work inconsistently, sometimes at Levels 1 to 3, and sometimes at Levels 4 and 5. Such inconsistency is therapeutically unhelpful in that it leaves clients not knowing from one moment to the next who has the power to decide what happens or what things mean in the therapeutic relationship.

Writing about interpretation Rogers (1951) quotes, approvingly, the views of Otto Fenichel (1897–1946), a psychoanalyst, who pointed out that the final criterion for the 'correctness' of an interpretation is the patient's reaction over time or, as Rogers puts it: 'if in the long run an interpretation is not experienced by the patient as meaningful and true, then it is not correct' (pp. 221–2). This echoes what we summarised above about the significance of the sixth condition: the value and the impact of a particular interpretation or of any 'intervention', is in the eye of the beholder, the client.

Resistance

For traditional psychoanalytic therapists, any action that opposes the possibility of making conscious that which is unconscious is evidence of resistance. The power to name or interpret the resistance lies, of course, with the therapist. Person-centred therapists, however, trust that their clients are organismically motivated to seek the truth. The idea that clients would be resistant, and that resistant would be a negative way to be, is a nonsense. Speierer, for instance, (1990) sees 'resistance as an error of empathy on the therapist's side' (p. 343). Patterson (2000a) sees that clients may experience therapists' interventions as threats, and that resistance is an appropriate defence against threat. 'Client-centered therapy', he says, 'minimizes resistance by minimizing threat' (p. 187). Tudor and Merry (2002) view resistance as 'a response to overzealous interpretation or intervention by the therapist, which is neither a desirable nor constructive part of therapy' (p. 124).

Transference

For psychoanalytic therapists the concept of transference is key to their understanding of the therapeutic relationship. Transference literally means 'carrying across', and usually refers to the process by which clients carry across ideas, experiences and beliefs from their past and relive them in the present with their therapist or others. Such transference may be affectionate (positive) or hostile (negative). Whilst the resulting behaviour towards and fantasies about the therapist may not be accurate to the therapist's perception of present-centred actuality, such re-livings become the stuff of psychoanalytic therapy because they offer the therapist a way in to an exploration of the client's unconscious. Thus, following Freud, psychoanalytic therapists work on the basis that analysis without transference is an impossibility. If person-centred therapists are to address the phenomenon of transference, we need both to respond to this argument and to advance our own. Shlien's 'countertheory' (see below) is one example of such a response.

Rogers (1951) acknowledges the existence of what he referred to as 'transference *attitudes*' (p. 200). The question at issue for person-centred practitioners is how to respond to them. Paraphrasing Fenichel, Rogers (1951) says that the therapist's response to a client's transference attitudes 'is the same as to any other attitude of the client: he endeavors to understand and accept' (p. 203). This understanding and acceptance often dissolves or sidesteps the transferential attitudes and so the relationship does not come to depend for its effectiveness on the transference and its interpretation. Empathic understanding and acceptance of presently felt and presently expressed phenomena encourage a present-centred relationship. Rogers also makes the point that if there is no obvious evidence for the client's transferential fantasies about the therapist, and if the therapist is acceptant and understanding, then there is little or nothing to sustain the transference. This, in turn, has the therapeutic advantage that the client has an opportunity to 'own' and explore their own fantasies, and to engage in a relationship of present-centred mutuality.

A countertheory of transference

Shlien's (1984) countertheory of transference is perhaps the most sustained, and certainly the most passionate, person-centred response to any of the psychodynamic concepts. He begins by asserting that transference 'is a fiction, invented and maintained by therapists to protect themselves from the consequences of their own behavior' (p. 153). He traces the development of transference theory in the early work of Freud and Breuer, most notably in the documented work with the patient Anna O. Taking into account the historical, social, economic and cultural milieu, he shows how and why Freud evolved the idea. He uses the personality of Freud as a poignant reminder that all theories have at source the personality of their 'father', and he believes that the development of transference theory reflects this especially. Shlien proposes that Freud tended to protect himself from strong emotional feelings and quotes Freud's assertion that he had never done a mean thing. This sets the scene for confirmation of the idea that patients are responsible for doing transference to the therapist, rather than that the therapist has any influence on the here-and-now experiencing of the patient or client. 'What matters here', says Shlien, 'is the analyst's proclamation of innocence – a stance that permeates transference theory throughout' (p. 164).

Shlien's counter to the long established theory of transference is that the phenomena that transference describes could as easily be the result of a client's experience of his therapist's behaviour. A client who felt deeply and accurately understood would tend to behave in ways which an analyst might talk about as positive transference. A client who felt deeply misunderstood would tend to behave in ways which an analyst might talk about as negative transference. Shlien suggests that client responses to therapists are a direct result of being understood, or not, and that these are the issues which cause the success, or otherwise, of therapy. These are natural human responses, he says, and we do not need to theorise about them:

> ... the therapist is responsible for two fundamental behaviors – understanding and misunderstanding – which account for love, or for hate, and their associated affects. These, as well as other behaviors and the situation and personality of the therapist, may account – should first be held accountable – for the whole of what passes for transference. (p. 177)

This counter to the theory clearly implicates the therapist in the creation of transference and in the outcome of the therapeutic process. It also offers a position of equality to clients, a sharing of power in the process of healing and change. It allows for therapist and client each to influence the other, and it relieves the client of sole responsibility for what happens between her and her therapist. In all of these ways it enshrines person-centred principles of transparency and mutuality and reflects the approach's belief in and commitment to the integrity and trustworthiness of the client's tendency to actualise.

In many ways the dialogue between the psychoanalytic and person-centred models of therapy has only just begun. The respective philosophies and principles underpinning the two approaches seem some way apart, and may indeed represent incompatible paradigms. Nevertheless, we think it's helpful, and consistent with person-centred principles, to work towards an empathic understanding of psychoanalytic terms, concepts and colleagues. The comparative strand of this present work constitutes our contribution to that process.

We want to end this chapter with a comment on the similarities and differences between therapeutic relationships and other relationships. The therapeutic relationship is clearly a particular kind of relationship. Therapist and client meet for a particular kind of engagement, characterised by the particular needs of the client and the particular attitudes and skills of the therapist. Other relationships arise in different circumstances, meet different needs, and follow different paths. In a paper originally published in 1975, Rogers (1980) agrees, and suggests that different kinds of relationships call for different attitudes. In what he calls 'the ordinary interactions of life', by which he means the relationships between, lovers, friends and colleagues, between teachers and their students, and between employers and employees, 'congruence is probably the most important element' (p. 160). In other relationships, 'between parent and infant, therapist and mute psychotic, physician and very ill patient', the most significant attitude may be one of 'caring, or prizing' (*ibid.*). And then there are relationships where one 'person is hurting, confused, troubled, anxious, alienated, terrified'. In that relationship, which we think most closely approximates the therapy relationship, 'understanding is called for' (*ibid.*). The person who offers understanding in this kind of relationship, says Rogers, 'must, of course, possess the other two attitudes' (*ibid.*). We look at a history of relationships in Chapter 8, and at other particular relationships in Chapters 9, 10 and 15.

Having discussed the person in therapy in this chapter, in the next chapter we turn our attention to the person of the therapist and their development in offering what Rogers originally referred to as 'relationship therapy'.

SUMMARY

- The person-centred approach differs from analytical and behavioural models of therapy in the importance it accords the therapeutic relationship.
- The actualising tendency is, more accurately and more helpfully, a 'tendency to actualise'.
- Rogers developed a theory of therapy based on six necessary and sufficient conditions for constructive growth.
- Rogers' process model of psychotherapy describes a movement from 'fixity' to 'fluidity'.
- The practice of psychotherapy has a context and boundaries.
- The person-centred approach has ways of describing the conditions, process and outcomes of therapy, which differ from psychoanalytic understandings of the same phenomena.

On Becoming
a Therapist

Our title for this chapter alludes to Rogers' (1961/1967b) volume, *On Becoming A Person*. Here we look at the processes of becoming a therapist, being a therapist, and belonging as a therapist. We hope that what we have to say will be relevant to trainers, to therapists, to therapists in training, and to anyone considering whether to train as a therapist.

Becoming a therapist

One of the themes of this book has been the idea that person-centred principles constitute a functional approach to many areas of life. In this chapter we want to look at what happens when we bring those principles to bear on the task of helping people to become therapists. We also want to look at the implications of a person-centred approach to training for both trainers and for their students.

We begin with the idea that there's a difference between, on the one hand, training to be a person-centred therapist, and, on the other, a person-centred training to be a therapist. The first sets out to train people to be person-centred therapists. The second sets out to offer a person-centred training to people who want to become therapists. The difference is crucial. In a similar vein, Villas-Boas Bowen (1986) describes two distinct types of supervision: 'form-oriented', where 'the primary commitment is to the preservation of a single mode of doing psychotherapy' (p. 292); and 'philosophy-of-life-oriented', where the supervisor offers a relationship consistent with her own philosophical values and theoretical orientation, whatever her supervisee's practise. This catches the difference we want to explore.

We would argue that a training course which sets out to train therapists to be person-centred is, in itself, inconsistent with person-centred principles. No student, says Rogers (1951), 'can or should be trained to become a client-centred therapist' (p. 432). This is a provocative and mischievous way of making the same point, and deserves some unpacking. The logic of it goes something like this. Rogers held consistently that human beings, in any sphere, could be trusted, and that they could therefore be allowed maximum freedom to follow their own promptings and to explore whatever seemed to matter to them in the moment. He believed that this was the only way anybody would or could learn anything worth learning. He described, developed and practised a therapy that was consistent with these beliefs, a therapy that was trusting, permissive and non-directive. Given equivalent freedom and permission in their training, therapists in training are likely to explore and discover their own deeply held beliefs and attitudes, and to move towards working in a way that is consistent with what they discover. Some of these therapists will find that their beliefs, their attitudes and their ways of working will sit comfortably with person-centred principles. Some will not. This is probably inevitable, and, for reasons we'll explore shortly, not necessarily a problem.

If we take it seriously and follow it through, though, this argument does have implications for the training process. Perhaps the most significant of these is that individual therapists in training would be left free to discover for themselves what kind of therapists they were and what kind of therapy they wanted to practice. A corollary of this is that there would be neither trainings nor any externally awarded qualifications in person-centred therapy, as both would entail the pre-establishment of a curriculum or set of standards in response to the needs of an awarding body rather than the learner's curiosity. Approaching this from a different angle, House (1997) challenges and critiques the myth that there's any causal relationship between the training of therapists and their competence to practise. He suggests that a person's choice to become a therapist may well be 'the crucial variable in competence' (p. 101), and that it's that, rather than the 'training per se that somehow transforms non-counsellors into competent practitioners' (p. 101).

All of this leaves us, in effect, with a person-centred training in therapy, and that's what we're interested to explore now.

Characteristics of a person-centred training

Extrapolating from what Rogers wrote (1951, 1961/1967b), and drawing on more recent work by Combs (1986/2000), Mearns (1997), Patterson

(2000b,c) and Natiello (2001a,b), we suggest that a person-centred training deals distinctively with the following elements: personal development, skills, practice, supervision, assessment, and course structure.

We consider each of these elements in turn, explore distinctively person-centred thinking about them, and examine how they fit with current professional trends both in the organisation of counselling and psychotherapy, and in the training of counsellors and psychotherapists. These elements can also become questions prospective students might ask when they consider training courses, look at prospectuses and interview the trainers.

Personal development

A person-centred training puts the person of the individual therapist-to-be at the heart of the training process. This is consistent both with a client-centred approach to therapy, which puts the client at the centre of the process, and with Rogers' belief that the person of the therapist is significant in the therapeutic process: 'In any psychotherapy, the therapist himself is a highly important part of the human equation. What he does, the attitude he holds, his basic concept of his role, all influence therapy to a marked degree' (Rogers, 1951, p. 19). In practice, and amongst other things, this means that a person-centred training pays a great deal of attention to students' personal development. Training courses from different traditions pay different levels of attention to the personal development of the student. Even where some priority is given to it within the hours of the training, many traditions expect that students will do much of their personal development work in private with their own therapist. A person-centred training, however, sees that the personal development of the student *is* the training, and for this reason gives it the highest priority. One justification for this comes from Combs (1986/2000). Starting from the premise that what a person does is a consequence or a symptom of what he believes, Combs argues that the process of training therapists should therefore attend primarily to what students believe and to the values they hold. He sees this as more important than skills development for the training of effective therapists.

The most effective therapists seem to be those whose own personal philosophies embrace naturally, for themselves and for others, such values as respect and authenticity, and who then live those values most fully in their relationships with their clients. A therapist's personal beliefs, therefore, need to be congruent with the way she practises. It is nonsense to expect a therapist who believes that human beings are anarchic and need to be controlled to try to practise a permissive and non-controlling therapy. It's also nonsense to try to force a therapist, or anybody, for that matter, either to change his or her attitudes, or to work in a way that is inconsistent with them. It's in this sense that no one can or should be taught to be a person-centred therapist.

If the most effective therapists are those whose values are most therapeutic and whose practice is consistent with their values, it follows that the most effective person-centred therapists are those whose values sit most comfortably with the philosophical values of the person-centred approach, and who find ways of living those values most fully in their relationships with their clients. For this reason, it seems essential that a person-centred training be geared towards helping individual students find, articulate and then implement their own values. It's at this point that skills and techniques become important. Having flexible, facilitative and therapeutic values is one thing. Living them articulately in the moment-to-moment encounter with a client is another. Rogers (1951) puts it this way:

> In our experience, the counselor who tries to use a 'method' is doomed to be unsuccessful unless this method is genuinely in line with his own attitudes. On the other hand, the counselor whose attitudes are of the type which facilitate therapy may be only partially successful, because his attitudes are inadequately implemented by appropriate methods and techniques. (p. 19)

This argument justifies both the teaching of techniques and the development of skills. It also gives skills and techniques a place in the training process: *subsequent* to the exploration of attitudes and values, but important nonetheless.

Skills

The current educational trend in favour of measurable outcomes and definable competencies skews many training courses away from the exploration of attitudes and towards the teaching of observable skills. Trainers running courses which they want to be externally accredited, academically validated, or both, will probably have to wrestle with this dilemma at some point, and either come to some compromise between philosophical integrity and commercial viability, or find a way of maintaining both.

Although we believe that Rogers and others have been clear about the secondary importance of skills and techniques, the person-centred approach seems susceptible to a training based on the acquisition of surface competencies. Rogers focused primarily on the process of therapy as experienced by the client and left a gap in which others could describe, and ultimately prescribe, the process or method of the therapist. This gap allowed writers such as Robert Carkhuff, Charles Truax (Truax and Carkhuff, 1967; Carkhuff, 1969a,b) and Gerard Egan (Egan, 1997) to put forward models of therapy based predominantly on separated *skills* rather than integrated values, such as: specificity in emphasising emotional experiencing; concreteness in problem-solving; the ability to confront; the ability to interpret the helping relationship; assessment; identifying and clarifying problem situations; developing preferred scenarios; formulating strategies and plans; goal-setting; overcoming awkwardness in clients; probing; managing resistance and reluctance; challenging.

Some approaches to counselling and psychotherapy, and some training courses in these and other helping professions, make an artificial separation between skills and theory. This is particularly marked in people who and on courses which adopt Egan's work, and assert that he and they are person-centred. Egan is not person-centred and, as far as we know, does not claim to be. The separation of skills from theory is problematical in that it allows therapists to incorporate into their practice any skills or techniques they may have learned without reference to any underlying or organising theory of why they're doing what they're doing, or of why what they do works or fails to work. This leads to therapists who are reactive rather than responsive, and eclectic rather than deeply settled in a coherent way of working. It also discourages therapists from thinking systematically about their work, and from developing a deeply reflective practice.

In our view, skills and techniques are relevant only in so far as they embody or articulate an individual therapist's values and attitudes. They are a therapist's philosophy in evidence. Rogers (1957/1990) says it well: 'one cannot engage in psychotherapy without giving operational evidence of an underlying value orientation and view of human nature' (p. 402).

It follows that skills training in a person-centred context means the process of facilitating people to find increasingly accurate, comprehensive and satisfying ways of implementing their personal values.

Practice

Rogers (1951) argues 'that the practice of therapy should be a part of the training experience from the earliest practicable moment' (p. 433). Although we could debate when 'the earliest practicable moment' would be and how we'd recognise it, we think it's fairly clear that Rogers intends that students should see clients sooner rather than later. One of the advantages to this is that students can learn primarily from their own experiences as well as from what are to them second-hand sources: written material, presentations of theoretical material or video presentations. This flows from and is consistent with Rogers' conviction (1953/1967b) that personal experience is the highest authority: 'neither the Bible nor the prophets – neither Freud nor research – neither the revelations of God nor man – can take precedence over my own direct experience' (p. 24). It also mirrors the history of his own learning, to which we've alluded in Chapter 2.

Another advantage is that this kind of experience exposes therapists in training to the difficulties and challenges of the work, and gives them an immediate opportunity to identify their own learning needs precisely and quickly. If Combs (1986/2000) is right, and if 'people learn best when they have a need to know' (p. 272), then any experience by which they can discover exactly what they need to know is important.

We agree that most students should practise as therapists from early on in their training. In the current climate, this is difficult to achieve. Many voluntary and statutory agencies won't consider students for a counselling placement until they've completed at least the first year of their training. We see some problems with this policy. In so far as we understand it, it's probably designed to protect vulnerable clients from beginning, and there-fore apparently inexperienced, therapists. However, the first problem we see is that it's based on a questionable assumption. Beginning therapists, although inexperienced as therapists, are often highly experienced as human beings. The assumption that their technical inexperience is neces-sarily an impediment to their practice as therapists fails to take account of their life experience, psychological maturity and personal readiness. We're not saying that any therapist, however inexperienced, is competent to work with any client, vulnerable or robust. We are saying that the blanket assumption that beginning therapists don't and shouldn't see clients until they've reached at least a certain point in their training is at best a blunt and only partially effective protection. It deprives some clients of the help they need, and some therapists of the practice that would quickly help them become competent and skilled practitioners. Although it may protect some vulnerable clients, it also protects beginning therapists from some of the experiences that would most enhance their development. Our view is that clients need protecting not from inexperienced therapists, but from unskilled or unscrupulous ones. On the question of trainees working with 'difficult' clients, we agree with Mearns (1997) when he advocates additional supervision: 'instead of dismissing the client we invested more resources in support of the counselor to continue his work with the client' (p. 93).

One obvious alternative to working for a voluntary or statutory agency is to work in private practice. The British Association for Counselling (1996) (now The British Association for Counselling and Psychotherapy (BACP)), however, argues that most students should not work in private practice until they have qualified. Again, the motives for this caution are probably to do with protection and safety. Agencies offer two apparent advantages:

- The support that comes with belonging to a team of close colleagues, with the possibility of formal and informal supervision as soon as it's needed; and
- More experienced practitioners who will assess clients and allocate them appropriately.

We call these advantages *apparent* for a number of reasons:

- The first is that we're not convinced that they are genuinely advantageous.
- The second is that in our experience, many agencies actually offer few of the advantages that all agencies could potentially offer.
- The third is that we think it's possible to build in to a private practice whatever is genuinely advantageous in the agency set-up.

Let's look at each of these apparent advantages. Working as a therapist can be lonely work. It's probably incontrovertible that a network of colleagues is important. In that sense, a well run agency placement offers a genuine advantage to individual therapists. Not all agencies, however, are well run. We know of beginning therapists in placements who have seen clients on their own in lonely buildings late into the evening without anyone else around. We think that this is more than the lack of an advantage; we think it's positively harmful to a therapist's morale and a potential risk to his safety. In favour of private practice, we'd argue that it's possible for therapists to grow their own network of close and supportive colleagues. It's not automatically in place, but it's not automatically in place in an agency either just because it's an agency. Practitioners who want to work privately have both the capacity and the responsibility to put in place around them the support they need and, in our view, it is preferable to do this during training when they may be both supported and challenged to do so.

The second apparent advantage concerns the assessment and allocation of clients. Therapists working privately have no filter between them and the world outside. Who knows what kinds of clients might present themselves, with what kinds of issues and dilemmas? Although we understand this concern, we question the logic that says that more experienced practitioners should take this responsibility. Even if a client sees an experienced therapist who assesses him before allocating him to a beginning therapist, common sense and ethical protocol suggest that beginning therapist must still make some assessment *for herself* as to whether she feels competent and willing to work with this particular client, at this particular time. It's naïve, unethical and infantilising to assume that somebody else's assessment absolves her of that responsibility. For more on this, see also Mearns (1997). It's also common for clients to choose to reveal greater problems or more painful experiences in the context of an established relationship, rather than at an initial meeting within the context of an assessment.

Another aspect of this debate is that clients who approach particular agencies for help are, by definition, likely to be in some particular crisis: bereavement, addiction, illness, or breakdown. Therapists of any experience, and beginning therapists especially, may feel the weight and immediacy of some of these concerns as particularly demanding. The majority of clients in our various private practices are self-referring and self-supporting. They're not necessarily in crisis and are often functioning relatively well in their lives. So although it's true that therapists in private practice shoulder the responsibility of assessment themselves, there's also the possibility that their clients are less likely to be in immediate crisis than those who approach counselling agencies or General Practitioners.

If agencies won't offer placements until the start of the second year of training, and private practice is disallowed, most courses wanting to provide students with the experience of *being* therapists offer them the opportunity to practise counselling with each other, often in a triad with an observer who then gives feedback. Rogers (1951) endorses this: 'one of the most useful early training experiences has been for students to counsel with each other' (p. 470). We differ from Rogers in this and have doubts about the value of such triad work for a number of reasons.

Most ethical frameworks proscribe, or at least discourage, dual relationships. It is, for instance, generally thought unethical to be therapist and friend, or therapist and trainer, to the same person. Yet the triad generates exactly that kind of dual relationship. The participating students are primarily peers, colleagues in an often intense and accelerated learning process, and are here expected to behave towards each other as if they were client and therapist. If the expectation is that the client brings real and current concerns, then the duality of the relationship is that much more problematical.

If the client is expected to play a role, then the potential for authenticity is compromised. And in this instance, says Combs (1986/2000), where 'the problem is unreal, attention becomes focused on methods so that both parties concentrate upon symptoms rather than the dynamics of the counseling process' (p. 273).

Our second concern has to do with the observer. In traditional triad work, the observer's task is to offer feedback. We question the wisdom and validity of this for a number of reasons. At its best, a person-centred training supports individual students finding and working from their own internal locus of evaluation. However close an observer might be to the counselling relationship, she is still external to it. Moreover, the expectation that the observer gives the counsellor feedback encourages the opposite: an external locus of evaluation. Also, because the observer is neither the counsellor nor the client, she can offer feedback only on what's visible or audible, and not on what's happening internally for either counsellor or client. To put it another way, an observer can offer feedback only on the therapist's behaviour, and not on her attitudes or beliefs. A therapist might use such feedback to reflect on her attitudes and beliefs, but that seems to us an unnecessarily complicated way to further that process. One final reservation about the observer's feedback is that it can deflect the therapist from noticing the feedback that might be genuinely useful: the feedback that comes from the client, based on the sixth, 'assumed condition' (Rogers, 1958/1967).

For all of these reasons, and whenever students do practise counselling in triads, we suggest that the 'observer' be given a different brief. We take the view that the client's feedback is the most important for the counsellor to hear, and so we suggest that the observer's role should be to learn for herself whatever she can from what she sees, and to facilitate the exchange of feedback from client to counsellor. Logically, of course, the observer does not even need to have observed the counselling session in order to do this second task. Whether she observes or not, the task becomes one like supervision, and one that students can usefully begin to practise. We find the method of interpersonal process recall (IPR), as developed by Norman Kagan (1931–1994), also useful in helping the observer or, more accurately and usefully, the facilitator, to facilitate the counsellor's recall of their process. Briefly, Kagan developed a protocol whereby one person helps another explore his own work on audio or video tape through a series of questions about what he was noticing *while* he worked. The person exploring his work is in control of the process, in the sense that he decides exactly which moments to explore, and when he wants to move on. For a further description of this in relation to person-centred supervision, see Allen (2004).

Supervision

Supervision is a process in which therapists or other practitioners talk about their work with another colleague, whose function it is to help them explore their relationships with their clients. At its best, supervision offers support, challenge and professional refreshment. It's a place where therapists can talk about the joys and difficulties of their work, revisit familiar theoretical concepts, test new ones, explore ethical dilemmas and agree a course of action. It's one of the ways in which therapists live with and learn to thrive among the paradoxes, uncertainties and intangibles of their work.

Those of us who are therapists are committed to our own supervision, and agree without reservation that it's a necessary and desirable element of a psychotherapist's practice. We do, though, have a critique about the way supervision is often organised. In the United Kingdom, in most training institutions and under most ethical guidelines, regular supervision is mandatory. We are critical of that, and think that it's consistent with the principle of trust in their tendency to actualise that supervision should be readily and quickly *available* to beginning therapists rather than imposed on them. The costs of imposition are high. If students don't assess for themselves when they might need supervision they may not easily develop trust in their internal locus of evaluation.

The same logic that protects vulnerable clients from beginning therapists by having a more senior therapist assess and allocate clients determines not only the fact of supervision but also the amount of it. Given that it's the same logic, many of our critiques are equally relevant, and we won't rehearse the arguments again here. It seems to us that therapists who are finding their work particularly demanding, however experienced they are, simply need access to more frequent supervision. The risk of imposing a minimum monthly requirement, as the BACP does, or a minimum ratio of supervision hours to client hours, as many training courses do, is that some therapists will work to that minimum. The lowest common denominator becomes the norm. Deregulation seems counter-intuitive, but we suspect it would bear fruit. Therapists and their clients compose an infinitely varied series of demands, dilemmas, difficulties and delights. Any attempt to put a number on the hours of supervision a particular therapist should have, even if that number is advertised as a minimum, is at best inadequate in the face of such complexity and variety.

One counter to our critique about the imposition of supervision is to ask whether we could not trust therapists to decide for themselves how much supervision they needed, whether there's a prescribed minimum or not.

This is a fair comment. Mandatory supervision, though, sets the process off on the wrong foot and is antithetical to the conditions which best promote best practice.

Assessment

We've already identified in this chapter what seems like an inevitable tension between the apparent need for some degree of external evaluation and the philosophical principle of respect for a student's self-awareness, self-knowing and autonomy. In any training process, this tension is at its keenest at the points of assessment, and the intensity of keenness rises or falls with the perceived importance of each point of assessment. Rogers (1959/1967) is ruthlessly clear about this:

> I believe that the testing of the student's achievements in order to see if he meets some criterion held by the teacher, is directly contrary to the implications of therapy for significant learning. In therapy, the examinations are set by life. The client meets them sometimes passing, sometimes failing. He finds that he can use the resources of the therapeutic relationship and his experience in it to organize himself so that he can meet life's tests more satisfyingly next time. I see this as a paradigm for education also. (p. 290)

The implications of what Rogers is saying are profound. Taken seriously, they would entail separating the training of therapists from the assessment of them, allowing life, in the form of a therapist's practice with clients, to set the examinations. While some of us are philosophically and educationally in favour of this, we recognise that it's unlikely to happen. We think there is room for movement, though, especially in the area of Rogers' phrase about students 'meeting some criteria *held by the teacher*' (our emphasis). If those who train also devise and maintain the criteria against which students are assessed, the locus of evaluation stays thoroughly external. The process of assessment becomes a much more person-centred affair if students themselves are involved in drawing up the criteria against which they're to be assessed, and if they are then a full part of that assessment. Different training courses will weigh variously the assessments of trainers, peers and students themselves. We're arguing that, whatever balance they come to, they should give student self-assessment a weight at least equal to any other component. One specific example of this concerns the assessment of congruence. On many traditional trainings, tutors assess whether a particular student is 'being congruent', or not. More recently, some trainings include the student herself in this assessment. We take the view that the *only* person who can know how congruent she is in any given moment or inter-action is the student herself. Taking Wilkins' point (1997, p. 41) that any incongruence is probably visible, external observers or assessors might, at best, assess whether a particular therapist is behaving incongruently.

Course structure

Rogers (1951), Combs (1986/2000) and Mearns (1997) have all described some of the practical implications of person-centred principles for the run-ning of training courses. If individual students are central to the process of their own learning, then it's a short and sensible step to argue that they should also be involved in discussions and decisions relating to the wider structure of the course. In practice this means, at least, that course meetings include student representatives and that all students have access through these representatives to both the agendas and the minutes of those meet-ings. In that way they can influence decisions that may affect them, they have a way of putting their own concerns on the agenda and subsequent access to a record of what happens. Other organisations have evolved other options. Within the NHS, for instance, open Board Meetings allow anyone to attend and sit round as in a theatre whilst the Board conduct their busi-ness in the middle. Members of the 'audience' can put items onto the agenda in advance and may be invited to ask questions at certain points. Minutes of meetings posted on the internet and web meetings or discussion groups prove fruitful in some circumstances. The person-centred movement has a history of using large group processes to facilitate the involvement of a whole conference or body of students (see Chapter 14), and there are a number of national and international person-centred discussion groups meet-ing both live and electronically (see Tudor and Merry, 2002 for contacts).

Student representatives have been included at course meetings from the founding of Temenos and our experience of this shows a number of things. The presence of changing representatives both slows meetings down and, in the short term, can complicate them. They bring other voices and other concerns to what can sometimes seem an already full agenda. Their pres-ence, though, is also a continuous reminder of our primary task, and so helps us stay close to what we set out to offer. Their feedback, as recipients of the training we offer, is invaluable and, because of their position within the organisation, they often articulate both concerns and solutions that we the trainers have not seen. None of this means that the process is always easy or smooth. Our different needs, agendas and concerns mean that we sometimes disagree. Student representatives often ask questions that expose philosophical differences within the trainers' group. While all of this takes time, there is at least one profoundly helpful consequence, and that is that we all learn and learn again the need to allow time for dialogue and process, and the benefits of listening thoroughly, to ourselves and to each other.

Given all that we've said so far, we want to suggest that a person-centred trainer has two main tasks. The first of these is to help students find ways of identifying for themselves what they need to learn. The second is then to help them find ways of meeting those needs.

If as trainers we're going to help students identify for themselves what they most need to learn, and what they need to learn next, we probably need to start without fixed ideas of our own about what they should learn. In phenomenological language, we need to bracket our assumptions about what people need to learn, however useful those assumptions may have been to us in the past and however reliable or extensive the experiences on which we've based them. This goes against the popular notion that teachers convey from their own store the knowledge that their students need to know, and points instead to a way of teaching that is facilitative or educative rather than instructive. The verb 'to educate' derives etymologically from the Latin *educere* meaning to bring forth or to lead out, and that's how we use the word here. Our job is to offer students opportunities that will invite them out of what they already know and into a dialogue of curiosity and experiment with what they don't yet know. This is not always as easy as it sounds. It demands of person-centred trainers a profound humility, and a willingness on their part for students to learn what they most need to learn, when they most need to learn it, and from sources both including and other than the trainer.

Once students have identified what they need to learn, a person-centred trainer's role is to help them find or develop ways of meeting those needs. Again, this is a demanding process. If we're following a curriculum, we need know only what's on the curriculum. At times, even, we need be only one step ahead of where our students are. If, instead, we're facilitating people to identify what they need to learn, there's always a chance that they'll identify needs that we are not immediately able to meet. At such times, we need to be confident enough in our own skills, experiences and resources to be able to say that we don't have the answers. Our role then is to help students find what they need from the resources around them: from books and other training materials, from other trainers and practitioners, and from each other. Just as a person-centred therapist works alongside his client, so a person-centred trainer engages in the learning process alongside her trainees as both facilitator and co-learner, open to and welcoming new learning.

This way of educating is an unusual one. As we've shown, it runs counter to some current models of teaching and places great demands on any trainers aspiring to train in a person-centred way. It also taxes the student, and that's what we want to look at now. Most students training to be therapists are adults. Most adults have experienced relatively traditional, transmissional schooling, based on the 'banking' concept of education which we discuss more fully in Chapter 10. Many will experience the person-centred training we've described as a challenge to their experiences to date and to their expectations. We need to stay sensitive to this so that the intensity of the challenge itself doesn't compromise the learning process.

Another aspect of the challenge of training to be a therapist is that learning involves change. Kosko (1994) puts it even more strongly: 'To learn is to change. And to change is to learn. You can learn well or badly. But you cannot learn without changing or change without learning' (p. 205). People training to be therapists learn many things about themselves, about the values that matter to them and about their relationships with others. They explore their own thoughts and feelings about issues such as gender, sexual abuse, suicide, spirituality, culture, violence and bereavement. They will probably question their own assumptions about, say, sexuality, and may want to explore their own sexuality in new ways. They will, in Mearns' words (1997), be 'shocked to see the extent [to] which relationships in "real life" are constructed upon incongruence' (p. 108). Any or all of these learnings will, almost inevitably, challenge the stability of life outside training. Friendships and relationships that once felt satisfying now may feel stale or restrictive. Situations that once felt tolerable may now feel untenable. Students form intense and often satisfying relationships with each other, a process which can threaten outside friends and partners and expose existing problems in those relationships. Understandably, some students choose to stay with the status quo, and train up to a certain point and no further. Those who stay the course often risk re-writing the story of their lives, with consequences that are, in the short term, at least, unsettling or worse for those around them. We have sympathy with the practice of some analytic training courses where the trainers interview both prospective students and their partners. This allows them to ask the partners whether they know what they're letting themselves and their relationship in for.

Being a therapist

As we said above, being and remaining a therapist can be a lonely business, even within a well-organised and supportive agency or practice. In the nature of their work therapists hear more than their share of distress, despair and confusion, and the ethical principle of confidentiality dictates that they don't talk much about what they hear. They are, also, often hearing and responding to experiences about which they can *do* nothing. Therapists cannot bring a lover back from the dead, or persuade a husband not to leave. They cannot arbitrate for a couple disagreeing about whether or not to have children, or reassure a client that a chronic illness will go as mysteriously as it came. The invitation to feel powerless is strong. 'What do you do when you don't know what to do?' asks Laing (1986), immediately before pointing out that 'there are more suicides among psychiatrists than in any other profession' (p. 126).

For all of these reasons, it seems essential that therapists who want to remain effective in their work and happy in the rest of their lives should attend to their own needs for support, intimacy, solitude, variety and rest. There isn't a distinctively person-centred line about any of this. It follows, though, that the more closely a therapist listens to what she is experiencing, and the more deeply she trusts the wisdom of her organism, the more likely it is that she'll both know and do what she needs to do to stay resourced in her work.

We've made the point above that from a person-centred point of view the personal development of the therapist *is* the training. It follows that the distinction between personal development and professional development is an arbitrary one. The BACP's (2002) *Ethical Framework* says that all therapists subscribing to the Framework 'should consider carefully their own need for continuing professional development and engage in appropriate educational activities' (p. 6, para. 9). Currently in the UK both the BACP and the United Kingdom Council for Psychotherapy (UKCP) require evidence of continuing professional development for continuing accreditation, and registration, respectively. On the one hand this is understandable, even laudable. We agree that therapists should take their professional development seriously, and if, as we've argued, the distinction between the personal and the professional *is* arbitrary, then a well chosen professional workshop is likely to be of personal benefit as well. On the other hand, the arguments against the imposition of supervision hold here too. Where an activity that doesn't need to be mandatory *is* mandatory, the imposition of that activity carries a message that therapists are not individually trustworthy, and can breed a culture of repression followed by resentful compliance or covert rebellion. One relatively immediate and obvious way of making sense of this state of affairs is to think that those who run the relevant sections of the BACP and the UKCP believe that professional development needs to be mandatory because therapists wouldn't engage in it if it weren't. This takes us right back to the discussion in the previous chapter about the Freudian view of human nature, and is another instance of the degree to which that view is embedded not only in the wider culture, but also in the professional culture of counselling and psychotherapy.

Belonging as a therapist

In the final part of this chapter we explore some of the issues of belonging as a therapist, in terms of both our professional and our personal identity. Who am I now I am a therapist: a professional; an employee or employer; working on my own in private practice; a partner or single; a friend, a relative, a citizen? Increasingly, the emerging therapist has more roles in life to mediate. In all of this it is important to find a way to belong and to have a sense of belonging. Indeed, some consider that having a sense of belonging and social support are crucial to positive mental health and well-being (Joubert and Raeburn, 1998).

Personal belonging

There are social and professional implications for therapists who want to continue relations with old friends or to meet new ones when those people have ideas about what you can 'do to them' now you are a 'therapist'. People often emerge from their training on a path that is different to the one they were on when they entered the process. Their perceptions of themselves and their old social contexts change; as a result, they often make further changes in their social and professional lives. We all share the experience of losing friends or partners we were once close to as a direct result of training to be a therapist. We have all met people in social settings who, on hearing the words 'counsellor' or 'psychotherapist' pour out their hearts, and others who avoid any contact. In our experience and particularly, we think, when individuals choose to be involved in the person-centred approach, these experiences and moments extend beyond the world of therapy to wider arenas in life. If we believe that we are engaged in an *approach* to life, then we subject ourselves to scrutiny, are subject to scrutiny from others, and, arguably, need more personal support for our chosen way of being.

Belonging in this context begins as a student in the peer group during the training course, perhaps especially informally, in breaks, at lunchtimes and socially. If students are close to their peers, experience a sense of group cohesion, and develop friendships during this process, it is likely that they will experience a greater sense of loss at the end of the year and the course. Forming close, trusting and facilitative relationships with others engaged in the same or similar work can act as an invaluable source of support, and continuing personal as well as professional development. This is different from having a network of colleagues to whom we might refer. Forming a network or a community, within which we feel held and supported, is a vital task for us all; and in Chapter 14 we look at the concepts of networks, networking and community in a broader social and political sense.

Professional belonging

Historically, and perhaps especially in the current climate of professionalisation, accreditation and regulation, we have the option to belong to one or more of several professional bodies or associations, depending, of course, on whether we fulfil their entry and membership requirements. These include the BACP, the UKCP and the Independent Practitioners Network (IPN). Relevant particularly to the person-centred approach, there is a British Association for the Person-Centred Approach (BAPCA) and two international associations: the Association for the Development of the Person-Centered Approach (ADPCA), and the World Association for Person-Centered and Experiential Psychotherapy and Counselling (WAP-CEPC). Other associations and organisations represent specific professional interests, such as the Association of Humanistic Psychology Practitioners (AHPP), Psychotherapists and Counsellors for Social Responsibility (PCSR) and Pink Therapy. (Contacts and websites for all these organisations may be found in the list of References.) One point we make in identifying these associations is that there are many ways of belonging. Although the BACP is the largest and most influential national organisation of individual members in the United Kingdom in its field, it is run and influenced by a relatively small number of people, and does not have a monopoly on the truth.

These and other organisations offer a variety of services, which usually include some form of benefit for membership, ethical and professional guidelines, frameworks or codes, complaints procedures and publications. Most professional associations also organise conferences which offer an opportunity for members and other professionals to keep up-to-date with ideas and developments in the field; to meet colleagues and to expand their networks; and sometimes to find like-minded people who contribute to a sense of community. Membership of professional bodies also brings with it certain obligations and responsibilities. Although we are supportive of professional bodies, we have concerns about professional hegemonies, and we encourage therapists at all stages of their career to investigate alternative bodies, to explore the terms and conditions of membership prior to joining, and to participate actively and critically in the life and work of whatever body or association you decide to join.

SUMMARY

- Training person-centred therapists is different from person-centred trainings to be a therapist.
- Person-centred training deals distinctively with personal development, skills, practice, supervision, assessment and course structure.
- The separation of skills from practice is problematic.
- Skills are relevant only in so far as they embody the therapist's values and attitude.
- Supervision is one of the ways therapists live with and learn to thrive among the paradoxes, uncertainties and intangibles of their work.
- A person-centred trainer has two main tasks: to help students identify for themselves what they need to learn, and to help them find ways of meeting those needs.
- For therapists to 'belong' in a community raises personal and professional issues of identification, association, membership and accreditation.

The Person

The person lies at the heart of the person-centred approach. In Part II we address the subject of the person. We look at the development of the person; at a person's continuing developmental needs; at personality; and at the significance of context.

On Becoming
a Person

We have taken the title of this chapter from Rogers' third book *On Becoming a Person* (Rogers, 1961/1967b). It is the second of three books which outline the fundamental philosophy, theory and practice of the person-centred approach (see also Rogers, 1951, 1980a). This chapter addresses the process of being and becoming: initially and literally, the emergence of the human being into her social world, and her continuing process of development. In the next chapter we consider how these ideas are relevant to the notion of personality, including what happens when a person has a breakdown and their personality becomes 'disordered' or in some way fragile.

The use of the term 'being' in the person-centred approach derives from existential philosophy and its emphasis on the active existence or existing of humans. This, in turn and in practice, leads to a focus on being in the present, and an acceptance of who and how we are. As organisms and human *beings* we are in a constant process of becoming, a term which reflects the *process* as distinct from the *outcome* of human potentiality. The distinction between the ongoing and unfolding process of life and the more linear approaches of 'stage theories', as well as those which focus on ends and outcomes, is a theme which runs through both this chapter and the next. It is also one which, as we shall see, clarifies the differences between what Rogers calls the *actualising tendency* and Maslow's (1954) notion of 'self-actualisation' (see Chapter 2).

The emphasis in the person-centred approach on being and becoming has led to a focus on the present and the future, and perhaps a certain scepticism about any focus on the past. Some say that psychoanalysts have the best tunes on the psychology of the past and on our individual development.

Some take a partisan stance and ignore that canon of literature. Others are suspicious of the need for a theory of child development. Given the emphasis in the person-centred approach on the present, it is certainly worth asking whether we need this particular piece of theory, and if so, why. This chapter seeks both to fill what we see as a gap in person-centred theory and, in doing so, to make the case for the relevance of such theory for our current understanding of human beings in process: being and becoming.

'The child is father of the man' (William Wordsworth)

At some point in our lives many of us become aware of patterns of feelings, thoughts and actions which, with the benefit of hindsight, we realise have not served our own or others' best interests. If, through reflection or therapy, we trace the patterns back through our lives, we often find their roots in childhood or infancy. The understanding which follows this discovery often helps us begin to change how we feel, think or behave now. Where we come from and whom we come from are fundamental human inquiries. The abundance of theories about the development of the human infant and child testify to our need to make meaning and sense of our experience. We can view such theories as stories or narratives derived from our experiences, sometimes supplemented by scientific enquiry, which serve us in this endeavour. All theories of child development are retrospective in that they focus on the past from the position of the present, and on the child from the position of the adult. All attempt to describe something about the child, including its pre-verbal expression, from the position of a sophisticated and verbal adult. This is further complicated by the fact that all such adult observers have themselves been children and are therefore informed by their own childhoods. In this sense all such theories are 'adulterated'. The Jungian analytic psychologist James Hillman is one exception to this. He writes eloquently about the seeds of the future being present in the child if only we dare to see and acknowledge them (Hillman, 1997). Until recently one of the hottest debates in the field of psychology has been whether nature (genes) or nurture (the environment, family, society), has more influence on the development of the individual. Thanks to recent research in the field of neuroscience, we now have evidence that, in the words of the neuroscientist and psychoanalyst, Allan Schore (2002), the development of a child is '100% nature and 100% nurture'. The child usually has her full complement of human abilities and inherited characteristics, talents, limitations and preferences and these will develop to their fullest potential only if she has the necessary stimulation and opportunity during crucial periods of maximum neurological development. If such stimulation and opportunities are absent during these times it is, again as Schore puts it, 'a case of use it or lose it': some potential neurological development will fail to take place or will begin only for neurons to die for lack of connection.

All schools of psychology and therapy have a theory of human development, usually identified as 'stages' or 'phases' of child and (sometimes) adult development, based on some schema: psycho-sexual development (S. Freud, 1905/1977; A. Freud, 1936/1966), developmental progression in response to unconscious phantasy (Klein, 1932/1975, 1952), the concept of individuation (Jung, 1939; Mahler, 1968), psycho-social development (Erikson, 1951/1965, 1968), cognitive development (Piaget, 1964) and, in the same tradition, moral development (Kohlberg, 1976, 1981). These theories have in common the fact that they are all stage theories: they propose a number of stages of development which the human infant/child has in some way to 'work through' and leave behind. Consistent with the rest of his theoretical framework, and in constrast with stage models, Rogers proposed a *process* model of development, in which the individual:

1   Is continously changing and growing;
2   Revisits developmental issues continuously in different ways and at different times; and
3   Has the capacity to be ever-changing in the light of her experience, a quality Rogers (1958/1967) refers to as 'fluidity'.

Before focusing on what Rogers said about human development and expanding this, we offer a brief and necessarily superficial summary of the historical background of ideas against which he wrote and thought.

The grandfathers and grandmothers: stage theories of child development

Sigmund Freud first proposed a linear progression through various stages, from infancy (about which he said relatively little), to adult maturity. After likening the neonate, or newborn, to 'a bird's egg', dominated by physiological rather than social or psychological concerns, he described the stages in this way:

▪   Oral – a time of fixation on the mouth as the primary sensory organ with which the child explores the world.

- Anal – a stage in which dealing with the process of elimination of urine and faeces is dominant in the child's inner and outer reality.
- Oedipal – in which the child becomes aware of genital and gender differences, and wishes both to engage the attention of the parent of the opposite sex and to usurp the parent of the same sex.
- Latency – from about 7 to 10, in which children prefer the company of same gender companions and appear unconcerned with sexuality.
- Adolescence – ruled by gender-specific concerns and the development of secondary sexual characteristics.
- Adult maturity.

To be 'arrested' at any stage of this development or to regress to a developmentally earlier stage was seen as immaturity.

Like Rogers, Freud was as scientific in his methods as his era allowed. He made most of his hypotheses on the basis of his observations and on the reports of his adult patients and his own children, probably the only ones available to him for this purpose. Freud's primary concern was to draw a map of the mind. He was less concerned with curing his patients. This is in contrast to, and was a point of disagreement with, his daughter, Anna Freud (1895–1982). She was the second person to offer child analysis, the first being the often unacknowledged Hermine Hug-Hellmuth (1871–1924). Anna Freud recognised that children were not 'mini adults' and that this had implications for theory and practice. The first of these is that the psychological processes which her father described as 'transference' did not operate in the same way. As we discussed in Chapter 3, transference literally means the 'carrying across' of emotions, thoughts and behaviours from the past to the present (and the person-centred approach has a different attitude to the subject). Anna Freud's point was that the child primarily loves the parents in the present and 'not only in fantasy as with the adult neurotic'. The second implication is that, since children are sent to analysis by their parents, they have to be 'won over' by the analyst. She was also concerned to ensure that the environment of the child, at home and at school, should support rather than undermine the good work of analysis, and that education should include preventive therapeutic work. These values were all in keeping with the liberal reformist circles the Freuds inhabited in Vienna in the 1920s and 30s. The other famous pioneering child analyst of this era was Melanie Klein, who fundamentally disagreed with Anna Freud in that she did not soften her language or adapt psychoanalytic techniques for the benefit of children. She both shocked and alarmed sections of the psychoanalytic community by the emphasis she placed on the sadistic, aggressive and cannibalistic phantasies[1] of the infant at the breast. Although her concern was largely with the inner phantasy life of the infant up to the age of two, she acknowledged that the response from the mother affects the inner dynamic of the child. Perhaps her own experiences, knowing herself to have been an unwanted child, and later as a mother who suffered postnatal depression, alerted her to the drama of the infant's relationship with himself and his environment.

In terms of the influence of these ideas and developments on Rogers, we know:

- That in his time in New York (1924–28) he was exposed to psychoanalysis and influenced by the work of William Healy, a Freudian (see Kirschenbaum, 1979).
- That he was influenced by the work of the psychoanalyst Otto Rank and the clinical psychologist Jessie Taft.
- That, in his years working in Rochester (1928–39), first in the Child Study Department and later in the Rochester (Child) Guidance Center, he was surrounded by psychodymanically-oriented professionals.
- That he was familiar with psychoanalytic ideas about working with children. Anna Freud is amongst a number of psychoanalysts cited in the bibliography of *The Clinical Treatment of the Problem Child* (Rogers, 1939).

We can see Sigmund Freud and these two women, arch rivals in psychoanalytic circles in early-mid twentieth century, as the founding father and mothers of modern British psychoanalysis. The passing of time and the natural generation of people and ideas means that they have since become the great-grandparents. So irreconcilable were their theoretical and technical disagreements that the profession split into Freudians, or the Viennese School as it was also known, and Kleinians. Those analysts who could see some merit in each and did not want to take an adversarial stance to either formed themselves into a group known as the Independents. Within each of these groups there have been many developments and regroupings over the years, but broadly simplified, this remains the structure of British psychoanalysis today. Jungian analytical psychologists are also a large and influential group but we have omitted them from this account because Jung

---

[1] Following psychoanalytic convention, we use the term 'phantasy' to refer to unconscious phantasy and 'fantasy' to refer to the conscious version.

did not develop his own theory of child development. He was interested in the regressed states in which people experience thoughts and feelings apparently familiar from an earlier time in their lives, and behave as if those thoughts and feelings are generated, rather than restimulated, by current events.

One of the most influential founding members of the Independent group of psychoanalysts was Donald Winnicott (1896–1971). He took an understanding of the human infant into the realms of relationship when he stated, perhaps somewhat mischievously, that 'there is no such thing as a baby' (Winnicott, 1952). He meant, in other words, that we need to consider the whole unit of mother and baby who affect and are affected by one another. An optimist, Winnicott was an unusual psychoanalyst in that he believed in the essential health and sociability of the child. He and others contributed to the development of 'object relations' which place relationship rather than biological drives at the heart of what it is be human. Object relations theory holds that our internal and external experiences affect and are continually affected by each other. Human beings are relational; the term 'object' refers to an 'other' needed to help us to experience 'I'. The 'object' might be a person, a concept such as home, an idea such as 'family', or a thing such as a house. Object relations theory flourished through the contributions of Ronald Fairbairn (1889–1964), Harry Guntrip (1901–74), Michael Balint (born Bergmann) (1896–1970) and, in the 1960s, that of John Bowlby (1907–90) and his far reaching theory of attachment.

Bowlby, along with his colleagues Mary Ainsworth, Mary Boston, James Robertson and Joyce Robertson, initiated the development of what is now referred to as 'attachment theory', drawing on knowledge from the disciplines of medicine, psychoanalysis, psychiatry and ethology (behavioural biology). He drew attention to the likelihood that the nature of the communication between mother and child which takes place through gazing into each other's eyes and through facial expression and bodily contact influences the security and sense of well-being which the child experiences. It had been suggested, and it was also Bowlby's observation through his work with adolescents, that children involved in long-term separations from their parents experienced serious long-term problems. In order to discover the process or dynamics involved, Bowlby and his colleagues began to study shorter and shorter transactions and separations of parents and children and, despite the fact that the work was ignored or derided in the 1940s and 1950s, from the 1960s onward the results of those studies have influenced policy in medicine and social care. We shall see later how the work begun by Bowlby, the theories of Rogers, and those of the developmental psychologist Daniel Stern (b. 1954), are converging in and being confirmed by current discoveries in neuroscience.

The conflict and consequent regrouping of British psychoanalysts described above helped dissolve the existing intellectual stasis. By the 1960s the affluence of America and Europe allowed people to use their resources for self-development and self-reflection. Socially this manifested most obviously in the 'hippie' movement, and professionally in the human potential or 'growth' movement. Kohut's (1971) work led to an interest in the psychology of the self and to a fundamental revision of psychoanalytic theory and practice, a revision which continues to this day in the light of ever more evidence about the nature of the mind, the body, and their relatedness. From the early 1950s, behaviourists too began to question the paucity of their thinking about the human mind, a questioning which led to what has been referred to as the 'cognitive revolution'. Postmodern cognitive theory and therapy take into account environmental influences on the self and the importance of the therapeutic relationship.

The next generation: process theories of child development

We distinguish the first generation of theories and theorists from the next generation by virtue of the narrative turn the theories took. Despite their differences, the common denominator is that this first generation developed 'stage theories' that describe the unfolding of an invariant sequence. Rogers, on the other hand, in his 'Postulated characteristics of the human infant' (written in 1956, although not published until 1959) and consistent with his overall theoretical framework, proposes a 'process model' of human development. Contemporaneously, in Britain, Bowlby began writing his famous trilogy *Attachment, Separation* and *Loss*, the three volumes of which were published between 1969 and 1980. He saw that biologically based factors dispose human beings toward relationship, the nature of which is governed by the individual's experience of their interaction with others in the environment. Bowlby stressed the life-long nature of the process of individual development through dealing with issues presented by bonding, attaching, separation and loss. Later, Stern (1985), from the tradition of self psychology and based on extensive infant observation, developed an intersubjective theory of human development. Although from different traditions, we see that Stern's work and the work of theorists developing and substantiating Bowlby's work, help develop our understanding of Rogers' postulated characteristics.

Rogers wrote relatively little about infant and child development. He published *The Clinical Treatment of the Problem Child* in 1939 after over a decade working with children with difficulties, or 'maladjustment' in the parlance of the time. If he had written it later, we imagine that Rogers would probably have talked about 'the child with problems', rather than the 'problem child'. In contrast, however, to the prevailing wisdom of the era, he writes in the first chapter:

> In this book we shall deal with the child, not with behaviour symptoms. One will look in vain for a chapter on stealing, thumb-sucking, or truancy, for such problems do not exist, nor can they be treated. There are children – boys and girls – with very different backgrounds and some of these children steal and some run away from school and some find satisfaction in sucking their thumbs, or in defying their parents or in saying obscene words, but in each case it is the child with whom we must deal, not the generalization which we make about his behaviour. (pp. 3–4)

In further challenges to the psychological establishment of the time, Rogers argues that there were other qualities at least as important as theoretical knowledge in determining the success of the helping relationship:

-   A 'capacity for sympathy which will not be overdone' (p. 281). This prefigures his later thinking about both congruence and empathy.
-   A 'deep-seated respect for the child's integrity' (p. 282). This prefigures the condition Rogers came to call unconditional positive regard.
-   The therapist should have 'a sound understanding of himself, of his outstanding emotional patterns, and of his own limitations and shortcomings' (p. 283). This prefigures the notion of congruence and provides an early argument for the necessity of therapist's personal development (see Chapter 5).

We saw in Chapter 3 how Rogers and others developed and applied these ideas. After this, and perhaps because for most of his working life he was engaged in helping adults, Rogers wrote nothing specifically about children or development other than his 'postulated characteristics' and a theory of the development of the self. Despite the apparent simplicity of the postulated characteristics, they foreshadow the later findings, also derived from observation, of developmental psychologists such as Stern and, more recently, that of neuroscientists such as Schore. In the next part of this chapter we examine Rogers' postulations in the light of some of this more recent research and thinking. Many of the hitherto accepted divisions between disciplines such as ethology, behavioural psychology and developmental psychology, as well as the more hotly debated distinctions between differing psychotherapeutic orientations, are becoming less relevant. Knowledge of processes involved in child development and the interplay between nature and nurture is expanding and, at the same time, there seems to be firmer scientific evidence for some of the earliest tenets of psychotherapy.

Postulated characteristics of the human infant

Rogers (1959) postulates that the human infant has at least six characteristics:

1   He perceives his *experience* as reality. His *experience* is his reality.
    a. As a consequence he has greater potential *awareness* of what reality is for him than does anyone else, since no one else can completely assume his *internal frame of reference.*
2   He has an inherent tendency toward *actualizing* his organism.
3   He interacts with his reality in terms of his basic *actualizing* tendency. Thus his behaviour is the goal-directed attempt of the organism to satisfy the experienced needs for *actualization* in the reality as *perceived.*
4   In this interaction he behaves as an organised whole, as a gestalt.
5   He engages in an *organismic valuing process*, valuing *experience* with reference to the *actualizing tendency* as a criterion. *Experiences* which are *perceived* as maintaining or enhancing the organism are valued positively. Those which are *perceived* as negating such maintenance or enhancement are valued negatively.
6   He behaves with adience toward positively valued *experiences* and with avoidance toward those negatively valued. (p. 222)

We have seen students and therapists alike struggle with this series of statements. We offer here our understanding of these postulations. These characteristics are assumed to be common to all human infants, whatever individual genetic or environmental factors also apply.

Everything the infant perceives is part of her experience. This is the only reality she knows, and she makes coherent sense of her individual experiences (1st postulation). Since no-one else has these particular experiences and certainly not in the same constellations, she is the only one who develops her specific view of the world. It follows that no-one can completely and fully see the world through her eyes. To put this another way, each person has a unique view of the world and is unable fully to understand the view any other person forms as a result of his own unique experiences (3rd postulation). The infant has physical and psychological needs of which she is aware and which she attempts to meet through interaction with her environment (2nd and 3rd postulations). The infant knows what feels comfortable and satisfying and what feels uncomfortable and unsatisfying. This knowledge constitutes her self-regulatory system. She demonstrates a natural preference for experiences which she perceives as pleasant over those which she perceives as unpleasant. In this as in all matters, her thoughts, feelings and behaviour are consistent with each other (4th, 5th and 6th postulations).

Rogers sees that along with all living things, the infant has an 'inherent motivational system'. Forty years on there is speculation that the attempt to minimise unpleasant feelings and to maximise pleasant ones is the driving force in human motivation (Schore, 2002). We can see pictures of the foetus responding to the stimuli of sound and light before the age at which the central nervous system is fully developed. A newborn baby will respond to an object moved above him, and it seems to be the movement itself, rather than the qualities of particular objects, to which he responds (Turnbull, 2003). We can see the whole body responding: feet, arms, nose.

The brain of the prenate and of the infant lacks a developed pre-frontal cortex with which to think in a linear pattern or to remember sequentially, but the infant does mediate its experience through sensation, feeling tone and felt levels of experience. This makes sense in that those parts of the brain which store memory related to emotional events, the amygdala and basal ganglia, develop in utero. However, it is not until later, at around 18 months and again at three years, when verbal expression is possible, that the brain develops the capacity for narrative memory. An interesting aside here is Pally's (2000) speculation that people who do not remember their childhood may have lacked explicit memory processing during their early years. They may not ever, for example, have sat with a parent at bedtime and talked about the day's events. There is some debate about the age from which infants can remember sensations and emotions. There is documented and anecdotal evidence that some adults can remember something of their births and very early events in their lives. On the other hand, Lewis, Amini and Lannon (2000) dispute this. They suggest that 'people cannot retain event memories before the age of two' (p. 114).

Assuming a full genetic inheritance and no organic damage to the infant, the capacity for organising these experiences into a coherent whole, for making patterns and perhaps predictions, continues to develop throughout life (Stern, 1985). An example from early life, translated into words, could be something like: 'When I move my eyelids it gets darker.' This capacity to create something whole or new from existing fragments manifests in the everyday and the sublime, from cooking a meal or organising a desk to composing an opera or designing a building. From the start, from conception, the prenate not only organises her experience, but 'behaves as an organised whole' with each experience or capacity affecting others. Before a child might have learned about social rules or felt the effects of conditions of worth ('I don't like you when you do that'), this organised whole is observable in most interactions. In the baby's and the toddler's full-bodied and full-voiced communications of delight or displeasure, there seem few if any discrepancies between thought and feeling and totally clear, focused communication.

Rogers' (1959) first postulation is that the infant's experience is his reality, that no-one can completely assume his internal frame of reference, and that what matters to the infant is his experience and perception, rather than any notion of an externally consensual reality. Rogers acknowledges that this is challenging for some people. He gives as an example an infant picked up by 'a friendly and affectionate person' and suggests that it is the infant's *perception*, rather than what an external adult might call the 'real' situation, which will regulate his response. Even if, over time, the infant learns that this is a friendly, affectionate person, and changes his response from fear to delight, we can observe that it is still the infant's experience or perception of the person's friendliness and affection which leads to the change in response. Whatever the adult may do to reassure and engage the infant, it is the child's perception and not the adult's which ultimately informs the child and his response.

The infant is likely to develop a preference for this person because he offers her something she values. Our increasingly familiar stranger engages with the child in a riotous game of 'throw you at the ceiling' or 'running fingers up your legs to tickle your tummy'. If the adult experienced such engagement as a child himself, he is able, with learned intuitiveness, to arouse the infant to a point of high, but bearable excitement, and to take the cue from the infant – a split second turning away of the head, or a change in the pitch of her sound – to alter the level of excitement of the game so that it stays within bearable and enjoyable limits. This is the time-honoured way that adults relate to babies. Although the general form of such games is present with few variations across cultures, there are as many particular variations as there are infant and adult pairs. In this sense these interactions are both universal and particular. In order that neither tire of this game, the adult will, almost automatically, if she has had this experience herself as a baby, vary the timing, the emphasis, the volume, or some part of the action, with each repetition. The adult might seem to have initiated this pleasurable game, but it might as often be the child's pleased greeting or insistent vocalising which has prompted it. The sensitive adult continually modifies his level of stimulation subtly in the light of the child's response and so it continues until one or both tire of the co-created game. Although it is a game and fun, such experiences are also necessary for the development of the infant's ability to self-regulate her emotions. She acquires much experience of dealing with her own excitement and of being helped to deal with it. Stern (1985) refers to this as a way in which the infant learns 'an early coping function' (p. 76). There is another important but unplanned benefit. The child learns that parts of an interaction can change whilst others remain constant, and it is still the same *kind* of interaction. This is a very useful social skill. For example: 'Hello', 'Hi', 'Everything OK?', 'Good morning', 'Alright?', 'Good afternoon', 'How are you?', 'Evening!': all are greetings, and all may be uttered in a dozen different tones and inflections and still stay recognisable within one local culture.

Stern made these observations as part of his research into how an infant develops a sense of self. He finds that a child discovers who she is and who she can become primarily through her dealings with her environment and, especially, through her relationships with significant adults. This confirms Rogers' (1959) earlier speculation that 'in line with the tendency toward differentiation which is part of the *actualizing tendency*, a portion of the individual's *experience* becomes differentiated and *symbolized* in an *awareness* of being, *awareness* of functioning. Such awareness may be described as *self-experience*' (p. 223).

The social, self-regulating infant

Stern (1985) also suggests that these jointly created experiences of adult-child relationships affect the child's development of a sense of self and come to be owned by the child. There is evidence that at ten months infants have the capacity to abstract and represent experience (Stern, 1985). When you hear the word 'holiday', for instance, you are likely to experience a series of images, thoughts and feelings in quick succession, representing a generalised sense of the experience of 'holiday'. These are unlikely to be sequential in place or time and may not correspond at all to any one particular holiday, but will have elements of many holiday experiences. The word evokes something immediately and in a generalised way. Even the pre-verbal and, argues Stern, the very young infant, develops this capacity of an organised response, or a generalised sense, as a response to repeated experiences. Describing interpersonal interactions between adults and infants, Stern found it useful to name them 'representations of interactions that have been generalised', or RIGs. He describes these as 'flexible structures that average several actual instances and form a prototype to represent them all. A RIG is something that never happened before exactly that way, yet it takes into account nothing that did not actually happen once' (Stern, 1985). The acts or the events of being cared for lead to the formation of episodic memories, but it is the *manner* of the picking up, feeding, playing with, the particular, more or less consistent qualities (joy and excitement, haste, absence through preoccupation or depression, tenderness, patience or frustration) which the child experiences, with which she forms RIGs.

To stay with the example of a game, but bearing in mind that the following point will have relevance for the whole variety of experiences, the infant who has a history of co-created happy experiences in which she was helped to manage her excitement will have a different RIG of 'the fingers marching up your body' game from one whose primary care giver has rarely played such games or has been unable to respond to her cues. The child who lacks the experience of negotiating with confidence the emotional highs and lows of this type of interaction is likely to need to interrupt the game early. She will therefore not benefit from this particular opportunity by having a different experience, even if she interacts with someone more able to attune psychologically to the shifts in her emotions. As Rogers understands it, this happens because the child moves away from negatively valued experiences, and, as Stern would suggest, because the child has a RIG characterised by discomfort and uncertainty.

Nature and nurture

Before moving on to consider the conditions thought by Rogers to be decisive in the continuing development of the child, we want to consider this statement of Rogers (1959):

> … no attempt has been made to supply a complete catalogue of the equipment with which the infant faces the world. Whether he possesses instinct, or an innate sucking reflex, or an innate need for affection, are interesting questions to pursue, but the answers seem peripheral rather than essential to a theory of personality. (p. 223)

We now know that the discoveries made by neurobiologists and other scientists about the brain of the neonate, far from peripheral, are essential to a comprehensive understanding of the development of a human personality (Schore, 1994; Solms, 1994, 1998; Panskepp, 1998; Kaplan-Solms and

Solms, 2000). Until recently, there has been a polarity between the 'nature' and 'nurture' sides of the debate about human nature, with a majority of psychotherapists and counsellors favouring, indeed developing, nurture or environmental theories. Interestingly, Freud (1885/1966) studied neurology and attempted to synthesise psychology with knowledge of the physical workings of the brain in his 'Project for a scientific psychology'. He prophesied that this work would be possible in the future, and that the disciplines of psychology and neuroscience would each aid the development of the other. Furthermore, the implications of neuroscientific research explain phenomena and help to predict the consequences of both nature and nuture. Robertson's (1952) film *A Two-Year-Old Goes to Hospital* influenced changes in childcare practices in hospitals. More recent infancy studies show some of the effects on children placed in orphanages (Provence and Lipton, 1962; Ames, 1997; Rutter, 1998).

These studies confirm that children deprived of stimulation and of regular, loving, physical contact suffer developmental arrest which is less likely to be reversible the longer the period spent in institutional care. This is so in all the following variables which have been studied: head circumference; height; weight; motor skills; sensory responsiveness and initiation; language development; reactions to people; impulse control; ability to deal with 'ordinary' changes and transitions; and ability to think both logically and generally. Most of the children studied lived in conditions of bleakness unimaginable to most of us: a bland unvarying diet; almost total physical confinement in cots in rooms with many other identical cots; attended to by uniformed staff too hurried and burdened to perform all the necessary tasks of feeding and toileting, let alone any considered 'extra' such as playing, singing, talking, or cuddling. A lack of visitors, no noise other than that generated by pain and misery, and no objects or possessions, further contributed to their deprivation. There are accounts of individual children lucky enough to receive, often by an accident of the position of their cot, a small extra amount of attention. The developmental impairment of these children has been in some way lessened. All of this seems to indicate that the current focus of developmental psychologists and neuroscientists on the role of positive experiences of communication, laughter, joy and contentment, and on the relationship of these experiences to the realisation of the fullest potential later, is well placed. It is clear that somethings need to happen in the child's environment to facilitate the development of the brain and to enable the full development of human potential and that, in some respect, timing is of the essence. Whilst some children in 'ordinary' circumstances learn to walk or talk before others, the variation in timing is not that great, although it may seem so to the first-time parent. Our human genetic inheritance ensures that unless a child sustains brain damage, pre- or neonatally, a programme of skills and capacities manifests in predetermined patterns, given a loving enough and stimulating enough environment. Black and Greenough (1986) describe two forms of interaction with the environment: *experience expectant* such as walking and talking, which will happen if the child has opportunities and stimulation during the critical periods; and *experience dependent*, which are idiosyncratic to each child and can continue throughout a lifetime. Examples of this latter type of experience might include learning a musical instrument or a second language, excelling in a sport or a craft or being good at telling jokes. Many or fewer possibilities will be inherited, but all need opportunities to flourish if they are to develop to the fullest potential. The story of *Billy Elliot* illustrates this well. The film tells the story of a young boy from a mining family who, against his family's wishes and the expectations of his class and culture, discovers his talent for dancing and is eventually accepted at a ballet school.

Long before our current understanding of the development and working of the brain, psychologists noted that many changes seem to happen around the end of the first year of life. The period of vertical locomotion coincides with what Mahler and her colleagues have named the 'practicing phase' (Mahler, Pine and Bergman, 1975), in which the child explores the world physically, moving away from the primary caregiver for longer periods and for greater distances than formerly, returning now and then for brief, reassuring contact. This coincides with one period of rapid brain development, between approximately eight months and 18 months to two years. In this period the development of the child's sense of herself in all aspects of her experience is unfolding and its particular qualities, strengths and weaknesses are modified, enhanced, or limited by the qualities of the relationships available to her, especially, but not exclusively, that with the primary care giver.

In the next chapter we review the needs and conditions under which the child develops further and the experience and structure of the human personality.

SUMMARY

- The person-centred approach offers a process model of human development and potentiality. This contrasts with other linear, progress or 'stage' models.
- Rogers developed his ideas about child and human development against a background of psychoanalytic thinking.

SUMMARY (cont'd)

- Other, more recent process theories, specifically those of Bowlby and Stern, complement Rogers' ideas.
- Rogers' early work with children provides the key element of his later theory of the conditions required for therapeutic change.
- Attachment theory and more recent research in developmental psychology and neuroscience support Rogers' postulated characteristics of the human infant.
- The human infant is social and self-regulating.
- In the light of recent research, the 'nature or nurture' debate seems to be redundant.

Personality

6

In this chapter, we continue our re-presentation of the developing or becoming person by considering other needs human beings have in order to develop. In the second part of the chapter we review person-centred personality theory and its importance for understanding people both when they are healthy and integrated, and when they are less so.

Other human needs and developments

Following his postulated characteristics of the human infant and comments on the development of the self, Rogers (1959) describes the conditions required for the development of personality. Much of what follows is as applicable to the adult as it is to the infant in that the development both of the organism and of the individual's sense of self is open to adaptation and adjustment from moment to moment, according to what a person is experiencing and integrating at whatever age or 'stage'.

The need for positive regard

Rogers (1959) writes: 'as the awareness of self emerges, the individual develops a *need for positive regard*. This need is universal in human beings, and in the individual is pervasive, and persistent' (p. 223). He speculates about whether the need is inherent or learned and makes several points about the nature of positive regard. It is interesting to read this statement in the light of modern knowledge of the role that hormones play in human relationships: 'It is reciprocal in that when an individual discriminates himself as satisfying another's need for *positive regard*, he necessarily experiences satisfaction in his own need for *positive regard*' (p. 223). Brazier (1993) too argues that the primary need is to *give* positive regard rather than to receive it.

We now know that oxytocin is a hormone which is released when nurturing physical contact takes place, whether it is a crying baby being picked up or an adult receiving a massage. It is also present in elevated levels post-coitus and in new mothers. It has been demonstrated that the endocrinal system of a baby responds directly to that of the mother (Schore, 1994). The mother feels love for the baby, experiences this as satisfying and oxytocin is released into her body. She demonstrates this sense of love and well-being in the way she handles and responds to her baby who then also feels good and whose body, in response, also releases oxytocin. The mother experiencing the baby's pleasure and satisfaction, experiences herself as a good mother and is able to feel more love for the baby, and so the cycle continues. It does not take much imagination to picture the cumulative effect of such moments which may occur in the whole variety of human interaction. As the child grows secure in her intrinsic belovedness she remains open and trusting and is likely to continue to elicit a loving response from others.

Rogers (1959) acknowledges another aspect of the potency of positive regard: '...the *positive regard* of any social other is communicated to the total *regard complex* which the individual associates with that social other' (p. 224). What he means is that a child who experiences positive regard in relation to a particular action or quality generalises that experience into a picture of how the other feels about her in total. From moment to moment the infant and small child is aware of the face of the primary care giver. Robson (1967) tells us that eye-to-eye contact plays a role in attachment between mother and child, and Winnicott (1971, p. 112) notes the importance of the maternal gaze as a mirror: '...the mother is looking at the baby and what she looks like is related to what she sees there.' After the second month the infant becomes more engaged with the mother's eyes (Maurer and Salapatek, 1976). Pupil size, taken as an indicator of interest, is often increased in women at the sight of an infant, and the sight of an infant with increased pupil size disposes a woman to care for a child. Significantly, larger pupils trigger an enlarged pupil in response (Hess, 1965). The child's ability to tolerate higher levels of emotional arousal increases throughout the first year and is supported by the pleasurable experiences of mutual gazing and, consequently, of mutual physiologically aroused states (Klaus and Kennell, 1976). The stimulation of mutual gaze, says Schore (1994), 'is an essential component in a growth promoting environment. The mother's emotionally expressive face is the most potent source of visuoaffective information, and in face-to-face interactions it serves as a visual imprinting stimulus for the infant's developing nervous system' (p. 91). By the time the child has become mobile she is able to 'read' the expression of the mother in a fraction of a second. Whatever she believes she sees there affects her continually so that she forms an opinion, subject to change as the caregiver's face changes, about what we may call her loveableness. A toddler soon learns that smiles please, and that certain behaviours earn disapproval, and so she learns to modify her behaviour. Stern (1985) argues that the child senses the other's experience of her and out of specific responses to specific events develops a view of how the other regards her as a whole person.

The development of the need for self-regard

Out of experiences of positive regard, its presence, absence, or intermittent presence, the child begins to be aware of a need for self-regard, a need to feel good about himself, and maybe even proud of aspects of himself. Initially, as we have noted, the child forms a view of himself as a mirror almost to the view he believes to be that of the significant adults in his life. Later, he begins to develop his own self-evaluative system, and although it is his own independent view, its formation and the ways in which he can or cannot allow it to be modified by current experiences depend to a large degree on the positive regard he received as an infant and small child: 'The individual thus comes to *experience positive regard*, or loss of *positive regard* independently of transactions with any social other. He becomes in a sense his own significant other' (Rogers, 1959, p. 224).

The development of conditions of worth

When people who are significant to the child appear to value some aspects of her more than others, the child learns to do likewise. A child who is praised particularly for being strong and assertive will come to value that aspect of himself more than he values an aspect which does not attract such positive attention, such as his sensitivity. He may seek opportunities to demonstrate his strength and assertiveness and attempt to avoid or minimise expression of unrewarded sensitivity. He will almost certainly avoid revealing qualities for which he has received negative attention.

When the child seeks some experiences or avoids others because she has learned to regard herself in a certain way, Rogers describes the individual as having acquired a 'condition of worth'. If a child is angry and is ignored, chastised or told he doesn't really feel as he says he does, he may try to please those around him, or at least avoid displeasing them, by trying to hide his angry feelings. He may do this despite the fact that expressing anger may feel satisfying and releasing, mentally and physically. Receiving positive regard from the significant other becomes more important than satisfying other needs of the organism: the need for approval and acceptance from his parents is in this case greater than his organismic need to express angry feelings. According to Rogers, no conditions of worth would develop if the infant always felt prized. Although some behaviour would have to be prohibited, for safety's sake and out of consideration for others, the attitude of valuing and the practice of acknowledging the child's feelings as well as those of the adult would result in the child feeling as if he had a genuine choice about his behaviour. Rogers (1959) suggests that the response of a carer to a child who had been hitting his brother might carry a message such as this:

> I can understand how satisfying it is for you to hit your baby brother … and I love you and am quite willing for you to have these feelings. But I am quite willing for me to have my feelings too, and I am very distressed when your brother is hurt … and so I do not let you hit him. Both your feelings and mine are important and each of us can freely have his own. (p. 225)

The development of discrepancies between self and experience

A child has to decide which of several possible satisfactions is most important at any one time. It could be pleasing Dad, or it could be drawing on the wall. In practice, the clarity of Rogers' response above is extremely hard to achieve consistently, and probably no-one does. To allow a toddler to choose her actions and to know their consequences has implications for the time available; for the parents' patience, which, however abundant, is always finite; for the child's safety; and for social acceptance. The parents also have their own satisfactions to weigh up: 'Am I going to parent the way I do at home or shall I consider how Grandma would feel about what might happen if he doesn't make the choice I hope for?'; 'I'd like to take more time with this and not be hurrying him up, but I'm already late for work.' Our hypothetical child, positively regarded in all aspects, and with a parent who has been fully present and responsive in the relationship, and who has been able to say: 'No. Wait. Yes … if', and to act on the consequence if the condition is not met, will have been supported in the fullest expression of herself that is consonant with appropriate consideration of others. She will therefore be aware of the many facets of herself. There are, of course, degrees of imperfection and disappointment. This is the range in which parents operate and in which children learn (see Chapter 9).

Consider again the boy whose parents disallow the expression of angry feelings or perhaps even the fact of his anger: 'That's horrible. I don't want to see that expression on your face again' or 'You can't be angry about it, she didn't mean it.' The boy learns from his parents to hold a negative value about anger, and develops a picture of himself as a person who does not feel angry or who does not show his anger. In order to maintain his self-regard, he then needs to find ways to deal with experiences which threaten the view he has of himself. When he cannot manage this, he feels anxious and is in a state of inner conflict, which Rogers describes as incongruence. A part of his experience is at odds with his beliefs about how he should be. If he is successful in suppressing anger, his family may describe him as 'placid', 'patient' or 'always in a good mood'. He may come to view himself in this light or, as Rogers would say, to adopt an external frame of reference, increasingly trusting others' opinions and evaluations above his own, and learning to disregard his own intuition, feelings and assessment. He comes to depend on his patience and buoyant mood for self-acceptance and for acceptance from others. Perhaps as he gets older, and is involved in some small conflict, others may notice that he has withdrawn and ask if he is angry. He may experience the enquiry as an accusation and deny it, or he may deny it because he does not experience as anger what others interpret as such. He may experience no change in his inner world, or a change which he attributes to some other factors. Rogers (1959) suggests that: 'experiences which run contrary to the *conditions of worth* are *perceived* selectively and distortedly, as if in accordance with the *conditions of worth* or are in part or whole, *denied to awareness*' (p. 226). So, while some children might say that they felt angry, the child in our example would not recognize the physiological phenomena of flushing and increased heart rate as clues towards what he was feeling. He would not incorporate them into his idea or picture of himself such that he could say 'I am angry.' He might say: 'I'm not like that' or 'I don't know what came over me.' This is now no longer a matter of preference or choice, but a strategy necessary to maintain emotional or psychological equilibrium. Consequently, he is no longer functioning as he was in infancy, as a whole in which all elements of his organism are consistent with each other. There is now tension and division between, in this example, an organismic or bodily felt experience, and a belief that both his own self-acceptance and the acceptance and approval of others are threatened if he conceptualises or symbolises that experience as 'anger'. This describes the development of incongruence between a person's organismic experience and his allowed picture of himself. This incongruence may manifest in varying degrees of vulnerability, tension or anxiety and in this sense is the beginning of a person-centred understanding of psychopathology and disorder. A person may also experience a tension between his experience ('I don't like this') and the idea that he imagines others have of him ('He's a good chap, he won't mind'). This threatens to undermine the integrity and stability of his self-concept. Rogers suggests that this tension generates anxiety and an increase in defences such as selective perception or a denial of all or part of the experience in order to shore up a person's sense of himself as worthy of the good opinion of himself and others. The person may come to be perceived by others as rigid, having fixed views and behaviours, or as unreliable, having an apparently distorted perception of events. Most of us have introjected more than one condition of worth and may be more or less defensive in different aspects of our experiencing. We may, for example, feel relatively comfortable talking about the end of a long and significant relationship, and not at all comfortable talking about failing an exam.

The development of discrepancies in behaviour

We could say that a boy who enjoys sport and plays football regularly is behaving in such a way as to maintain and develop his self-concept. Rogers (1959) would describe his behaviour as 'accurately symbolized in awareness' (p. 227). He enjoys playing football, he knows that he enjoys it, and he plays whenever he can. If he believes that he isn't sporty, but more of an intellectual type, and yet continues to play football regularly, we could understand his behaviour as a response to perceived conditions of worth, and as enhancing 'those aspects of the experience of the organism which are not assimilated into the self-structure' (p. 227). He may perceive his participation in a way which is more compatible with his view of himself. He may distort or select perceptions to support his self-concept: 'I only play because they can't find any one else to keep goal,' 'It's just to keep fit' or 'I'm not really part of the team.' At worst, he may even deny the experience of playing.

The experience of threat and the process of defence

A woman conceives of herself as compassionate and kind. She shops for her elderly neighbours and this both supports and extends that idea of herself. Again, Rogers would describe her behaviour as 'accurately symbolized in awareness' (p. 227). If this woman is also physically violent to her partner or her children, she risks transgressing the condition of worth that says she is acceptable only in so far as she is kind and compassionate, and threatens her self-concept, which depends for its stability on her meeting those conditions. She would become anxious if she were to allow herself to experience the discrepancy between her belief about herself: 'I'm kind and compassionate' and her experience: 'Sometimes I lash out at the people I love the most and I hurt them.' She may instead defend herself from these threatening and destabilising experiences in a number of ways. She may acknowledge only part of her experience: 'They provoked me. It was all too much.' She may distort her experience: 'I wasn't really violent. It was just a little tap.' Or she may deny her experience, in whole or in part: 'I'm not violent. Everybody knows how kind I am.' All of these processes serve to keep her awareness of her experience consistent with her self-concept, and within the bounds dictated by her conditions of worth.

This example shows some of the more common defences such as rationalisation and discounting. Rogers (1959) recognised that more extreme defences such as compensation; fantasy ('I am the Queen, so I am always right'); projection ('The neighbours are telling me to kill my father'); compulsions; phobias; as well as psychotic behaviours may also be employed to cope with the experience of threat. Essentially, Rogers (1951, 1959) construed all such defence mechanisms as taking the form of either denial, or distortion, or both denial and distortion, of some portion of our organismic experience.

The process of breakdown and disorganisation

Through common, everyday examples we have illustrated processes to which we are all subject to a greater or lesser extent. However, in some situations a person's defences may fail them and they may become extremely distressed and ultimately destabilised. Rogers (1959) notes a number of processes which occur under specific conditions:

1 If a person experiences a large or significant degree of incongruence or if it occurs suddenly, then the effectiveness of their defence is reduced or shattered. A man discloses to his sister that he remembers their father abusing him as a child; his sister realises that she has never wanted to admit that her father abused her too. She cannot reconcile this with her other memories of her father as loving and kind man. Her defences fail her and she has a breakdown.

2 'The degree of *anxiety* [experienced] is dependent on the extent of the *self-structure* which is *threatened*... a state of disorganization results' (p. 229). A man in his mid 50s has been a successful businessman all his life and provided well for his family. He is well respected in his community

and is involved with a number of local charities. He is made redundant and has little prospect of re-employment. He and his family have to sell their house and reduce the extravagances of their lifestyle. He is devastated; he begins to drink heavily and generally lets himself go. He feels like he's no longer a 'real man'.

3   In such a state of disorganisation, the person may well vacillate between, on the one hand, behaviours which are compatible and consistent with past or current experiences (such as feeling angry and scared about having being abused, or angry about having worked hard for an ungrateful company); and, on the other hand, behaviours which uphold a certain image to self and others (maintaining a universally positive memory of a father who abused, or keeping hold of the company car). The resulting behaviour may appear inconsistent and irrational, and may well be bewildering for both the individuals concerned and for those who care about them.

The process of reintegration

In order to reverse such a process of defence and breakdown Rogers (1959) argues that we need to decrease the conditions of worth and to increase unconditional self-regard. He suggests that 'the communicated *unconditional positive regard* of a significant other is one way of achieving these conditions' (p. 230), and that such communication must be in the context of empathic understanding. In this process of reintegration Rogers emphasises the significance and impact of relationship.

In this and the previous chapter we have summarised a person-centred approach to human development. More often, in our practice in whatever field of application (as therapists, teachers, consultants, receptionists, nurses, managers, and so on), we see the adult 'warts an' all'. In the second part of this chapter we consider how person-centred psychology understands personality. This is especially important and topical in the context of debates about people with personality disorders and changing legislation regarding their 'treatment'.

Personality theory

Rogers presented his ideas on personality in his book *Client-Centered Therapy* (Rogers, 1951) in a chapter entitled 'A Theory of Personality and Behavior'. The chapter comprises nineteen propositions (which we refer to throughout this book) and a schematic presentation of the 'total personality'.

The propositions are worth reading in their own right and have been 'translated' in an accessible article by Harkness (1998).

One of the definitions of personality is 'that quality which makes a being personal' (Onions, 1933/1973, p. 1561). Personality then is personal, distinctive and unique. For us this means that an individual's personality is organismic and has the qualities of the organism (see Chapter 2). In terms of personality theory, this may be represented as when a person's sense of herself is in accord with or congruent with her experience (see Figure 6.1).

At any point in our lives, arguably from conception onwards (see Piontelli, 1992), when a person is in psychological tension she is doing one of three things:

i   Distorting something about herself ('I don't want to do that; I'm so lazy').
ii Denying some aspect of our experience (having a headache and saying 'It's nothing,' or having a migraine and saying 'It's only a headache').
iii Or both.

In this case the personality may be represented as in Figure 6.2.

The overlapping area represents that part of the personality which is congruent and integrated (as in Figure 6.3).

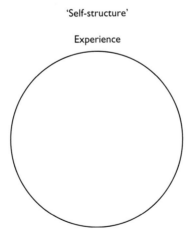

'Self-structure'

Experience

Figure 6.1   The total personality
Source: based on Rogers (1951)

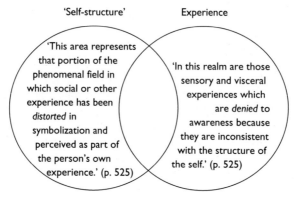

'Self-structure'   Experience

'This area represents that portion of the phenomenal field in which social or other experience has been *distorted* in symbolization and perceived as part of the person's own experience.' (p. 525)

'In this realm are those sensory and visceral experiences which are *denied* to awareness because they are inconsistent with the structure of the self.' (p. 525)

Figure 6.2 The total personality in tension
Source: Rogers (1951)

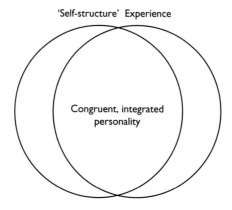

'Self-structure' Experience

Congruent, integrated personality

Figure 6.3 The total personality in some tension
Source: Rogers (1951)

This representation explains all tensions in the personality, as well as personality traits, adaptations and 'maladjustments', and, ultimately, personality 'disorder'. Furthermore, as this is a dynamic representation of 'personality dynamics', it may reflect greater or less tension (Figures 6.3 and 6.4).

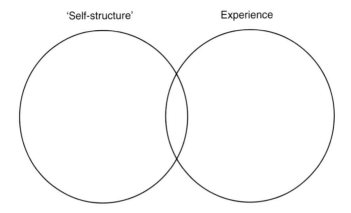

Figure 6.4 The total personality in considerable tension
Source: Rogers (1951)

Personality traits, adaptations and disorders, and the problem of diagnosis

In its *Diagnostic and Statistical Manual of Mental Disorders* (now in its fourth edition) (hence *DSM-IV*), the American Psychiatric Association (APA) (1994) distinguishes between personality *traits* and personality *disorders*:

> Personality traits are enduring patterns of perceiving, relating to, and think-ing about the environment and oneself that are exhibited in a wide range of social and personal contexts. Only when personality traits are inflexible and maladaptive and cause significant functional impairment or subjective distress do they constitute Personality Disorders. The essential feature of a Personality Disorder is an enduring pattern of inner experience and behavior that deviates markedly from the expectations of the individual's culture. (p. 630)

Other writers, such as Ware (1983) also consider personality *adaptations*, which represent a common characteristic and adaptational pattern to which the individual returns when under stress. On the basis of certain criteria, research and symptom pictures, both the APA (1994) and Ware (1983) then go on to identify and classify personality disorders and adaptations, respectively, and hence the terms and diagnosis of 'borderline personality disorder' and 'passive-aggressive personality adaptation'.

From a person-centred perspective, there are a number of problems with such diagnostic classifications:

- By focusing on the illness or 'disorder' they imply a certain health and 'order' to personality.

▪ They are based on a medical/psychiatric model of diagnosis–treatment–cure and therefore a certain prescription and differential treatment.

Furthermore, the process of diagnosis is problematic as:

▪ It places the locus of evaluation in the hands of experts which, in turn, leads to a dependency in clients.
▪ It has undesirable social and philosophical implications, to do with people (usually doctors) having undue responsibility for and control over people's lives (see Rogers, 1951).

Over the years since 1951 when Rogers responded to questions raised by other viewpoints, including the question of diagnosis, there has been much debate in person-centred circles about this subject (see Cain, 1989b). Summarising this, Tudor and Merry (2002) identify three strands of thinking in person-centred literature and practice:

1   To eschew diagnosis altogether as, for instance, Shlien (1989) does (see also Chapter 7).
2   To seek to understand other systems of psychology and medicine and, in effect, to translate their approaches to diagnosis into person-centred theory and constructs, a perspective reflected in the work of Speierer (1990).
3   To develop a person-centred approach to illness, psychodiagnosis and assessment; this is reflected in the work of Fischer (1989), Warner (1991, 1998, 2000), Speierer (1996) and Biermann-Ratjen (1998).

Moving away from diagnosis and prescription, in terms of a person-centred approach to personality, personality traits, adaptations and disorders may be understood as describing different degrees of distorted perceptions and/or denied awareness (see Figures 6.3 and 6.4). Rogers' (1951) view of psychological maladjustment is important in developing a person-centred approach to mental illness/disorder: 'psychological maladjustment exists when the organism denies to awareness significant sensory and visceral experiences, which consequently are not symbolized and organized into the gestalt of the self-structure. When this situation exists, there is a basic or potential psychological tension' (p. 510 [Proposition XIV]). We understand this basic or potential tension as incongruence. Developing this, Speierer (1990) argues that incongruence is the central construct of a client-centred concept of illness. Rogers describes three process elements of incongruence: vulnerability, anxiety and awareness. Firstly, 'When the individual has no awareness of such incongruence in himself [*sic*], then he is merely vulnerable to possibility of anxiety and disorganization' (Rogers, 1957, p. 97). Secondly, if the individual dimly perceives, or subceives some incongruence then they develop a tension or anxiety. The third process is when the individual is aware of his or her incongruence, such as 'some element of their experience which is sharp contradiction to his self-concept' (*ibid.*, p. 233). Furthermore, self-concept is not only a problem or incongruence with self, but may also be understood as incongruence with self-in-context, in relation to family, environment and culture. These three processes help us to develop a person-centred approach to mental illness/disorder. Working backwards, our awareness of our incongruence, Speierer (1990) assumes, 'is much more frequently followed by coping free of neurotic and psychosomatic consequences' (p. 339). At worst, at this level of process our incongruence may reflect a patterned incongruence (or personality trait). Secondly, if in response to some dimly perceived (or subceived) incongruence, we develop a tension or anxiety, we are likely to (mal)adjust to the situation in the way/s we used to (personality adaptation). Finally, on this schema, the individual's lack of awareness and vulnerability to anxiety and disorganisation (of the self) may be described in the clinical model as 'personality disorder'. From a person-centred perspective, it is not a question of not believing in mental illness or distress, anymore than not believing in transference (see Chapter 3), it's that we have a different perspective based on different philosophical perspectives and principles.

This view of personality 'disorder' is particularly important as, according to current mental health legislation in England and Wales (the Mental Health Act 1983), people with personality disorders are viewed as 'untreatable'. However, they are only regarded as such because they do not fall within the remit of the Act: a case of the legislative tail wagging the medical dog. In fact, people with personality disorders are eminently 'treatable' and there is a wealth of psychotherapeutic literature to support this. The prospect is that the category of 'personality disorder' will be included, in England and Wales, within the next Mental Health Act (see www.doh.gov.uk/mentalhealth.htm). In March 2003 the Scottish Parliament passed the Mental Health (Care and Treatment) (Scotland) Act 2003 which includes personality disorder under mental disorder (see www.scotland-legislation.hmso.gov.uk/legislation/scotland/acts2003/20030013.htm). The logic of this is that, overnight, people with personality disorders in England and Wales will become treatable and, in Scotland, they have already become so! The danger, of course, is that such treatment will be medical rather than therapeutic.

Having discussed the person in personality, we now, in Chapter 7, widen our focus and consider the person in context.

SUMMARY

- The person-centred approach has a theory of human development from infancy onwards.
- Rogers' assertion that positive regard is a universal need is supported by more recent evidence and research from infant psychology and neuroscience.
- A child develops conditions of worth in accordance with her perception of the values others ascribe to her various qualities and behaviours.
- Discrepancies occur between a person's experience and her beliefs about herself, leading to the establishment of defences or defensive processes.
- In particular circumstances, a person's defences may fail them, resulting in disorganisation and breakdown.
- In order to reverse these processes, Rogers advocates that a diminution of conditions of worth and an increase in positive regard facilitate an increase in positive self-regard and, ultimately, reintegration.
- Rogers developed a theory of personality and behaviour based on the experiencing organism.
- The person-centred approach generally has a critical view of diagnosis.

The Person
in Context

In this chapter we discuss the interplay between person and environment principally in terms of individual psychology. We focus especially on the significance of a person's context and environment, and their perception of it. In addressing the person in context, we take up the developmental theme of differentiation and integration begun in Part I (Chapters 2 and 3) and continued in the previous two chapters. Here we consider the problem of internalising negative introjects about such contextual/environmental issues as gender and sexuality. We follow this with a discussion and critique of oppression, and a review of the person-centred concept of personal power. We regard this as especially important in the light of critiques of the person-centred approach for not taking sufficient account of the impact of context or commonality of experience (for example Waterhouse, 1993).

Human beings in context: context in human beings

They say you can take the boy from the street
But you can't take the street from the boy.

In many ways the above lines sum up the dialogue between person and context: we can take an organism out of its original environment, and put it or ourselves in another environment. However, given that the organism has taken in its environment (literally, in the case of a baby at its mother's breast) and that that becomes part of who it is, we cannot take the environment out of the individual, nor can we remove an individual from environment. Organisms, people, are always in relationship with the context and environment within which they exist. This is not to say that we are determined or condemned by our environment. We are creative beings and we can and do change our perceptions about the particular streets of our childhood. This provides a more sophisticated view than the humanistic mantra: 'It's never too late to have a happy childhood.' As an adult it *is* too late to have a happy childhood, but it's never too late to change our *perception* of that unhappy childhood, or to change what we took or learned from it. Angyal (1941), whose work echoes throughout Rogers' 1957 and 1959 papers, offers a systems hypothesis for the way in which we may come to see our own history differently.

Here we consider the relationship between the environment or context and the organism.

Organism and context

Within the person-centred approach we often talk about 'organism' as if it is something that exists separate from the person, in the same way that the 'actualising tendency' has taken on an identity of its own. This is why we prefer the active concept and formulation that human beings, and indeed all other life forms, have a 'tendency to actualise' (see Chapter 2). Similarly, if we reify the organism or separate it from the whole person, we are in danger of imposing an artificial differentiation from our own frame of reference, and compromising our empathic understanding of the complex organisms that are human organisms. The organism is the visceral body. Our view of that body, whether our own or someone else's, is informed by history, context, society and family.

We use the terms 'context' and 'environment' interchangably. Traditionally we think about environment as the physical world about us. However, within the person-centred approach, we also talk about 'creating an environment'. This usually refers to the creation of relationship, characterised by certain distinct attitudinal qualities: contact, congruence, unconditional positive regard and empathy. Environment and context also encompass those things such as: geography, weather, politics, legal systems, economics, class, colour, race, familial circumstances and relational experiences, physical atributes, gender, sexuality, language, ability and disability, and, of course, our individual experiences and perceptions of all of the above. Whatever our original family and social contextual realities are, we have some relationship with them: easy or complicated, resolved or not. Our experience of where we come from, and the context in us, informs how we view the world, how we behave in it, and how we relate to others.

Differentiation, integration and introjection

Differentiation is the process whereby a portion of the individual's experience of their context becomes symbolised in an awareness of being, and of functioning as, a separate person. In other words we ascribe meaning to our experiences to make sense of ourselves as individuals. Such differentiation is one part of our tendency to actualise and it is central to the development of the self. Therein lies a problem. While we all need to differentiate, we also all need to be part of a whole and to experience ourselves as whole, holistic organisms, with a sense of belonging. Angyal (1941) calls this homonymy, and sees it in relation to our need to be separate and self-directing, which he calls autonomy. Most of us probably spend much of our lives exploring and coming to terms with the tensions involved in this psychological 'pull push', this tension between autonomy and homonymy. How can I be me and you be you? How can we be separate *and* together? At times we want to be a part (of each other), and at other times we want to be apart (from each other). We explore this dynamic with regard to relationships in the next chapter.

Differentiation has another significant outcome. Those who differentiate themselves, or who are differentiated, from cultural or societal norms to too great a degree, or in too provocative a domain, risk being marginalised, neglected, abused or oppressed by the undifferentiated majority.

Some people differentiate themselves, and are differentiated, from their context as female, Black or working class, for instance. For some, this is the most significant symbolised experience in their lives. For others who are also female, Black or working class, that particular difference is not as significant. Whether the 'difference' is personally significant to an individual or not, that individual still risks the consequences of being seen as different. Person-centred practice values *unconditional* acceptance, and therefore does not collude with such marginalisation or oppression. For that reason we look at anti-oppressive practice as one example of a person-centred stance.

In the literature on context, otherness, difference and oppression, and with particular reference to the field of counselling and psychotherapy, we discern three distinct strands:

1   The first is the plethora of articles, chapters and books on increasingly specialist subjects, usually in relation to different population groups, such as counselling Hispanic men (Valdés, Barón and Ponce, 1987). It's not that such articles are not interesting or informative, although despite their specialisation, they often contain problematic generalisations. The point is that they represent *only* a movement towards increasing differentiation.

From an organismic perspective, the problem with such differentiations is that they address only one aspect of somebody's identity. At the same time as we support people's right to identify as they choose, we also think it's important to see the whole person in his relational field, and to acknowledge the tendency towards homonymy as well as the tendency towards autonomy.

2   Secondly, such differences and articulations are symbolised *both* by the individual, as identity, and by society. Not all differences, of course, are equal or are *experienced* or *perceived* as equal. Historically, socially, politically and in personal relationships, 'difference' has been and still is the object of discrimination and oppression. Our ability to tolerate, accept and understand 'difference' is linked to our ability to be empathic towards ourselves and others. The second strand of literature represents this and examines a particular 'difference' such as gender, race or sexuality, and then relates ideas from that field to a particular activity such as education, therapy, or organisational work. Again, the problem with much of this analysis, from an organismic perspective, is that it tends to differentiate and separate people and issues (at times to the point of separatism). Texts on feminist therapy or gay affirmative therapy, for instance, tend to advocate and promote particular ways of working with particular groups. However, as we have seen (in Chapter 3), in the context of a discussion about diagnosis, Shlien (1989) argues that client-centred therapy has only one 'treatment' for all clients. Any special treatment or method used as a result of the differentiation or compartmentalisation of people is, therefore, antithetical to the person-centred approach. Talking about a different set of diagnostic categories, Bozarth (1998c) makes a similar point. The other problem with basing work on oppression is how to deal with the subsequent and complex relationships between different oppressions (class, sexuality or disability, for instance). This has led a number of authors to consider the implications of and for people experiencing what is referred to as double, triple and multiple jeopardy (see Moodley, 2003).

3   The third strand (which challenges both the above) comprises literature which attempts to understand difference, otherness and oppression with a view to a better understanding of the whole person, group, organisation or society. This is represented in psychology by the concept of 'cultural intentionality' (Shweder, 1990), an example of which is an article by Singh and Tudor (1997) who consider Rogers' (1957, 1959) therapeutic conditions from a cultural perspective. Whilst often critical of the subject under analysis, the direction of such work is towards holistic

understanding of a particular field. Merry (2002) captures the dilemma: 'The problem, then, is one of balancing the need to know and understand factors affecting discrimination and oppression with the need to remain consistent with one's theory and philosophy of counselling' (p. 8).

A number of ideas follow from this third perspective:

- Everyone may benefit from knowledge and awareness of both their own culture and other cultures (see Rogers, 1951).
  As we gain insight and information about other cultures and experience the ways in which different peoples live, we can begin to know and identify our own culture, a 'culture' that we may have no idea we have until we are able to compare and contrast it with the 'other'. A personal experience of one of the authors illustrates this. When living in Australia for a year, he was surprised to discover that maps of the world placed Australia in the centre, with Europe to the left and the Americas to the right. This challenged his concept that the UK and Europe were in fact at the centre of the world.

- Anti-oppressive practice is good practice for all, not just for some (see, for instance, Lago and Smith, 2003).
  Anti-oppressive practice is relevant to all, not only to the oppressed 'other' who is obviously different to ourselves. We have heard people argue, for instance that Black people, by virtue of their experience of racism, need 'more empathy'. In our view this patronises the particular person or group concerned; minimises the extent of racism, and carries a sense of personalising the solution (if only that individual felt more understood, then perhaps they wouldn't experience so much racism); and raises the question of what is 'more' empathy. For us, anti-oppressive practice is an attitude that recognises difference and separateness in each individual, even if they share a culture, skin colour or sexuality; and honours differences between as well as similarities across cultures.

- The point of any differentiation is to enable the helper to understand the experience of the person, group or organisation being helped. Mearns (1997) reminds us that 'the theory will not give a detailed understanding – only empathy can do that' (p. 46).
  This highlights the need for personal development and, for each of us, the need for an ever-deepening understanding of ourselves as the individuals that we are. It's something of paradox that, in order to understand the 'other', we must first have a degree of understanding of

ourselves as separate, different from, and not the same as the other. Having positive self-regard is a prerequisite of our regard and empathy for others (see Rogers, 1959 and Chapters 5 and 6).

Differentation and integration are usual (a word we prefer to 'normal') processes in human development. When we take something in from our environment – some learning, for instance, or an attitude – we evaluate it in relation to our internal valuing process. This process of integration defines the congruent, mature personality in the person-centred approach (see Rogers, 1951, 1959; Seeman, 1959, 1983). Conversely, when we take in something that doesn't 'fit' we may reject it and spit it out, or we may deny some other aspect of our experience, or distort our perception of ourself in some way (see Chapter 6). This kind of internalisation is often referred to as 'introjection', whereby an individual takes in the negative values and judgements of others, makes them their own, and renders them a part of their personality.

Perhaps the earliest, most significant example of the active interchange between organism and environment concerns gender and our gendered bodies. Through relationship with those around us we learn that we are boy or girl, male or female. This apparently simple learning carries with it a host of potential other learnings, not all of which are as simple. We may learn, for instance that boys are not allowed to cry, that girls are not allowed to be clever, and that boys and girls are expected to play differently, dress differently and learn different skills. Over time, these learnings become embedded or internalised, to the degree that we may think of them as fact rather than belief or construction. This is, in effect, a person-centred perspective on the process of internalising any limitation on organismic experiencing and expression.

Oppression

Just as resistance may be viewed as a failure of empathy on the part of the therapist (see Speierer, 1990 and Chapter 3), so we view oppression on a psychological level as an empathic failure towards oneself or another. This failure of empathy occurs not only between individuals but also between groups, organisations, and across cultures and nations.

We don't want to suggest that oppression is merely an internal experience or perception. There are external 'realities' too, marked by social trends and reflected in, for example, familial, racial, political, legal and religious systems. For instance, slavery was only abolished in Brazil as recently as 1888; the end of apartheid in South Africa came in 1994, less than ten years ago; in Britain, the legal age of consent for homosexuals in Britain was only made equitable with the age of consent for heterosexuals in January 2001. These external realities both express and maintain internal realities.

In this part of the chapter we consider external and internal oppression, in turn, taking as an example the issue of homophobia. We look at this in some detail in order to reflect the degree to which the law impinges on sexual conduct, and the extent of the struggle to change oppressive and intrusive legislation.

Oppression: the external reality

There appears to be no political or legal definition of oppression. The law defines discrimination, which is currently unlawful on grounds of race, sex and disability, but only in employment and the provision of services. From December 2003, the UK was due to become subject to a European Union directive that outlaws discrimination on grounds of sexual orientation and religion, but only in employment. It would then be unlawful not to employ someone because they are gay, but not unlawful not to sell them accomodation in a hotel. The same will apply to discrimination on grounds of age from 2006. Oppression, however, is wider than disrimination.

In Britain, gay sex was partially decriminalised in 1967. The age of consent for gay men was set at 21, not at 16, as it was for heterosexuals and lesbians. This inequality signalled society's disapproval of male homosexuality. Gay male sex was still seen as immoral, dangerous and to be discouraged.

Stonewall, the gay rights organisation, launched the first major legal challenge at the European Court of Human Rights (ECHR). Three young men, who were all aged 18, claimed that the unequal age of consent was a breach of their right to privacy. Stonewall followed this challenge with packed meetings and vigils at the House of Commons with celebrities, politicians, and thousands of gay men and lesbians all making the case for equality. John Major, the then Prime Minister, agreed that there would be time for a free vote on the age of consent in the course of the Criminal Justice and Public Order Bill; Edwina Currie, a backbench Conservative MP, moved the amendment. The vote for equality was lost by fourteen votes, but the age of consent was reduced to 18 for gay men. Stonewall launched its second challenge to the ECHR, *Sutherland* v *UK*. Euan Sutherland was 16 and worked with Stonewall in the campaign. Euan's case was heard by the Commission of the ECHR in May 1996 which held that the unequal age of consent was a breach of human rights. In 1997 when a Labour government was elected in the UK, the new Home Secretary gave an undertaking to Stonewall to introduce legislation in Parliament and the final hearing of Euan's case was stayed while Parliament considered the issues. In 1998 Ann Keene, MP moved an amendment to equalise the age of consent. It passed in the Commons but was defeated in the House of Lords by an alliance of hereditary peers led by Lady Young. In 1999 the government introduced a Sexual Offences Bill equalising the age of consent. Again this passed in the Commons, but was defeated in the Lords. The government then decided to use the Parliament Act 1911, which gives the Commons power to pass Bills that have been defeated in the Lords. In 2000 another Sexual Offences Bill was introduced, and when it was again defeated in the Lords the Parliament Act was used, and an equal age of consent became law in January 2001. In Scotland the Scottish Parliament voted for an equal age of consent and agreed that the Westminster Bill should extend to Scotland. (For further information see www.stonewall.co.uk.)

Taking another example – of racism – the report of The Stephen Lawrence Enquiry (referred to as the Macpherson Report after its author), identifies what it refers to as 'institutional racism'. The Report itself has no legal force, but it has been influential in shaping legislation, and in particular, the Race Relations Amendment Act 2000. The report defines institutional racism as follows:

> The collective failure of an organisation to provide an appropriate and professional service to people because of their colour, culture or ethnic origin. It can be seen in or detected in processes, attitudes and behaviour which amount to discrimination through unwitting prejudice, ignorance, thoughtlessness and racial stereotyping which disadvantages minority ethnic people. (Macpherson, 1999)

This applies equally to discrimination on the grounds of sexuality, class and disability. For instance, it has taken 25 years of debate and struggle to have Section 28 of the Local Government Act 1988 repealed, legislation which had made it illegal to promote gay relationships and 'pretended family' relationships constituted by gay people and children. This paragraph is interesting in that it refers to 'processes', which we could also call systems or 'contexts', and then moves on to 'attitudes and behaviour'. In our own definition of oppression as 'an empathic failure', we can begin to see how attitudes and behaviour become important. If the person-centred approach is an attitudinal stance, which we adopt towards another, and if our attitude or our 'reality as we perceive it', impacts our behaviour, then we live and act on what we believe. Furthermore, that we may not have considered our attitudes or beliefs towards others will impact our ability to understand them empathically, and may lead us to 'unwitting prejudice' through our 'igrorance', 'thoughtlessness' or 'racial stereotyping'.

Oppression – internalising a negative external 'reality'

We carry our context with us, in our concept of the life we have experienced and perceived as our 'reality'. This may be unproblematic, positive, or even a source of pride. A working class student goes to university, retains his accent, and returns home after graduating. A woman living far from home continues to follow her home football team. A second generation British Asian man in his thirties starts to go on holiday to India. Seamus Heaney tells of James Joyce, far from Ireland, still able to recite the names of the shops on O'Connell Street in Dublin.

The context we carry may also be less positive and even undermining. One particularly pernicious example of this is internalised oppression, whereby the subject of societal oppression oppresses himself. In other words, a person introjects a negative perception, a process which is supported by a hostile environment or the perception of hostility. This perception becomes part of a distorted self-concept and, in order to maintain this concept, the person concerned perpetuates the experience of being oppressed. Some gay men and lesbians don't 'come out' as such because of their own internalised oppression.

A man introjects negative images and beliefs about homosexuality and experiences teasing and bullying for being different, although he denies the impact of this to himself. He then comes to realise that he is gay. He experiences the choice between being true to himself, in accord with organismic valuing, or perpetuating a lie which he can no longer deny to himself. This is an organismic tension. Simply to 'come out' is not easy. He fears physical violence, rejection, homelessness, withdrawal of love from parents, family and friends. He fears being arrested as he is below the legal age of consent. The tension becomes unbearable. His organismic tendency to actualise eventually finds expression in coming out to family and friends, some of whom are supportive.

These two realities of oppression – the external and the internal – are inextricably linked: they fuel and maintain each other. From a tradition of radical psychiatry, Costello, Roy and Steiner (1988) put this well:

> In capitalist society, the leading ideological edge of Internalized Oppression is Individualism – the set of beliefs which places the individual above the collective. Behavior inspired by individualism takes a certain form as well, and that form is competition. Together, individualism and competition represent the special way our Internalized Oppression is organized, and the vehicle for its perpetuation. (p. 55)

Equal opportunities and anti-oppressive practice

For some, particularly in the public sector, the response to oppression and oppressive practice, in the form of exclusion or jokes, for instance, has been to develop forms of 'anti-oppressive practice'. This is the most recent of a number of terms and initiatives which began with legislative attempts to ensure equal opportunites for all (see Smith and Tudor, 2003).

Equal opportunities

We acknowledge and support the advances made by working class struggles, the women's movement, Black consciousness, gay liberation and disability politics in raising people's awareness and challenging the worst excesses of sexism, racism and other oppressions. However, we are critical of the political correctness of the 'equal opportunities' industry, particularly rife in local authorities and the voluntary sector, which simply adds another 'oppression' to the list, whilst doing little or nothing to make their services equally accessible. Political correctness has become an issue of compliance, and compliance breeds resentment. The 'tick list' approach to equal opportunities has put oppression on the map. The map, however, is not the territory, and in many instances this particular map has become a means of silencing debate and stifling communication. At worst, political correctness interrupts our capacity to be empathic with one another and leaves everyone less understood and less able to express themselves. Genuine encounter, which involves really meeting the 'other', is impossible if people are oppressed *and also* if people are defensive. Political correctness also labels, generalises and demeans people's experience. Not everything is to do with oppression.

> Over several years of tolerating loud parties, slamming doors, shouting and generally noisy and inconsiderate behaviour, and after several attempts to talk with his Black neighbours, during one of which he was physically

> **(cont'd)**
>
> threatened, a man went to his housing association. He asked it to fulfil its contractual obligations to install soundproofing between the flats. The 'neighbours from Hell', against the terms of their contract, refused to cooperate. Finally, he 'lost it' and, one night, took his stereo system outside and played it at full volume. The next day the neighbours went to the housing association and complained that they had been the subject of a racist attack. The original complainant neutralised this complaint by saying, in turn, that the neighbours were homophobic.

This is an example of how some people may use an accusation of oppression to deflect genuine communication. Labelling something as oppressive does not make it so. Furthermore, it locates power, and the solution to a problem, in the external world, and denies personal power (which we explore below). Generalising an incident or experience as oppressive denies the experience of both self and other. Significantly, in the above example, the claim of homophobia was a deliberate manoeuvre in response to the claim of racism, and, of course, it stopped this particular game of 'oppression'. Worst of all, such games demean people's experiences. In the above example we imagine that the Black couple concerned may well have had experiences of being oppressed. Moreover, it trivialises the real impact of racism and homophobia. In this context, we may read Ali G's refrain: 'Is it 'cos I is Black?' as an ironic commentary on the trivialising of oppression. Finally, political correctness, which, by definition, proposes a 'correct' way of being and doing things, does not allow for fluidity, process or dialogue. It implies and proposes a fixity, a stasis and an orthodoxy.

Anti-oppressive practice

Anti-oppressive practice is the current term which describes practice that in some way counters the experience of hardship and injustice. It is distinguished from anti-discriminatory practice which has a legal underpinning (see Burke and Dalrymple, 1995). In many ways the origins of anti-oppressive practice can be traced back to equal opportunities legislation, beginning in the UK in the 60s with the several Race Relations Acts (1965, 1968, 1976), the Equal Pay Act 1970 and the Sex Discrimination Act 1975. This area of law is highly complex and particularly complicated, not least involving differences within the UK (in Northern Ireland) and between the UK and the

European Union. In response to this, the Centre for Public Law (2002) conducted an independent review into UK anti-discrimination legislation, and published a draft Equality Bill and proposed a single Equality Act. Alongside social and legal developments over the past quarter of a century, terms have changed, reflecting changing ideas and ideology about the impact of oppression and discrimination, and responses to these forces.

- Equal opportunities training – Based on a view of discrimination as the unequal distribution of power, rights and resources, and encompassing discrimination on the grounds of sex, race and disability, this type of training aims to inform people participating about the relevant legislative framework, as well as local policy.
- Awareness training – In order to promote equality of consideration, some training courses are designed to promote multiculturalism. This may take the form of learning about other [*sic*] cultures, customs, food, dress and festivals. Interestingly, while this has been extended to disability awareness (see Wood, 1990), it was illegal under Section 28 of the Local Government Act 1988 to promote positive awareness of different sexualities and their culture (this Section was repealed in September 2003 as this book was going to press). However, such training has been criticised for minimising the extent and impact of institutional oppression, reducing structural inequalities to cultural 'difference', and even perpetuating stereotypes. See Gurnah (1984) and Sivanandan (1985) on race awareness training, and French (1996) on disability awareness training.
- 'Anti' training – This refers to and encompasses the various trainings which take on the particular oppression and present particular views and strategies on anti-racism, anti-sexism and so on.
  Both this and awareness training are also open to the pedagogical point that such courses are: 'often imposed (through compulsory attendance) ... [and] also promote one (right) way of "teaching" and "being aware" over more student- or participant-centred, facilitated learning' (Smith and Tudor, 2003, p. 137). These courses often induce guilt rather than genuine change on a personal, collective and institutional level.
- Anti-oppressive practice – This most recent term refers to the commonality of all forms of oppression. Also, by focusing on 'oppression' we think that it encompasses both external and internal oppression, and the relation between the two. Again, it is open to criticism, summarised by the question Wilson and Beresford (2000) pose as to whether anti-oppressive practice constitutes emancipation, or another appropriation of dissent and

resistance. Even psychotherapy, which we might expect to be unequivo-cally freeing of the individual, can be oppressive. Its history is littered with examples of ways in which social and sexual radicals and dissenters have been marginalised, pathologised, excluded and oppressed (see Robinson, 1969; Schwartz, 2000). Both therapists and clients are affected by issues of power within the therapeutic relationship. These issues are not always or satisfactorily addressed by 'equal opportunities policy' or necessarily by 'anti-oppressive practice'. For us the concept and practice of 'personal power' (Rogers, 1978b; Natiello, 1987) is a more comprehensive way of approaching and tackling these issues.

Personal power

Natiello (1987) describes the concept of personal power as: 'the ability to act effectively under one's own volition rather than under external control ... The individual is aware of and can act upon his or her own feelings, needs, and values rather than looking to others for direction' (p. 210).

This statement refers to the operation of a locus of evaluation that is internal rather than external. When individuals can trust their own experi-encing as a referent and resource in decision-making processes, they are operating from an internal locus of evaluation and are personally powerful.

Personal power is an obvious theme to emerge from the person-centred approach. It is a product of engaging in the personal development work that is involved in fully understanding concepts and theory of the approach and is one of the results of people experiencing the relational conditions in ther-apy, training, group work or living.

To have power and to be powerful are often see as contentious. However, in the person-centred approach, power and personal power are political and pertinent issues. This is encapsulated by the feminist slogan of the 1970s that 'the personal is political'. The reverse, of course, is also true: the political is personal. A number of person-centred writers (Rogers, 1978; Natiello, 1990, 2001c; Tudor, 1997) have explored the dialogue between the two halves of this statement. Within the world of counselling and therapy, Rogers moved the power away from the expertise of the therapist and privileged instead the organismic wisdom of the client. This was a move that he did not recognise as political until writing *Carl Rogers On Personal Power* (Rogers, 1978b). He opens Chapter 1 with the acknowledgement that 'this was the beginning – perhaps a late beginning – of my education regarding the politics of interper-sonal relationships' (p. 3). He goes on to say: 'I've been practising and teaching politics all my professional life and never realized it fully until now' (p. 4). Rogers had changed the role of the therapist from 'expert' to servant (see Chapter 15 of the present book). This is the result of his underlying belief in the organism and its tendency to actualise, and his trust in this tendency as a constructive and pro-social force. It follows from this belief that the therapist has no need to influence, control, diagnose or lead. She needs only to create an environment in which the organism can actualise with congruence:

> The politics of the person-centred approach is a conscious renunciation and avoidance by the therapist of all control over, or decision-making for, the client. It is the facilitation of self-ownership by the client and the strategies by which this can be achieved; the placing of the locus of decision-making and responsibility for the effects of these decisions. It is politically centred in the client. (Rogers, 1978, p. 14)

Individuals who are personally powerful are autonomous and self-directed, influenced by their own experience of the reality in which they exist, and not overly influenced by external pressures. People with power have no need to control, overpower or get their own way at the expense or cost of another. They are more likely to desire cooperation, collaboration and the organismic actualisation of the other. They are open to the experiential process of being with another, listening and understanding without feeling threatened. They are also more willing to see what will emerge from any process when no final result is required other than the one which does emerge. They're more free to choose to engage or not with another, without being driven by external pressures or introjected ideas and expectations, or the 'oughts and shoulds' of a self-concept that is incongruent with the organism. Personal power is about congruence and integration, a congruence and integration between self-concept and organismic experiencing, and ultimately is about a capacity to be empathic with oneself and another. The following is one person's experience in therapy and training over several years.

Personal power is also collaborative power, which Natiello (1990) describes as characterised by:

1   Openness (all information is fully shared).
2   Responsiveness (all needs and ideas are carefully heard).
3   Dignity (everyone is respected and considered).
4   Personal empowerment (each person has both freedom and responsibility to participate fully).
5   Alternating influence (the impact on process is shared).
6   Cooperation rather than competition.

I can track the emergence of my own power, my own shift away from the concerns of others to being more concerned about myself. This process was an extraordinarily liberating experience, as I became more aware of myself and the referents I used to live my life by. I became more and more aware of how uncentred I was/had been all my life: looking after those around me before I would or could look after myself. It was this motivation that (ironically) brought me to train as a counsellor some ten years ago. What a shock I got in the training group when 'me, myself and I' were the focus of the work! I emerged, I actualised, liberated from and dissolving self-concepts that were in conflict with my organismic experiencing, I became more of myself. Not more selfish, as I had imagined, but more accepting of myself and consequently more accepting of others. I became more open to the process of living and moved away from trying to control everything and everybody around me. My life changed in ways that I had not imagined possible. I trust myself, my own experiencing and am open to trust the experiencing of those around me. I am more moved to work with people, both as a therapist and as a trainer and experience my work as a privilege. Being witness to the emergent personal power of those I am in contact with moves me, as they come into close contact with themselves and trust in their own organismic experiencing and are too more of themselves is, for me, wonderful. The impact of the approach has been for me a revelation, an evolution and a revolution.

For us this is a person-centred approach to anti-discriminatory practice at a personal, psychological and social level, one which engages the person in their social and cultural context.

SUMMARY

- Organisms, people, are always in relationship with the environment and social context within which they exist.
- The organism is the whole visceral person, our view of which is informed by history, context, society and family.
- Our experience of where we come from, and the context in us, informs how we view the world, how we behave in it, and how we relate to others.
- Differentiation is the process whereby a portion of the individual's experience of their context becomes symbolised in an awareness of being, and of functioning, as a separate person.

SUMMARY (cont'd)

- Differentiation and integration are usual processes in human development.
- We view oppression, on a psychological level, as an empathic failure towards oneself or another.
- Oppression is both an internal experience and an external reality.
- Political correctness interrupts our capacity to be empathic with one another and leaves everyone less understood and able to express themselves.
- To have power and to be powerful are often seen as contentious issues.
- Power and personal power in the person-centred approach are political and pertinent issues.
- If individuals are personally powerful then they are autonomous, pro-social and collaborative.

Implications and Applications

III

Based on its core principles, person-centred psychology as an *approach* to life has many implications and applications, as Rogers originally suggested and indicated in his major formulation of the client-centred framework (Rogers, 1959). In this part of the book we explore four applications which have their origins in the concerns of Rogers and his colleagues: relationships, focused particularly on those between adult partners; relationships between parents and children; learning and education; and the contribution the approach makes to our understanding of the engaged and involved citizen, especially in the arenas of justice and peace.

Person to Person

We take the title of this chapter from a book first published in 1967 and written by Rogers with the gestalt therapist Barry Stevens (Rogers and Stevens, 1967/1973), with contributions from Eugene Gendlin, John Shlien (1918–2002) and Wilson Van Dusen. Rogers contributed papers on values, freedom and interpersonal relationships. In this chapter we explore these themes in the context of relationships between partners. We begin the chapter with a brief and necessarily selective history of the concept of relationship.

A brief history of relationship

All cultures over time have supported a variety of social arrangements whereby people connect, relate, form and dissolve relationships. Taking an historical view, most cultures value *relatedness* to family, tribe or community more highly than individuality: 'we' cultures have a longer history than the 'me' culture of postindustrial and postmodern affluent societies. Psychologically, we need relationships: they are the only context in which we can satisfy our human needs to love and to be loved. These needs may therefore more accurately be viewed and expressed as inter-human needs: my need to express love meets your need to feel validated, affirmed and significant, and so on (see Erskine, 1998). The *process* of relating is more significant than any one fixed idea of relationship. This emphasises what is between people, and what we create together in that dialogic relationship: it does indeed take two to tango!

As we've discussed in earlier chapters, the organism is pro-social. Rogers' (1959) view of human development as an ongoing process of differentiation also depends on our being in relationship: we cannot be fully human without being in relationship. Just as the organism cannot be understood apart from its environment and the individual cannot be known outside of his social context, neither can 'relationship' be understood outside of its social, historical context and changing construction.

As a state of being related and of kinship, 'relationship' is culturally and socially determined and historically located. For many, related means being related by blood and relationship entails some form of legal marriage. For others marriage is a relatively modern phenomenon in the history of man (*sic*), and associated with the rise of patriarchy and patrilinear societies and the defeat of matrilinear, collective societies: 'the overthrow of mother-right was the *world-historic defeat of the female sex*' (Engels, 1891/1968, p. 488, emphasis in original). The rise of patriarchy and the emergence of different forms of social organisation of relationships through different periods of history is well documented (see, for instance, Engels, *ibid.*, and Reed, 1975). For many cultures land cannot be owned, and from resources held in common for generations 'property' became the object of ownership by the individual. Private property rights were claimed through the blood lines of individual families and hence the importance of men's possession and ownership of women and children through marriage. This was, and is, further compounded by the influence of capital and class:

> In economically advanced societies, though the kinship exchange system still operates in a residual way, other forms of economic exchange – i.e. commodity exchange – dominate and class, not kinship structures prevail. It would seem that it is against a background of the remoteness of the kinship system that the ideology of the biological family comes into its own. In other words, that the relationship between two parents and their children assumes a dominant role when the complexity of a class society forces the kinship system to recede. (Mitchell, 1975, p. 378)

Significantly, the word 'family' comes from the Latin *familia* which meant the totality of slaves belonging to an individual. Thus the origin of the concept of the family lies in relationships of slavery and serfdom. Mitchell (1975) identifies four key structures involved in the subordination of women: production, reproduction (of children), sexuality and the socialisation of children; and argues that for women to achieve liberation all four structures need to be transformed. Through the centuries marriage laws have generally entailed the husband having custody of his wife's person, exclusive control and guardianship of their children, the sole ownership of her property, and the absolute right to the product of her industry. The economic benefit to men is echoed by the psychological advantage which marriage brings: in other words, both marriage and relationship are good for men's health (Kurdek, 1991), and bad for women's health (Bernard, 1976). Some of the difficulties and dissatisfactions couples experience in relationship both reflect and are due to the historical antagonisms inherent in the social organisation of family and marriage, of role, responsibility and child-rearing.

Marriage

The commonplace image of monogamous and permanent or at least serial heterosexual marriage is both limited and inaccurate. An anthropological, historical and cross-cultural view of relationships reveals a multitude of kinship relationships, including cohabitation and various marriage arrangements: between siblings and other relatives, group marriages and leviratic or 'ghost' marriages where a surviving relative took responsibility for a widow and her family and which, in some cultures, took the form of marriages between women (Reed, 1975). In Britain in the early nineteenth century, some people expressed their mutual commitment in ways that were independent and critical of the institution of marriage, which they viewed as representing laws which were clearly against natural justice (Bernard, 1976). This dissenting tradition has, in its modern expression, given rise to more personal forms of commitment and ceremony, facilitated by the Marriage Act 1994 and the Marriages (Approved Premises) Regulations 1995, which made provision for local authorities to approve premises for marriage and thus make it possible for heterosexual couples to get married in places other than churches and registry offices.

Despite the fact that the marriage rate is falling – in the 20 years between 1981 and 2001 from 49.6 per cent (per 1000 unmarried persons) to 25.6 per cent (ONS, 2002) – marriage is still popular. In 2001, 29 per cent of all marriages involved one or both parties who had been married before (Registrar General of Marriages, Divorces and Adoptions, 2001), and the institution of marriage is proving adaptable to changing social mores. The change in legislation allowing heterosexual couples to get married on licensed premises other than a registry office or church appears to have made marriage more accessible to a wider population. Also, a number of countries and states are changing laws to allow gay men and lesbians either to marry or to enjoy the same civil and fiscal benefits as those enjoyed by heterosexual couples:

- Marriage legislation, granting the full range of protections, responsibilities and benefits for same sex couples that come with civil marriage, has been adopted in Denmark (1989), Iceland and Greenland (1996), the Netherlands (2001), Finland (2002) and Belgium (2003).

- Domestic partnership registration which includes same-sex couples has been passed in Norway (1993), Sweden (1995), California (1999), Nova Scotia and Vermont (2000), Germany (2001) and the District of Columbia (2002), although there are differences in the legal and civil rights between such partnerships and marriages (see Stonewall, 1998).
- Other laws which explicitly recognize same-sex partnerships are in force in Manitoba and Quebec in Canada, in France, in some regions of Spain, and in two cantons of Switzerland.
- In 1997 in Hawaii, the Reciprocal Beneficiaries Law was enacted allowing any two single adults, including same-sex partners, blood relatives and friends to have access to a certain number of spousal rights on the state level, although none on the federal level. Although seen by some as a groundbreaking piece of legislation, several important benefits were eliminated by Hawaii's attorney general and there has been a relatively low take up (see www.buddybuddy.com).
- In February 1998 the Canadian province of British Columbia became the first jurisdiction in North America to give gay and lesbian couples the same privileges and obligations as heterosexual couples for child support, custody and access. Same sex couples already have equal rights for adoption and for access to cover under their partner's health insurance.

Add to this the increasing number of sustained and sustaining partnerships amongst heterosexuals, gay men, lesbians and bisexuals and the conclusions must be that relationship is viable, and that this viability does not depend on the institution of marriage. Such transcultural, transhistorical and modern perspectives may be viewed as attempts to reclaim genuine kinship and relationship, based on mutual relation or connection, with a degree of continuity or intended continuity, and expressed through some form of public statement of commitment.

Becoming partners: threads of permanence and enrichment

In 1973 Rogers published *Becoming Partners: Marriage and its Alternatives*. Based on interviews and people's own writing, this was Rogers' attempt to get inside the experience of partnership. In summary, Rogers identifies four threads or themes which he views as basic and 'binding', and which he defines as enriching rather than confining: dedication and commitment, communication, the dissolution of roles and becoming a separate self. We take these threads as a structure for this part of the chapter.

Dedication and commitment

Rogers clearly values dedication and commitment over permanence in relationships. Referring to marriage he comments:

> It is becoming increasingly clear that a man–woman relationship will have permanence only to the degree to which it satisfies the emotional, psychological, intellectual and physical needs of the partners. This means that the permanent marriage of the future will be even better than marriage in the present, because the ideals and goals for that marriage will be of a higher order. The partners will be demanding more of the relationship than they do today. (Rogers, 1973, p. 18)

Whereas permanence refers to a linear measurement of time and implies a certain longevity, dedication and commitment are concerned with working together in the present on the *process* of a relationship. In many ways ideals or values are the base on which couples build dedicated and committed relationships. Couples may live together for years without realising that, fundamentally, they do not share values about communication, sexuality, children, work, boundaries, emotions, or the meaning and direction of their lives. Differences discovered after years can be startling, hurtful and threatening to the fabric and future of the relationship:

> On the eve of her husband's retirement, a woman finds out not only that he hated his job but also that he feels his working life has been meaningless; he is now looking forward to spending more time with her at home. For her part, she thought that he enjoyed his job and also is worried about how much time they will be spending together. She worries that 'he will get under my feet'.

One problem with whirlwind romances and quick marriages can be that they allow partners little time to explore how compatible or incompatible their values are. In such instances couples may get 'married' before they are truly *engaged*.

We have referred already to the organismic valuing process (see Chapter 5) and this is relevant and present in a relationship also. From a person-centred perspective, values are simply the tendency of any organism – whether singular (an individual) or plural (a couple) – to show preference. Drawing on the work of Morris (1956), Rogers distinguishes between three types of values: *conceived, operative* and *objective.*

Conceived values

These are 'the preference of the individual for a symbolized object' (Rogers, 1964/1990, p. 170) such as the value of equality. Such values may be shared implicitly or agreed explicitly. Clearly a couple do not have to share or agree all their values, as successful relationships which encompass different faiths attest. Nevertheless, they do need to share, and probably agree, a conceived value about how to deal with difference: what are the 'bottom lines' in their relationship. In this sense, conceived values may be viewed as the bedrock of a dedicated and committed relationship.

A married couple have two young children: the wife is Roman Catholic; the husband describes himself as agnostic and has an active interest in Paganism. The wife wants to bring up both children in the Catholic faith; the husband does not. The children both want to be confirmed. The parents are stuck over the issue, there appears no acceptable compromise and they decide to see a couples counsellor. In deciding this and in their initial discussions, both parents agree on basic values of respect and the importance of communicating about and negotiating their differences. They then discuss the following options: both children could be confirmed in the Catholic faith; one child could be confirmed and the other not; the wife could forego that particular aspect of her religious beliefs and the tenets of the Catholic faith; the husband could convert to Catholicism. As they outline these options, the couple acknowledge that the last three options are non-viable in that they undermine the integrity of both the wife's and the husband's spiritual beliefs and, as regards the second option, the integrity of the family. In discussing his spiritual values, the husband decides that he is willing to negotiate and, after further discussion, they agree (i) that both children will attend church with their mother, be confirmed and receive communion, (ii) that the husband will introduce the children to other spiritual beliefs and values, and (iii) that each will support the other in these actions.

From the outset this vignette reflects the conceived value of mutual respect on the part of the couple, a respect which fuels their willingness to negotiate.

Operative values

These are values indicated by the organism behaviourally, and are often unspoken and even unknown. Rogers (1951) proposes that 'behavior is basically the goal-directed attempt of the organism to satisfy its needs as experienced, in the field as perceived' (p. 491). When such need satisfaction is mutual the couple appear compatible, about which Kaslow (1982) observes that:

> their well-being and harmony is apparent. They seem to exude tranquillity, a kind of inner peace, and liking of their place in the world. They may be quiet or effusive, but their confidence in loving and being loved and valued is unmistakable. They have an unselfconscious desire to please one another because there are sufficient shared paths, goals, and values … they seem to have each selected a partner with whom there is a good melding of symmetry and complimentarity [*sic*] in the relationship. (p. 523)

It is precisely this 'unselfconscious desire' which literally describes the organism's operative movement towards a mutually satisfying relationship – without necessarily much chat about it!

The person-centred approach to behaviour also provides us with an understanding of conflict and violence, whether expressed directly or indirectly. An illicit affair (as distinct from condoned or agreed relationships outside a partnership) can be understood as one individual satisfying his or her individual needs. At the same time, its effect on the partner can be devastating and traumatising. The affair may be a movement on the part of the *individual* organism towards a positively valued experience. However, as far as the organism that is *the couple* is concerned, it may well not express its tendency to actualise: the movement and 'energy' is focused outward rather than towards the partner and the relationship.

Violence is an extreme example of operative values. A man is violent. He may claim that it was an aberration: 'It wasn't me.' He may even apologise and say that he will not do it again and his partner may accept this. As regards values, violence, as an extreme behaviour, represents particular values or appraisals. Commonly, these are:

- That a man has a 'right' to violent expression, which often involves a confusion of anger with violence.

- That the man, ironically, perceives himself to be powerless: 'I couldn't help myself.'
- The partner is less important, which involves a devaluing and discounting of his or her physical, and often sexual, integrity and autonomy.

These values are all anti-organismic and anti-social. In person-centred terms, such operative values need to be explicated, probably through some separation, which takes the man out of the situation to ensure safety, followed perhaps by therapy.

Objective values

These are, literally, those values which are thought to be objectively preferable, whether or not people conceive of them as desirable. Unsurprisingly, given his commitment to subjectivity, Rogers has little to say about these values. They are most likely to be influenced, or even determined, by the dominant social organisation of relationships through marriage, heterosexuality and monogamy and by the image and experience of the relationships we take in and from which we learn: our parents, for example or images of relationships in the media. The beliefs they give rise to are, then, socially constructed. Many couples and relationships founder on the rocks of basic differences only uncovered after years. These may be differences of expectations based on personality, class, gender or culture. As surprising and distressing as such differences are, their seeds are, on reflection, often discernible in the first moments of the relationship.

> A middle class woman who had recently gone through an acrimonious separation from her partner does not understand her unwillingness to discuss and resolve their differences. In reviewing what had happened she remembers their first meeting and being slightly disappointed that her partner seemed shy and uncommunicative. For her part, her partner does not believe in counselling or in getting any outside professional or lay help, which she views with suspicion. Talking about the situation with a friend, she recognises that, in the early days of their courtship, she had not believed that the relationship would work or, indeed, that relationships are for her.

This vignette shows some differences which may be attributed to class and, ultimately, differences in values about expectations of and communication in relationship.

How people separate and maintain some degree of relationship has a profound impact on any children involved. The value of respect for differences is crucial in supporting rather than undermining each partner's separate and continuing relationship with the children, as well as the numerous decisions which still often need to be addressed jointly, such as access, education, holidays and maintenance. This value also extends to new partners who, by virtue of their 'step-parenting' role, have a relationship not only with their partner's child or children but also with their partner's ex-partner. It is also important that people understand their involvement in any relationship. Unless we have an understanding of the values we share (or not), agree (or not), and which are negotiable (or not), we do not learn from relationships and may then find it harder to integrate the experience of a 'failed' relationship with our view of ourselves: 'I just didn't realise what he was like'; 'How could I have had a relationship with someone who did that?' The sense we make of our experiences is important for whether and how we move into new relationships (or not), and for what we take into them.

In this section we have elaborated Rogers' (1973) views of dedication and commitment, underpinning them with a discussion of values. Certainly for Rogers the principal conceived value for relationship is a commitment to 'working together on the changing process of our present relationship' (p. 207). He goes on to quote Buber's (1937) view of the 'I–Thou' relationship. Buber used the phrase originally to describe the transcendent relationship between human beings and God: 'The primary word I–Thou can only be spoken with the whole being ... he takes his stand in relation ... no deception penetrates here' (pp. 3, 4, 7). Buber and Rogers met in public dialogue in 1957 and discussed the nature of relationship and, particularly, the possibilities of genuine mutuality in the therapeutic relationship (see Kirschenbaum and Henderson, 1990a; Anderson and Cissna, 1997). Rogers uses the phrase 'I–Thou' to describe the transcendent quality in relationships between people. Putting this together with his definition about working together, Rogers (1973) suggests that 'when dedication and commitment are defined in [this] manner ... then I believe they constitute the cradle in which a real, related, partnership can begin to grow' (p. 208).

Communication

If values are the bedrock of relationships, then communication may be viewed as its cement; and, of course, dedication, commitment and willingness to communicate are based on the conceived and shared value given to positive, respectful interactions. Of the four discussions in this part, this is the one about which most has already been written, as evidenced by the shelves of self-help books on relationship and communication. Here we discuss two areas of communication: gender and power, and the process of communication.

Gender and power

Much has been written within the different disciplines of linguistics, sociology, politics, biochemistry and psychology about the different ways men and women have of using language and of communicating. Focusing on heterosexual relationships, Tannen (1990) suggests that men's communication centres on 'report' whilst women's revolves around 'rapport'. More recently, this notion has found expression in a popular book *Men are from Mars, Women are from Venus* (Grey, 1993) in which the author develops the metaphor that, in their language and customs, men and women appear to be from different planets. Recent research suggests that differences in men's and women's brains affect their respective patterns of learning, language and communication. There are numerous examples of miscommunication which, according to research studies, are related to gender (see Eakins and Eakins, 1978). Couples in same-sex relationships, of course, also have difficulties in communication, but ones largely based on their learning and experience of gender roles.

Whilst all generalisations risk polarising and even reinforcing differences, there is also common recognition of these general(ised) truths. Nagging, for example, is a gender-specific term used predominantly by men of women. When a man calls a woman a nag, he usually means something like: 'I don't want to talk right now,' 'I don't want to talk anymore' or 'Leave me alone.' However, instead of making such direct statements, he labels, blames and pathologises her. This 'one-up, one-down' communication is an example of 'asymmetry' (Tannen, 1990), or the expression of men's power in relationship in the area of communication.

> Tom comes in from work; he has had a hard day, a stressful journey home in traffic and is tired. Harriet has been looking after their two young children all day. In addition she has done the cleaning, washing and shopping and has just put her feet up for the first time when Tom comes in and the

> baby starts crying:
>   **Harriet:** Will you see to her, Tom? I'm done in.
>   **Tom:** You're done in. What about me? It's all very well for you, being at
>   home all day. I've had a terrible time and I'm knackered. Can't you stop
>   her crying?

This conversation could develop in a number of ways, and could even escalate to violence. It is based on miscommunication and competition for the apparently scarce resource of rest or 'space'. Each makes assumptions about the kind of day the other has had and neither is empathic towards the other's tiredness and distress.

Although gender roles tend to remain strongly stereotypical, for some the concerns of communication between the sexes have generally moved on from the consciousness-raising of the 70s and the formulaic and politically correct language of the 80s to a more subtle appreciation of cultural complexity and diversity.

The process of communication

In response to such common miscommunication, there are numerous techniques, self-help or otherwise, which purport to help to establish or improve relationships. As such, however, they are merely the mechanical part of this particular science. Largely eschewing technique, Rogers (1959) describes the *process* of an improving relationship in which communication is characterised by:

- Increasing congruence or genuineness.
- Lack of vulnerability *in communication*.
- Increasingly accurate perceptions and
- Increasing empathy and positive regard.

He describes these processes as increasing in sensitivity, subtlety and scope as each party to the communication shows their willingness to be genuine, to understand and to show positive regard for the other. In a subsequent chapter on 'a general law of interpersonal relationship' Rogers (1961/1967a) also underlines congruence as fundamental to relationship, and in a later article on empathy (Rogers, 1975/1980) in which he discusses the interrelationship between the core conditions, he suggests that, in the ordinary interactions of life, congruence is probably the most important element.

Most self-help books on communication skills and techniques are no more than metaphorical elaborations of these qualities, values and conditions:

- *Increasing congruence*
  This requires each partner or party to be honest and straightforward in their communication. Rogers (1975/1980) identifies three elements to this:
  1 Letting the other person know 'where you are' emotionally: 'I'm tired, I'd really like a break. How can we manage that?'
  2 Confrontation, when necessary. This inevitably involves facing someone with something from a different frame of reference: 'I'm really angry you did that.' From a person-centred perspective, this is less problematic in a personal relationship than in a therapeutic one; for a discussion of confrontation in therapy, see Tudor and Merry (2002).
  3 'The straightforward expression of personally owned feelings' (Rogers, 1975/1980, p. 160).
  On this basis 'congruence is a basis for living together in a climate of realness' (*ibid.*, p. 160).

- *Lack of vulnerability in communication*
  This requires people to be positive in their communication rather than defensive: 'It's not my fault'; 'It was only because ...'; or competitive: 'Well, what about when you do ...?' When people interrupt and talk over each other, they have stopped listening, although we acknowledge also that there are cultural differences about 'interrupting' or 'overlapping' (Tannen, 1990), about which couples could usefully be aware. In addition, open and clear communication requires people to stay present-centred, to discuss the current issue without dragging past events into the present discussion, and to avoid name-calling. Of course, people are and do feel vulnerable in relationships, and a committed relationship is one in which each cares about the other's vulnerabilities and 'sore points' and does not exploit them, even or especially in moments of crisis and strain.

- *Increasingly accurate perceptions*
  This element of the process of improving relationships follows from openness in communication. As we listen, we extend and expand our understanding of the other's point of view, and are more likely to communicate accurately and specifically rather than generally. This is the basis of mediation and conflict resolution between people, cultures or

nations: being able to get alongside others and their point of view *especially* if we disagree with it (see Chapter 12). Rogers (1959) uses the phrase 'in an *extensional* manner', describing an expansive attitude which grows and includes others' perceptions and realities. This requires us to experience ourselves securely, in order that we can allow ourselves to 'enter in' to the world of the other. The problem with many attempts to resolve conflict, both personally and in the political arena, is that they often take place when one, both or all parties are feeling insecure or threatened.

Empathy or empathic understanding
This requires us to listen without necessarily or immediately responding with our own point of view. One way of developing this attitude is for partners simply to reflect back what the other has said. Often we hear what we want to hear or think we have heard. 'But you said ...' followed by 'No I didn't!' is a common sequence. Checking our understanding of what the other person has said and is meaning, and checking this *before* replying, saves a lot of time, energy and distress. It would also ruin the story lines of most television soaps! Empathy demands that we attempt to understand not only the meaning, but also the nuances of feeling, the value and the significance which the other person attaches to the subject under discussion.

Unconditional positive regard
This condition both follows from and enhances respectful communication and, as congruence, is a value as well as an attitude. One way of promoting this when a couple are not feeling very positive and are stuck in their communication is to agree a 'pause time'. Rows often entail people not listening to the other person's point of view. Instead of arguing a particular corner, a mutual agreement to listen and pause for five minutes or half an hour before responding often helps aid communication and understanding. It also has the effect of equalising unequal power relationships. In a heated argument, a man, for instance, may learn from pausing before offering a 'reasonable' reply. A woman, too, may learn from pausing before finding several ways to express her feelings.

Contact
All the previous elements or conditions require the couple to be in meaningful contact with each other, and to make time for communicating with other about the day-to-day minutiae of life as well as for more expansive discussions about the meaning and direction of their relationship. Many couples get into difficulties simply because they lose the

habit of making time for and with each other. In response, some have or make specific 'time for us', 'time to talk' or family meetings that are kept clear of interruptions.

The dissolution of roles

'To live by role expectations seems consistently in opposition to a marriage which is going somewhere, which is in process' (Rogers, 1973, p. 211). It is not roles as such but fixed roles to which Rogers objects or, more accurately, fixed attitudes to role, division and allocation. He goes on to argue that: 'to follow – more or less blindly – the expectations of one's parents, of one's religion, of one's culture, is to bring to disaster the ongoing, differentiating process of a developing partnership' (p. 211). There are a number of stage and process models which describe the development of relationships (see, for instance, Bader and Pearson, 1988). From a person-centred perspective, in which the purpose of any theory is to help an understanding of the client's experience, we are interested in those models which add to our understanding of the processes of differentiation and integration in relationship (see Chapters 5 and 6). We are also and especially interested in eliciting how the person in the relationship views roles:

- How they *experience* and *symbolise* roles in the relationship: traditional, oppressive, changing, negotiated.
- To what extent this is congruent with their own image of roles in relationship or to what extent they deny awareness or distort their perceptions.
- Where they are on a continuum from fixity to fluidity (see Walker, Rabin and Rogers, 1960; Rogers, 1958/1967).

Finally, we cannot understand roles in relationships outside of their social construction. Returning to the points Mitchell made in 1971 regarding the key structures involved in the subordination and liberation of women:

- Production – Whilst the means, patterns and nature of production have changed even in the past 30 years, and women are holding a greater variety of jobs, equal pay is still a crucial issue even in the world's leading economies. In Britain women earn 80 per cent of average full-time male hourly earnings (Equal Opportunities Commission, 1998). In the United States of America women earn on average $0.74 for every $1.00 a man earns and this worsens in terms of race: women of colour earn

$0.63 and Latinas only $0.56 (Center for Policy Alternatives, 2003). In the field of psychology, one survey showed that female psychologists were paid significantly less than their male counterparts (Burnside, 1986).

- Reproduction – This has changed dramatically with the advent of birth control and, whatever one thinks about the medical ethics, the technological advances in fertility treatment. However, in a global context, this is a partial view. For the majority of the world's women, control of their reproduction, their bodies and their lives, is disputed territory.

- Sexuality – Clearly most girls in our society are socialised into a heterosexual role. Insofar as they are offered few or no alternatives to this, their choices are limited and their autonomy compromised. This is exacerbated by Section 28 of the 1998 Local Government Act which prohibits the so-called promotion of homosexuality within local authorities, including schools.

- Socialisation of children – Despite legislation which seeks to protect children, they are still generally viewed as the property of their parents. As we discuss in the next chapter, the socialisation of children is largely a private family affair. It is arguable that increased financial support for nursery places widens the early influences on children. However, as we indicated in Chapter 5, this early schooling brings its own problems.

Becoming a separate self

Much of the discussion in the previous section also has an impact on becoming a separate self. In this section we elaborate this thread with reference to the boundaries of a relationship and then to the process of becoming a separate person in relationship.

The boundaries of the relationship

These refer to both the internal boundaries *within* a relationship, and the external boundary *around* the relationship which defines and describes it in relation to the outside world, and which provides a frame for separateness.

The boundary within the relationship describes the degree of closeness and distance between individuals. It concerns togetherness, intimacy and the mutual meeting of needs *and* separateness, solitude *and* privacy. Some cultures have neither a word nor a concept for what some would consider the luxury of privacy. If a relationship is *in process* the individuals within it stand separate *and* alongside each other, able to move apart, and come together in mutual connection and commitment.

A couple also need to address internal boundaries about issues such as sex, money and childcare. We consider it important that parents have and express to their children a clear boundary around their relationship to each other. In this way the children know that their parents have a prior and primary relationship, and that, whilst there may be differences, the parents communicate a certain consistency of parenting (Figure 8.1).

Following the breakdown in this couple's relationship, specifically due to differences in philosophy about and directions in life and consequent disagreements about work and parenting, the family constellation changed (Figure 8.2).

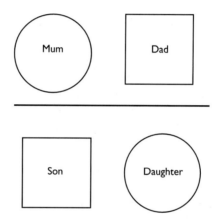

Figure 8.1 A family constellation, showing the boundary between a parent dyad and two children

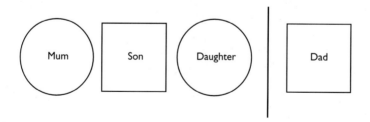

Figure 8.2 A family constellation, following breakdown in parent dyad relationship

This is how the family looked from the outside and was experienced from the inside, with the mother, son and daughter saying, partly proudly and partly resentfully: 'We're the family now,' and the father saying: 'What can I do?' The couple subsequently separated.

The problem with the new constellation is:

1   That the children come between the parents, denying and distorting aspects of the couple's relationship.
2   That it excludes the husband/father from the parenting relationship.
3   That, in elevating the children to being their mother's surrogate partner, it places them, and, in this instance, especially the son, in an inappropriate role with an inappropriate burden of responsibility.
4   That it communicates negative and disparaging ideas about men, fatherhood and relationships to the children, thereby distorting the perceptions of the next generation.

The boundary around the couple and family needs to be *definable* whilst not rigid, and *permeable* whilst not malleable. It defines the couple 'Adam and Andy' as distinct from 'AdamandAndy'. If two people only ever do things together or only ever relate to people as a couple, their relationship may be, and may be experienced as, rigid, inflexible and closed. On the other hand, two people who deny or distort their relationship or parts of it and, for instance, only ever go out separately, may not have a defined or definite relationship *as a couple*. The issue of permeability refers to how open the relationship, or family, is to outside influence. An impermeable external boundary not only excludes others but may indicate an incestuous relationship and family, in which 'privacy' masks unhealthy and inappropriate secrecy. A couple who exchange looks or use code words with each other and their children to change the subject may be unwilling to open their relationships to public comment or scrutiny by friends, neighbours or relatives. Such attitudes are, of course, supported by the traditional ideology of the private family who keep 'family secrets': 'We don't want people to know our business'; 'Don't wash your dirty linen in public'; 'We don't need help from strangers.' Authorities such as Social Services have increasing statutory powers to intervene in family lives. These powers rightly undermine such insular thinking, although they do so at a cost, as we have discussed in Chapter 3.

A couple with the kind of boundaries which nurture a committed relationship will tend to balance dependence and reliability with independence and autonomy. They are thus able to maintain an *interdependent* existence: although they are mutually supportive, one does not collapse emotionally when the other is away; although they share friends, interests and activities, they also each have their own. In short, they are both together and separate.

The process of becoming a separate self

It seems paradoxical to be describing this process in the context of a relationship but, as Rogers (1973) puts it succinctly: 'The more separate you become, the greater the chance for a strong union' (p. 212). He describes a number of themes in this process:

- Discovery of one's self – Essentially this is the discovery of one's organismic valuing process and the recognition that this is fluid and trustworthy, as distinct from holding a fixed position about one's self and one's role in a relationship. (In the first draft of this paragraph, the initial author typed 'one's elf'. The contribution of one's 'inner elf' to a relationship might warrant further discussion between partners!)
- Acceptance of self – This is movement towards accepting the changing complexity of what a person discovers about himself, whatever that might be.
- Dropping masks – In this process, the person moves away from her defences. Elsewhere, Rogers (1960/1967) suggests that clients typically move away from facades, from 'oughts', from meeting expectations, from pleasing others, and towards self-direction, 'being process' and 'being complexity'.
- Experiencing values – Each partner develops an 'internal locus of evaluation' (see earlier discussion on values).
- Growth for both – The process of becoming oneself gives permission and encouragement to one's partner.

Having discussed person-centred perspectives with regard to adult relationships, we turn in the next chapter to relationships between parent and child.

SUMMARY

- The human need for relatedness is distinct from relationship.
- Relationship – and marriage – have a social and historical context which is changing with new legislation with regard to registered partnerships.
- Rogers identifies four trends or themes with regard to relationship – dedication and commitment, communication, the dissolution of roles and becoming a separate self.
- Values are viewed as the bedrock of relationship, in which issues of gender and power are also significant.
- Rogers developed a theory and practice with regard to the process of communication and of an improving relationship.
- Sustainable relationships are ones in which roles are soluble and fluid, and in which, paradoxically, the individuals are separate and become separate selves.

Parent and Child

In Part II we looked at the developing person, and her personality, in context, on the basis that we cannot understand any person outside of or apart from her context. To paraphrase Winnicott's point about the baby and its environment we might say that there's no such thing as an individual person. Nevertheless, in order to comprehend the whole we need to have knowledge of its constituent parts: in order to understand the person we need to appreciate their environment. In this chapter we discuss the earliest relational context, that of our relationship with those who parent us and, in doing so, look at some of the implications for parenting of psychology, psychotherapy and the person-centred approach. In this chapter we use the term 'parent' to mean the primary carer of the child and do not assume primacy of biological parents.

Parenting: the adult is parent to the child

Parents and primary carers provide the environment in which children are raised, and with which they interact. This environment may encompass experiences of nurture, neglect, permission, evasion, stimulation, emotion, seduction, abuse and more. Parenting is the most important 'job' that many of us undertake in our lives. It has neither job description nor minimum entry standard. It requires no certificates of qualification, no formal education, and no preparation. Unless you are wanting to foster or adopt a child, you need no character references. It is also unpaid. In the absence of preparation, education or reflection, most new parents inevitably draw on their own experiences of being parented:

> Parents today rely almost universally on the same methods of raising children and dealing with problems in their families that were used by their own

parents, by their parents' parents, by their grandparents' parents. Unlike almost all other institutions of society, the parent-child relationship seems to have remained unchanged. Parents depend on methods used two thousand years ago! (Gordon, 1975, p. 4)

Writers on parenting such as Westman (1994) argue that introjected attitudes and beliefs are responsible for incompetent parenting which, amongst other things, uncritically supports smacking and hurting children 'for their own good' (see also Miller, 1983). Even parents who vow never to do it the way their own parents did are still reacting to their parents' ways of being, doing and thinking, and are not free from their influence. Parenting children is highly evocative. As Boukydis (1990) observes:

> The parent–infant relationship, based on all senses, can lead parents back to a more basic experience of self and may call forth early memories either at an explicit knowing level or an implicit 'felt in the body' level. What is felt, is felt in the body, at a level below ordinary awareness; before the distinction between body and mind. This kind of awareness can be disruptive. (pp. 797–8)

Despite the view that as human beings we should somehow 'know' how to parent or care for children, there is also a long history of social concern about parenting. Some of this pre-dates the (post)modern era, when fewer and fewer of us are raised in extended families or have brothers and sisters whose development we remember. There is legislation which defines child abuse and child neglect, and there are policies which determine the role of the state and its agents (social workers) in childcare. A number of psychological traditions have given rise to or informed various forms of parent education and training. In addition to all of this, parents are bombarded with advice on how to parent from numerous, popular parenting magazines. No wonder that parents, and not just new parents, can feel bewildered and undermined, struggling at critical points in their children's development to determine their own values and styles of parenting.

The impact of increasing legislation in the field of childcare, largely in response to the abuse of children mainly by parents and those *in loco parentis*, has meant that the parent–child relationship is now more than ever subject to official scrutiny and intervention. Whilst this is, arguably, motivated by the need to protect children, it breeds a professional distrust of parents. This is perhaps most clearly articulated in the work of Ayling (1930), whose view of parental ignorance and incompetence influenced professional social work significantly after the Second World War. Her solution to the perceived problem of parental incompetence was to limit the role of parents to a 'strictly bounded domain of usefulness' (p. 213) and to see the task of the child's socialisation as one for the helping professions. Winnicott (1944/1957) opposed this view, observing that 'doctors and nurses are often so impressed with the ignorance and stupidity of some of the parents that they fail to allow for the wisdom of others' (p. 138). He argued that good parenting, or 'good enough' parenting, was under threat from those who feared or envied this wisdom, a fear which appeared 'in the form of interferences such as petty regulations, legal restrictions, and all manner of stupidities' (*ibid.*, p. 138). Despite Winnicott's good offices, childcare legislation has increased and has created both defensiveness and paranoia in parents about their parenting, and a reaction against what is viewed as undue state interference in the private world of the family. We wonder whether this is in part responsible for the situation now in which many modern parents react aggressively rather than gratefully when strangers or acquaintances reprimand their children even mildly for inconsiderate or anti-social behaviour. In a book critical of *Paranoid Parenting*, Furedi (2001) discusses the effect of professional power on parental authority and knowledge: 'The very concept of parent education is founded on the premise that mothers and fathers are unlikely to understand their own needs and those of their children, and therefore need to learn these skills from specialists' (p. 169). Defensive childcare procedures regulate behaviour and attitudes. Some parents, extended family members, and especially foster parents, who are approved and therefore regulated by local authorities, are worried about hugging and comforting children for fear of misinterpretation and misrepresentation. Teachers report not feeling able to comfort a child who has fallen over in the playground and grazed her knee. Sound advice and guidelines aimed at increasing awareness of the meaning of interaction (such as forms of touching), in the context of a particular child's history (say, of abuse), become rigid rules which codify all behaviour to the point of being impersonal and anti-human. Some of the most vulnerable children are onto this and find permission in the culture of control to make or threaten allegations of inappropriate contact. We agree that guidelines are necessary, that children do need protection, and that relationships should be open to scrutiny. The current tendency, though, is to extrapolate rules and procedures from guidelines, which in themselves arise out of incidents and accidents. This codification discourages spontaneity, creativity and genuine nurturing, and offers only apparent protection from life's wounds. In person-centred terms, this culture provides an external locus of evaluation that encourages parents and those *in loco parentis* to mistrust their own experience, intuition and judgement.

Furedi is also concerned about what he sees as the paranoia of parents scared to let their children explore the world without them. Sensational reports in the media of child abductions and murder feed parents' worst fears that suffering and harm will befall their children. Most children who are murdered are killed by a parent or step-parent and most reported sexual, physical and emotional abuse of children is perpetrated in families by family members rather than strangers. This goes largely unnoted. It's not easy to contemplate that as many as one in ten of all children, from across the spectrum of wealth, class, professions and creeds, suffer in this way. This, too, doesn't make the headlines. Fear of the dangers lurking 'out there' leads parents to restrict their children's activities or to oversee them constantly. One of us knows of eight-year-old boys in two different families whose parents won't allow them to participate in any activities outside their own or someone else's home without the supervision of their own parents, even when other adults are around to supervise. It seems to us that these boys are learning that the world is a dangerous place, populated by untrustworthy people, and that their parents don't trust them to exercise their own judgement and control, or to seek help for themselves if needed.

Psychology, psychotherapy and parenting

The influence of psychology and psychotherapy on parents and parenting has a long history, dating back to the work of Alfred Adler (1870–1937) who, in the early 1930s, founded the first child guidance centres in Vienna, where doctors and psychologists worked together with parents and teachers. Adler's ideas have been developed into a psychoeducational approach to child guidance, classroom counselling and family counselling (see Oberst and Stewart, 2003 and Chapter 14 of this book). In terms of parenting this approach uses what it refers to as positive and active parenting: taking action instead of lecturing; encouraging; using natural and logical consequences instead of punishment; avoiding critical, no-win, situations; and using family councils to have formal discussions, and to agree rules. In his work Winnicott was concerned to translate the insights from object relations into ordinary language for the lay reader and, indeed, the lay listener: two of his books, *The Child and the Family* (Winnicott, 1957a) and *The Child and the Outside World* (Winnicott, 1957b), comprise talks originally broadcast on the radio by the BBC.

At the same time, the second 'force' of psychology, behaviourism, and specifically work based on the theories of B. F. Skinner, were also being applied to child-rearing and parenting. In the 1940s and 50s, feeding regimes, whereby the baby is fed at specific times and at specific intervals, and controlled crying, whereby the child is left to cry for a time before the parent responds, were both popular forms of behaviour modification, designed to increase the child's tolerance to waiting for food and to being left on his own. In effect, these practices conditioned or accustomed children to tolerate hunger and isolation. Modern science confirms that the issue of manipulation of the adult by the child does not arise, because the infant brain has no developed pre-frontal cortex and therefore lacks the equipment for such a sophisticated option. A child left to cry becomes increasingly desperate. Eventually, as a response to the stress, the brain produces cortisol, a steroid. In repeated and elevated levels this damages the development of the infant brain, affecting short-term memory and inhibiting the release of other chemicals vital to the capacity to feel interested and engaged in something. This has far-reaching consequences in later life. The infant needs physical contact which facilitates the release of oxytocin and other chemicals which help re-establish equilibrium. Rocking the buggy or talking to the infant is not enough. Although the infant may tire and become quiet, her heartbeat remains faster, from which we may speculate that she is still in distress.

Another behavioural technique is to teach manners by modelling, the intentional portrayal of what to do or how to be, with the implication that the child learns by copying. There is some evidence that children do learn more from what they see others do than from what others tell them. Parenting programmes based on the behavioural tradition tend to focus on rewards and punishments, rewarding the behaviour that the parent or adult desires, and punishing in order to modify and/or eliminate unwanted behaviour.

The humanistic tradition is reflected in parenting programmes based notably on the work of Bernard and Louise Guerney (B. Guerney, 1964, 1984; L. Guerney, 1977, 1978; Guerney and Guerney, 1989), Haim Ginott (1972/1988), and Thomas Gordon (1975), all of which we discuss below.

Parenting magazines reflect these different traditions, though mostly unknowingly. Much of their advice is based on a largely negative and suspicious view of children: that, in essence, they are 'nasty, brutish and short' and need taming and training. Articles and books on 'Daring to Discipline', 'Toddler Taming' and the seasonal 'How to Survive the Holidays' all reflect a negative view of children and a cynical and tired view of child–parent relationships. The good intentions of parents who implement some of these ideas are often misplaced because they have little or no knowledge of the developmental issues involved. An example is the fifteen-month-old told to eat up all her food or go to bed when she gets home. This not only undermines the child's developing sense of her own appetite; and fails to allow her to estimate her capacity; but also invokes a concept of the future, 'when we get home' which, developmentally, she does not have the capacity to understand fully.

In this context, and often working against it, we think it is particularly important to reclaim and represent a person-centred approach to this central human relationship. And although we focus on this relationship, much of what we say is equally relevant to any caring and responsible adult–child relationships.

Person-centred approaches to parenting

The person-centred approach, and more recent studies such as Stern's (1985) work, are important in this field because their process view of child development challenges the determinism of stage theories and the view that much of the child's future is determined in their early years. As Furedi (2001) points out:

> The proliferation of advice on every detail of a child's life has the double effect of undermining the confidence of parents and of promoting the authority of the professional. It is hard to trust yourself if you have been advised that a decision you make may have profound consequences for your child. (p. 168)

Political parties across the spectrum have used this determinism to further their own agendas by arguing that the origins of anti-social behaviour lie with poor parenting. Such supposedly causal connections fuel arguments for the licensing of parents (Westman, 1994; Campion, 1995) or the vetting of parents (National Society for the Prevention of Cruelty of Children, 1998). They also divert attention from the social, economic and political reasons for the neglect and abuse of children, abuse which can, and doesn't always, result in the neglect and abuse of the next generation.

Rogers' ideas about development and communication have influenced the education of parents mainly through the work of Thomas Gordon, who contributed a chapter on group-centred leadership and administration to *Client-Centered Therapy* (Rogers, 1951), and Bernard and Louise Guerney.

Gordon's parenting philosophy is based on what he calls the 'golden rule': 'Do unto others as you would like them to do unto you' and is reflected in his 'credo for relationships' (Box 9.1).

BOX 9.1   A CREDO FOR MY RELATIONSHIPS WITH OTHERS

You and I are in a relationship, which I value and want to keep. Yet each of us is a separate person with unique needs and the right to meet those needs.

When you are having problems meeting your needs I will listen with genuine acceptance so as to facilitate your finding your own solutions instead of depending on mine. I also will respect your right to choose your own beliefs and develop your own values, different though they may be from mine.

However, when your behavior interferes with what I must do to get my own needs met, I will tell you openly and honestly how your behavior affects me, trusting that you respect my needs and feelings enough to try to change the behavior that is unacceptable to me. Also, whenever some behavior of mine is unacceptable to you, I hope you will tell me openly and honestly so I can change my behavior.

At those times when one of us cannot change to meet the other's needs, let us acknowledge that we have a conflict and commit ourselves to resolve each such conflict without either of us resorting to the use of power to win at the expense of the other's losing. I respect your needs, but I also must respect my own. So let us always strive to search for a solution that will be acceptable to both of us. Your needs will be met, and so will mine – neither will lose, both will win.

In this way, you can continue to develop as a person through satisfying your needs, and so can I. Thus, ours can be a healthy relationship in which both of us can strive to become what we are capable of being. And we can continue to relate to each other with mutual respect, love and peace.

Thomas Gordon (1972/1978/1997)

Here we reflect on the elements and implications of Gordon's parenting philosophy, relate it directly to the theory and practice of the person-centred approach and look at other ideas about adult–child relationships.

Valuing relationship

One of the assumptions of the person-centred approach is the valuing of relationship itself. As we have seen in Chapters 1 and 2, the human organism is pro-social: we tend to move towards others, and are affected by others. As we have shown in this chapter, we develop and mature through relationship with others. The parent–child relationship is crucial at whatever age and 'stage' and is more important than 'ego', 'face' or 'discipline'. Gordon (1975) puts this well: 'I am now convinced that adolescents do not rebel against parents. They only rebel against certain destructive methods of discipline almost universally employed by parents' (p. 3).

Being separate
Although we are interrelated, we are also separate, and this is as true of parent–child relationships as of any other. Children have the right to meet their needs and to have their needs met, and so do parents. Overly controlling parenting and *laissez-faire* parenting alike deny the needs of both parent and child, and distort the relationship. Rogers' rhetorical question about whether we are secure enough to allow the other to be separate (see Chapter 1) helps us here. If a child wants to go out on a freezing day in only a t-shirt, and if he really doesn't feel cold, and doesn't get ill, whose problem is it?

Genuineness, acceptance and understanding
These conditions, which we elaborate in Chapter 7, are core to any interactive, healthy and growthful relationship. We learn them in relationship, either as children or as adults. Segrera (1984) makes the point that:

> ...a difficulty often arises when the first person (parent) has never experienced a caring relationship him/herself, and is therefore unable to offer one to a child. Many frustrations coming from the parent's life are either projected into the child or expected to be compensated through them, the result being in either case the denial of an independent development of the child's potentialities without interference of the parent's demands. (p. 21)

Many people are aware of what 'gets us going' about a particular interaction with a child: a difficult time of day, perhaps, a child at a 'difficult' age, or a particular issue. Some parents seem to know that they are more or less interested in their children at different ages. While we may recognize our behaviour, we may be less aware of its origins. For this reason we believe it is useful to reflect on this subject here. Just as many therapists are themselves in therapy, so too parents, potential parents, and their children, might benefit from having some space in which they could reflect on and understand the pain and distress of their own childhood. As Janov (1973) puts it: 'The only real protection a child has is for his parents to be healthy mentally and for this they need to be free of their own childhood pain.'

If we are feeling defensive or aggressive, acceptance and understanding are hard to find. If we also believe we have to be right, and be seen to be right, we can end up lecturing and haranguing. Ginnot (1972), a therapist and an influential parent educator, offers reassurance:

> Truth for its own sake can be a deadly weapon in family relations. Truth without compassion can destroy love. Some parents try too hard to prove exactly how, where and why they have been right. This approach cannot but bring bitterness and disappointment. When attitudes are hostile, facts are unconvincing. (p. 38)

In practical terms, Gordon (1975) advocates what he refers to as 'active listening' which helps both parent and child reflect on what's really going on, in or as soon as possible after a situation.

Organismic valuing
Key to the person-centred approach is a belief in the person's capacity to develop their own beliefs, based on 'organismic valuing' (see Chapters 2 and 5). In a discussion about values, Rogers (1964/1990) shows how they become preferences:

> The living human being has, at the outset, a clear approach to values. He prefers some things and experiences, and rejects others. We can infer from studying his behavior that he prefers those experiences which maintain, enhance, or actualize his organism, and rejects those which do not serve this end. (p. 171)

This leads to a flexible, changing valuing *process* and an internal locus of evaluation. Moreover, as the human organism is essentially pro-social, such internal valuing does not prove, as some would have it, a 'selfish gene' or, in this case, a selfish infant or child. It leads, rather, to a view that the other does matter and that 'a hurt to one is a hurt to all'. You only have to observe children's desire to love, to care and to be empathic to recognise this. In an older child, a well-developed sense of justice and fairness is further evidence.

This valuing is based on each person's subjective experience and experiencing of himself and his world. Ginott (1972) comments:

> ... first of all do not deny your teenager's perception. Do not argue with his experience. Do not disown his feelings. Specifically, do not try to convince him that what he sees or hears or feels or senses is not so. (p. 49)

Later, he says explicitly that 'our values should support faith in one's own feelings and the courage to stand alone when necessary' (p. 140). This is consistent with the values of the person-centred approach and Rogers' (1980c) view of 'the person of tomorrow'.

A parent or carer who uses 'I' language helps foster this validation of individual experience. 'I feel this, when you do that' helps children to recognise and empathise with the feelings of another and to relate these feelings to their own behaviour. 'You make me feel' only blames, and encourages a resentful and defensive response. Some of this draws on the work of Claude Steiner (1984) on what he called emotional literacy. Gordon (2001) views empathy as 'the root of emotional intelligence, maturity and self-discipline' (p. 1).

Behaviour
One of Rogers' most radical contributions to the field of psychology is the notion that all behaviour is the attempt of the human organism to get its needs met (Rogers, 1951). Children aren't bad, which is a theological construction, or naughty, which is a social one. They simply behave in ways that satisfy, or attempt to satisfy, their particular needs at that moment. Crying, spilling things, making a mess and throwing a tantrum are all attempts to get something, someone or somewhere. The difficulty of these behaviours often lies in the adult's lack of tolerance or understanding, and we include ourselves in that lack!

Resolving conflict
In any relationship, there will be conflict. The issues here are whether the parent or carer and child can tolerate the expression of difference and conflict, and whether they can resolve it. Gordon (1975) proposes a 'no-lose conflict resolution' method whereby the parent seeks to understand that the child wants to play and to make noise, acknowledges her own needs for quiet, and proposes options which satisfy both.

Filial therapy

Based on what they referred to as 'relationship enhancement therapy' (for further discussion of which see Chapter 13), Bernard and Louise Guerney developed 'filial therapy' which involves a therapist or parent educator 'teaching' the parents of often emotionally disturbed children particular therapeutic attitudes and skills including play therapy.[1] This approach to working with children has a long and distinguished history, dating back to Freud's (1909/1977) case study of 'Little Hans' in which he worked with

---

[1] We include discussion of filial therapy in this present chapter (rather than in Part IV) as it essentially involves the therapist or parent educator working with the parents who then 'work' with the children, as distinct from the therapist working therapeutically with both parties.

Hans' father and laid down the general lines of the treatment through the father. In filial therapy the parent becomes the child's primary therapeutic agent. Boukydis' (1990) model for consultation on the parent-infant relationship is another, different example of this approach. Currently we know of a number of therapists who positively refuse to work with children, preferring instead to work with the parents or carers on the basis that this best supports the child and the parent who is after all always *in loco* as a parent. In any case, in working therapeutically with children and young people who are most clearly enmeshed in a system or a number of systems (family, school), we adopt a systemic view (see Figure 9.1).

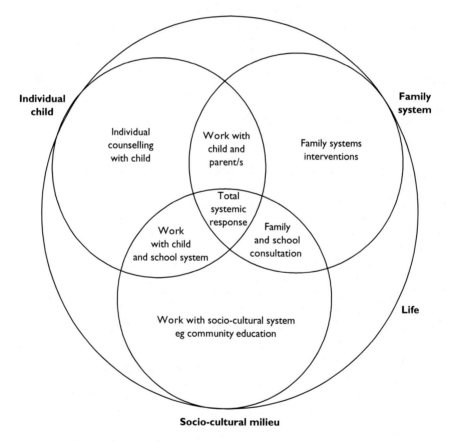

Figure 9.1   A model for systemic assessment in working with children

Source: based on Clarkson and Fish (1988)

This model for systemic assessment is based on three overlapping and inter-locking subsystems: the individual child, the family system (however defined), and the socio-cultural system – and all located within a wider, universal system of 'life'. One advantage of this model is that it locates the child within their immediate (family) context as well as their wider social context (family, culture, and so on). If a child is presented as 'the problem' or carrying the 'sick role' within the family, the therapist or educator, using this systemic model, has a wider perspective and at least seven options for planning their response. Minuchin (1974) compares 'a therapist working within the framework of systemic family therapy ... to a technician with a zoom lens. He can zoom in for a close-up whenever he wishes to study the intrapsychic field, but he can also observe with a broader focus' (p. 3). In this context filial therapy may be viewed as work with the family system, in this case with the parents.

In a contribution to a volume on client-centred therapy and the person-centred approach Guerney (1984) describes the attitudes and skills of structuring, empathy/warmth/acceptance, allowing self-direction, and setting/enforcing limits. Parents are taught primarily through demonstration and supervision of their play sessions with their own children, with sessions at the clinic being supervised live and home sessions supervised through the report of the parent/s. Teaching takes place with one or both parents or in and with groups of parents. Guerney (1984) is clear that the goals of filial therapy:

> go beyond the elimination of pathology. They include transformation of the relationship into a strong, positive one in which gains will be maintained over time ... Filial therapy is not only a non-threatening form of therapy, it is generally an inspiring form of therapy. (p. 262)

Filial therapy has been used especially in the training of foster parents (see for example Guerney, 1977); and with the parents of underachieving black elementary schoolchildren (Hatch, 1983). It has been extensively researched (see Guerney, 1984; Barrett-Lennard, 1998), and is the subject of at least two doctoral theses, with results showing significant reduction in symptomatology and other improvements, including, in one study, par-ental empathy and self-esteem, and the child's self-concept (Rennie and Landreth, 2000). Similarly, Boukydis' (1990) consultation model, starting from a respect for parents' experiencing, aims to enhance parental self-reflection and understanding the infant's process.

Having explored our earliest context, that of our relationship with our parents or carers, we next move beyond the home to the first broader context of education and school.

SUMMARY

- Parents/carers are the immediate environment for the developing child.
- Parents often parent on the basis of introjected attitudes and beliefs.
- Social concern and social policy about the safety and protection of children has subjected the parent-child relationship to more scrutiny and intervention than ever.
- Authors as diverse as Winnicott and Furedi promote positive, not paranoid, views of parenting.
- The influence of different psychological traditions on ideas about parenting may be discerned in the literature from academic books to articles in popular magazines.
- Person-centred principles may be applied to parenting.
- Filial therapy is a form of intervention whereby the parent becomes the child's primary therapeutic agent.

Freedom
to Learn

10

We take the title of this chapter from Rogers' (1969) groundbreaking work on education and learning, which he later revised (Rogers, 1983). In the first part of this chapter we introduce Rogers' ideas about education, linking these (as he himself did) with the work of the Brazilian educator and revolutionary Paolo Freire (1921–97) who worked with illiterate peasants before being expelled from Brazil following the military junta in 1964. Rogers' ideas on education have parallels with the work of Freire (1967/1976, 1972). We update these contributions in the light of recent developments in thinking about education. In the second part we present some contemporary critiques of schooling as distinct from education, critiques which are consistent with the challenge of the person-centred approach to education (see Chapter 5). As well as colliding with inequalities and inflexibility in our own educational experience, some of us have experienced inspired and inspiring teaching. We offer our critique of schooling as a contribution to the ongoing debates and in support of all teachers who sometimes feel that their creativity is constrained or drained by the requirements of educational policies and other systems. In the third part we consider life-long learning as an application of a person-centred approach to education.

Education: a person-centred perspective

The first thing that strikes us about the phrase 'freedom to learn' is that it contains two challenges to traditional views of education, teaching and training. The first challenge is that education is essentially about learning, which places the learner or student at the centre of the process, and not the teacher, the training or the curriculum. The second is that in order to learn we need freedom, a state and a process which encompasses social, political, physical and intellectual freedom. One of Freire's books, significantly begun in prison, is titled *Education as The Practice of Freedom* (Freire, 1967/1976). It is clear that if students have to learn particular bits of knowledge or skills, and if teachers are obliged to teach according to an externally determined and imposed curriculum, then no-one is genuinely free to learn, to teach, or to learn about freedom.

As with any of its applications, a person-centred approach to education is consistent with its principles (see Sanders, 2000 and our Introduction):

- It gives primacy to the student or trainee's tendency to actualise as they negotiate their learning.
- It asserts the necessity and sufficiency of the therapeutic or facilitative conditions in the learning environment, although Patterson (1989/ 2000) says that in teaching 'the relationship is necessary but not usually sufficient' (p. 96).
- It gives primacy to the non-directive attitude, at least in the content of education.

This approach 'represents a radical shift in educational philosophy and practice which is antithetical to concepts of education which create a dependent relationship between "expert" teacher and ignorant student, which are curriculum led, and which seek to "ambush" the student through formal examination' (Tudor and Merry, 2002, p. 45).

In his major theoretical formulation of the (then) 'client-centred framework' Rogers (1959) places at his centre of his theory of therapy the conditions, process and outcomes of therapy (see Chapter 7). He writes them in an 'If…, then …' formulation: 'If certain conditions are met, then a certain process ensues, and if this process develops, then certain outcomes will follow.' The same is true for the parallel process of learning. This changes the focus of education (and training) from outcomes and outcome measures to prioritising the creation and maintenance of necessary and sufficient conditions for a learning environment. Here, briefly, we consider the conditions, process and outcomes of education.

The necessary and sufficient conditions of and for learning

1 *That two persons are in contact*
   This reminds us that the quality of contact between the teacher or trainer and the pupil or student, and amongst the students themselves,

is crucial to the learning environment and process. Both the attitude of the teacher or facilitator and the ambience of the learning environment are important in this respect.

2   *That the first person, whom we shall term the student or participant, is curious*
    We have translated the notion of incongruence in this context as curiosity, as this more accurately represents the discrepancy between what the student currently knows and their desired state of knowledge, skills and experience. Whilst students may be anxious, they are not necessarily so. If they are genuinely free to learn, then they are more likely to be curious than anxious. Indeed, students who are anxious are less likely to be open to learning or less able to take in and process information and their experiences. This condition reminds us that the pupil, student, trainee or adult learner is almost certain to have had some previous experiences of education. Often these will have been based on a very different philosophy (to that of the person-centred approach) of 'being taught'. It may have been neglectful of that person's abilities, talents and skills, and may even have been abusive. In our experience as trainers this personal history of education often emerges initially as a certain suspicion on the part of the adult learner that 'training' can be student-led or that it can usefully focus on the process of learning. Close attention needs to be paid, especially in the first hours and days of a course or a school year, to building trust; to establishing what Steiner (1984) calls a 'cooperative social environment' in which vulnerabilities and anxieties may be understood; and to developing curiosity.

3   *That the second person, whom we shall term the therapist teacher, trainer or facilitator, is congruent in the relationship*
    This reminds us of the importance of openness, honesty and authenticity on the part of the facilitator. It's important, too, that she is not defensive, and that she is reflective about herself in the learning process. For us this is a key quality for all teachers and one which leads to being open to listening, to encouraging questions and questioning, to being willing to change the programme or syllabus in pursuit of learning, and to a willingness and openness to be challenged by the students.

4   *That the facilitator is experiencing unconditional positive regard toward the pupil, student or participant*
    This condition describes the attitude of the facilitator towards her students and towards the subject of learning, an attitude which needs to be perceived by both the individual recipient and by the rest of the group

if, more broadly, the teacher or facilitator is to co-create an acceptant climate of learning (see Rogers, 1951).

5 *That the trainer or facilitator is experiencing an empathic understanding of the participant's internal frame of reference*
The second of the two conditions which have to be perceived by the participants concerns the facilitator's ability to understand each participant's frame of reference regarding their work and the subject, as well as their prior and current experience of education, training and learning.

6 *That the student or participant perceives, at least to a minimal degree, conditions 4 and 5, that is, the unconditional positive regard and the empathic understanding of the facilitator*
This 'assumed condition' (Rogers, 1958/1967) reminds us that the customer, who in this case is the pupil, student or participant, is always right – even when he's wrong! (see Embleton Tudor and Tudor, 1996). In other words, the experiences and perceptions of the participants are the ultimate judge of the success (or otherwise) of a course, and of whether the facilitator has adapted the course or curriculum accurately to the needs of the students.

The process of education

Rogers uses the term 'process' to refer to the fluid and changing nature of organisms, including humans. He views 'being (in) process' as moving in a direction towards 'that self which one truly is' (Rogers, 1960/1967). The process of education, as that of therapy, is one in which the participant is increasingly free to express herself and, thereby, to move away from fixed and rigid attitudes (see Rogers, 1959). Consistent with this, Rogers (1983) identifies the aims of what he refers to as a 'more human education' as, typically, being a movement:

- Towards a climate of trust in the classroom.
- Towards a participatory mode of decision-making in all aspects of learning by all participants.
- Towards helping students prize themselves.
- Towards developing excitement and curiosity in intellectual and emotional discovery.
- Towards developing in teachers the attitudes in facilitating learning and helping them grow as persons.

Thus, any person-centred education pays attention to process, primarily through the attitude of the facilitators and, in practice, by means of some forms of 'check in' times such as 'circle time' which is established in some schools. Of course, attitude and ambience, conditions and process cannot be separate from context, and the current context is of a highly politicised education system and a curriculum-led schooling. In his searing critique of *schooling*, as distinct from education, the American radical John Gatto (2002) talks about seven lessons which pupils are, in effect, taught in school:

1 Confusion – where everything taught is taught from content.
2 Class position – primarily through numbering and ranking.
3 Indifference – through not caring too much about anything, as pupils have to switch their attention and concentration on and off when the bell rings.
4 Emotional dependency – through ticks, crosses and the giving and withholding of 'stars'.
5 Intellectual dependency – through encouraging reliance on an expert teacher for information about what to do and what to think.
6 Provisional self-esteem or conditions of worth – through constant evaluations and judgements.
7 There is no hiding place – through constant surveillance and having no private space or time.

Whilst many teachers would recognise some or all of these limitations of schooling and do not want to provide or reinforce a culture of competitive dependency, the context of most schools makes it extremely difficult to avoid the regular sacrifice of individual learning needs to the management of the classroom or to the demands of market forces. For example, a teacher might believe that six-year-olds have a long and stimulating enough school day, but feel compelled to set homework because some parents believe that their children need it in order to 'get on'. If the reputation of the school suffers, because 'it doesn't push the children enough', or because another school is pushing harder, teaching staff become subject to increased pressure to perform, sometimes with fewer resources being made avialable with which to accomplish an already complex and challenging task. The criteria for measuring performance are not set by the professionals who best know their students, their own strengths, and the local area and culture, but by government departments. The knowledge, professional and personal qualities of individual teachers are thus underutilised. This is particularly ironic in the light of the fact that teachers are now subject to the most rigorous scrutiny ever, and are working longer hours than ever.

Outcomes of education

In the person-centred approach, outcomes are linked more to the process of how students approach problems, think about situations, or find information than to specific, pre-theorised or predetermined ideas about what the student will have learned. From a person-centred perspective, growth and learning are not questions of being shaped according to external criteria, but are part of a process of becoming. Thus, for Rogers (1951), the outcome or goal of what he referred to as 'democratic education' includes assisting students to become individuals:

- Who are able to take self-initiated action and to be responsible for those actions.
- Who are capable of intelligent choice and self-direction.
- Who are critical learners, able to evaluate the contributions made by others.
- Who have acquired knowledge relevant to the solution of problems.
- Who, even more importantly, are able to adapt flexibly and intelligently to new problem situations.
- Who have internalised an adaptive mode of approach to problems, utilising all pertinent experience freely and creatively.
- Who are able to cooperate effectively with others in these various activities.
- Who work, not for the approval of others, but in terms of their own socialized purposes. (pp. 387–8)

If anything, these form the *process* learning outcomes of a course or an education.

Pedagogy and andragogy

Pedagogy describes the function of a pedagogue and refers to instruction, training and discipline, especially in relation to the teaching of children and young people. It carries the sense of expertise, communicated and delivered with the authority of a traditional teacher or instructor. By contrast, the term 'andragogy', first coined in 1833 by Alexander Kapp, a German grammar school teacher, refers to the person informed by and facilitating an integrated concept of adult learning. Here we summarise Freire's (1967/1976) key contributions to the theory and practice of education for freedom:

A critique of the banking concept of education
This concept refers to the traditional form of education which involves the 'banking' of knowledge by the teacher in the student. The student then has certain knowledge 'on deposit' which he can then, in effect, sell on to employers. This view of education as a commodity encourages consumer relations between student and teacher whereby the student expects to be 'taught' and, thereby, to come away having received a given body of necessary knowledge. Such consumerism involves buying and 'having' knowledge, rather than learning. In this pervasive model, the teacher is expert and also paid employee. Rather like his predecessor, the tutor to the aristocracy, the teacher is concerned about tenure and getting good grades from the institution, inspectors and even students. Knowledge becomes material, rather than the subject of curiosity and investigation. The teacher becomes the purveyor of knowledge as goods rather than facilitator and mediator of the relationship between the student and the world including the teacher. The pupil or student as consumer and customer is, in an increasingly litigious society, one with rights to sue if disappointed. The speed of technological innovation and the development of new 'knowledge' is so rapid that individual human beings can keep up with only a small fraction, even in specialist fields, leading to increased specialisation. Further, as Robinson (2001) points out: 'We are living in a period of spiralling academic inflation' (p. 50). In the last 20 years the number of graduates has doubled, but in the '90s the number of vacancies for graduates dropped by 35 per cent and there is still a large surplus of graduates forced to seek employment in positions for which they are overqualified. At the same time, worldwide, a large unemployed underclass is developing, and this increased surplus will be exacerbated by the increase in population. The success of headhunting agencies suggests that at the top there is a shortage of creative people. Employers report that they seek creativity, flexibility, the ability to innovate and to adapt to change, and that these qualities are more important than the paper qualifications which form the outcome of school and university curricula. The extent of disaffection among young people, particularly visible in Britain in the disproportionate numbers of young Black people in trouble with the law, and the continuing growth of the prison population, attests to the fact that large numbers of young people have withdrawn their intellectual assets from society.

▪ *Critical pedagogy*
Freire (1972) subverts the original meaning of pedagogy, turning it on its head by arguing that the instruction comes from the oppressed and that education as the practice of freedom can only be liberating when everyone claims knowledge as a field in which we all labour. hooks (1994) also makes the point that Freire was primarily concerned with the mind, and that Thich Nhat Hanh, the Vietnamese Buddhist monk, offers a way of thinking about pedagogy which emphasises wholeness:

> Progressive, holistic education, 'engaged pedagogy' is more demanding than conventional critical or feminist pedagogy. For, unlike these two teaching practices, it emphasises well-being. That means that teachers must be actively committed to a process of self-actualization that promotes their well-being if they are to teach in a manner that empowers students. (p. 15)

▪ *Critical consciousness* (conscientizaçao)
This is a term which refers to learning to perceive social, political and economic contradictions and, consequently, to take action against the oppressive elements in society. Comparing the work of Rogers and Freire, O'Hara (1989) describes the need for this kind of social consciousness-raising. It is not an end in itself but is joined by a meaningful praxis: action and reflection.

▪ *The importance of dialogue and praxis*
For Freire (1972), dialogue

> is the encounter between men, mediated by the world, in order to name the world. Hence, dialogue cannot occur between those who want to name the word and those who do not want this naming – between those who deny other men the right to speak their word and those whose right to speak has been denied them. (p. 61)

We note that, in this extract, Freire names only men, demonstrating the power of naming and language. In fact, the Women's Movement of the 1960s and '70s is an excellent example of the power of dialogue through consciousness-raising and debate, and of action, protest, representation and legislation. Within the word 'dialogue' is reflection and action and hence praxis: 'translating the term [conscientisation] to critical awareness and engagement, I entered the classroom with the conviction that it was crucial for me and every other student to be an active participant, not a passive consumer' (hooks, 1994, p. 14). Genuine dialogue between teacher and student about any and all aspects of education and training is crucial to a person-centred approach to education. One section of Rogers' (1983) *Freedom to Learn* is written for the teacher on innovation, facilitation and relationship and includes issues of power and the politics of education. This has echoes in Gatto's (2002) work in which he reports talking to students about the politics of the school.

Rogers (1978) acknowledges the similarities between his ideas and Freire's on education: both are subversive of authoritarian structures; in breaking the vertical, top-down 'banking' concept of education, both are statements about change in power relationships; and both propose a dia-logical, problem-posing, as distinct from a problem-solving, education. This is particularly pertinent in the context of the exponential rate of technolog-ical development in our society as many of the problems today's school-children will face are as yet unknown. It is therefore much more relevant to help children learn how to pose problems, and how to deal with the processes of development and relationship, than to focus them on 'being taught' to 'solve' problems. 'Any fool can answer a question,' said one of our teachers. 'It takes an intelligent fool to ask one!' Moreover, even those problems we can predict, such as the finite nature of the world's resources and the increasing number of ethical dilemmas over human reproduction, are problems rarely posed in today's schools. Neither do they prepare our children for the complexities of living in the postmodern world and the immense range of issues that are now part of our daily existence and that are brought to us at ever increasing speeds through multiple media.

Multiple intelligences

In order for children to learn, it is important to acknowledge both the uniqueness and the complexity of the human organism. The cellist Pablo Casals put this well:

> And what do we teach our children? We teach them that two and two make four, and that Paris is the capital of France. When will we also teach them what they are? We should say to each of them: Do you know what you are? You are a marvel. You are unique. In all the years that have passed, there has never been another child like you ... You have the capacity for anything. Yes, you are a marvel.

At the same time, from a person-centred perspective with an 'engaged pedagogy', it is important to emphasise wholeness alongside differentiation. This finds fertile ground in recent work on multiple intelligences.

Traditionally, education has measured students through tests, such as IQ tests, which are partial in that they examine only a small range of intelligence and are based on a particular and restricted definition of intelligence. Gardner's (1993) work on multiple intelligences widens this focus. Drawing on findings from research across a number of disciplines including evolutionary biology, developmental and cognitive psychology, neuroscience, neuropsychology and evolutionary psychology, Gardner identifies eight criteria by which potential 'candidate intelligences' may be assessed:

1   By their potential isolation by brain damage, which proves their relative autonomy from other human faculties.
2   By the existence of *idiots savants*, prodigies and other exceptional individuals, which proves the sparing of one ability over and against a background of others.
3   By an identifiable core operation or set of operations, such as a sensitivity to pitch or to imitation, which, Gardner argues, defines human intelligence as a neural mechanism.
4   By a distinctive developmental history, along with a definable set of expert 'end-state' performances, achieved through talent and training.
5   By an evolutionary history and evolutionary plausibility, 'including capacities (like bird song or primate social organization) that are shared with other organisms' (p. 65).
6   By support from experimental psychological tasks whereby we can study the details of an intelligence with specificity.
7   By support from psychometric findings, although Gardner is cautious about exaggerated claims for such tests.
8   By susceptibility to encoding in a symbolic system such as language, picturing or mathematics.

With these criteria in mind, Gardner identifies seven intelligences: linguistic, musical, logical-mathematical, spatial, bodily-kinesthetic, interpersonal and intrapersonal. This shifts debates about a person's intelligence and achievement from how smart they are, or are not, to the particular ways in which they are smart. Gardner suggests that the personal intelligences, which amount to information-processing capacities, the combination or fusion of which provides a sense of self, are in effect the intelligences with which we reflect on the other intelligences. This is why they are especially important. More recently he has identified an eighth, naturalist intelligence. Gardner's theory has ground-breaking implications for education, educationalists, policy-makers, children and parents:

- It offers a more comprehensive way of understanding and assessing an individual's learning style.
- As all intelligences are viewed as equally important, all education needs both to stimulate and to respond to all of them.
- A person's more developed intelligences can assist in understanding a subject which normally employs their less developed intelligences (see Lazear, 1992).
- By activating a wide band of intelligences, the educator inevitably facilitates a deeper understanding of the particular subject under discussion. This echoes Stern's (1985) point about the value of stimulating cross-model perception (see Chapter 5).
- It acknowledges complexity, through the differentiation of intelligence, and the fact that we are holistic human organisms.

The only danger with this framework is the tempation to 'fit' into it. As Gardner himself points out, there are many ways of being intelligent, and others as yet unrecognised and unnamed.

Having identified a number of strands in a person-centred approach to education we now consider the extent to which current schooling supports or frustrates this.

Education and schooling

Take at hazard one hundred children of several educated generations and one hundred uneducated children of the people and compare them in anything you please; in strength, in agility, in mind, in the ability to acquire knowledge, even in morality – and in all respects you are startled by the vast superiority on the side of the children of the uneducated. (Tolstoy, 1862)

Education has always been a parental responsibility. Historically, the children of families with wealth and connection were educated and cared for initially by governesses and tutors, later in fee-paying establishments, and after that through travel at home and abroad. From as early an age as they were able, the children of working people worked alongside their parents and others at whatever living was traditional or available, and either learned about the world and their craft directly from their parents, or were apprenticed elsewhere. The separation of home from learning is relatively modern and is a consequence of industrialisation. The early industrialists, some with a philanthropic intent, recognised that employees needed basic skills in order to perform their tasks, and thus education, at least to the level required by industry, became more widely available. The age for school attendance, initially between five and ten, was chosen to protect young children from exploitation in arduous and dangerous working conditions – but they could be exploited from eleven years of age! Despite evidence that the rates of literacy among children from countries which do not begin compulsory schooling until the age of seven are slightly higher than in Britain, the school starting age remains at five and although it is legal to 'flexi-school', that is to attend for only part of the day or part of the week, this is at the discretion of the individual school, is not generally encouraged, and happens rarely. The policy on school starting age also ignores the scientific evidence that boys have a testosterone rush at the age of around four and are disadvantaged in an environment that rewards children for sitting still and concentrating on activities requiring fine motor skills for extended periods. In any case, when male babies are born they are on average weeks behind female babies in development; generally this gap is still observable beyond the age of four or five. If a parent wants to secure a place at a particular school which is sought after, their child may have to begin when he or she is four and half in order to secure the place, rather than when they are ready for the separation from the parents and the challenges of school.

The education industry and the culture it fosters are now so established that many parents do not know that, according to the Education Act 1944, it is still the responsibility of parents to ensure that their children are educated 'in school *or otherwise*' (our emphasis). It is not the responsibility of the state to educate children. If a parent chooses state education, the state has an obligation to provide one. However, an increasing number of parents are choosing 'otherwise', usually in the form of home education. In Britain this involves an estimated 30,000 children and rising. In some parts of England an unofficial apartheid system has developed in which the large numbers of the population who can afford independent education have opted out of the state system. Seldom a day passes without a news item regarding education voicing and giving rise to widespread concern and dissatisfaction with many aspects of education provision in this country. There appears to be no consensus on what is wrong or how to tackle the issues. The national curriculum, and school league tables are viewed by politicians, and by some teachers and parents, as a solution which ensures continued high standards in education. At the same time the curriculum itself, together with a plethora of tests, increases anxiety all round and operates against genuine education. One survey of teachers reported that they felt that Scholastic Aptitude Tests (SATs) interfered with their teaching, and that they did not assist them to increase their knowledge of their pupils. The logic of tests is that, for the comparative purposes of longitudinal research, children are tested earlier and earlier. Thus, three-year-olds need to be able to count to three and to begin to write, no matter that many three-year-olds can count to ten or over, or that many lack the neuromuscular development to hold a pencil 'correctly'. (In any case this particular test is anachronistic in that this skill was originally developed in holding quill pens, and is not ergonomic in relation to modern writing implements.) Ironically, it seems that parents, who want 'only the best' for their children in an increasingly competitive world, have, in trusting the experts, become the driving force for league tables. As we write, the British government is under considerable pressure from teachers to abolish testing of the younger age group and, as we go to press, has made some concessions.

Other parents waiting at the school gates worry and grumble, but feel impotent. There are reports of teachers being threatened and even assaulted by parents for disciplining their children. Teachers report being pressurised by parents who want their children pushed harder to achieve, and being treated as free childcare by others. In a political climate of control, teachers and schools are subject to targets and policies which constantly change, and have to produce detailed evidence of everything they do. Teachers resent politicians and politicians mistrust teachers. At the time of writing, the current British Education Secretary declined the traditional invitation to attend an annual teachers' national conference for fear of being heckled and challenged. As teachers are all too aware this saps spontaneity and diverts energy from classroom activity, teaching and learning. Gardner's (1991) comments on the introduction of universal schooling in the United States one hundred years ago have a contemporary ring to them:

> Although few would have any reason to recognize it, a collision course was virtually inevitable. On the one hand, the demands being made on the school were increasing in virtually exponential fashion. On the other, the ways in which students learn and the kinds of conceptions and skills they bring to school were largely invisible to pedagogues, and even more unknown to those who set educational policy. Only the most optimistic assumption of a preestablished harmony between the student mind and the school curriculum would justify the prediction that the schools as constituted would succeed in their ambitious and ever expanding mission. (p. 144)

Today in primary schools in Britain, classroom assistants, with variable levels of training are allowed to supervise classes for up to three days in a term (Department for Education and Skills, 2002). Whilst this is supposed to alleviate some of the pressure on teachers, they pay a large hidden price in the time needed to prepare work in advance and to supervise the assistant. This also supports the view that the organisation of school is actually at least as much about the needs of parents to work, as it is about the needs and rights of children to an education. In the context of an increasingly litigious society, it is little wonder that the out-of-school activities which foster a sense of community, creativity, adventure and risk (such as clubs, sports, expeditions, visits and amateur dramatics) are threatened. It is a tribute to the dedication, generosity and courage of those teachers who do continue to offer their time and expertise that there are still school plays and trips, albeit fewer than formerly.

Many parents, including those who are confident and assertive people, feel powerless to voice all of their dissatisfactions for fear of repercussions whereby their children would be viewed as troublemakers and selected for unwelcome attention. Some parents are so affected by their own schooling that they fear being judged by their children's teachers as stupid, pushy or over-protective – feelings matched by the fact that many teachers feel judged and misjudged by parents. Where and to whom can parents safely take their concerns? If parents, themselves products of what is in essence the same education system, feel awed and anxious about taking up points of disagreement directly with schools, or facing their own difficulties, there is little chance of their children emerging as powerful and independent individuals. Holt (1967b) rejects the notion that children need to be beaten into submission or programmed to be geniuses, and calls on parents and educators to trust children. This is a radical notion indeed!

Products of the psychopathic school

Earlier we discussed Gatto's (2002) comments about what teachers and schools actually teach. Here we review eight characteristics he identifies of children who are products of state schooling or what he refers to as the 'psychopathic school'.

- *Indifference and hostility to the adult world*
  Adults are generally dismissed or seen as oppositional, not as potentially interesting people or as resources for learning. Holt (1967a) concludes that the system produces feelings of boredom, fear, humiliation and

confusion, and generally predestines children to failure. Home-educated teenagers starting school report bewilderment at the levels of hostility demonstrated to teachers by their peers, and sometimes experience difficulties in their own relationships with their peer group, resulting from their continued active involvement with adults as part of their own learning process. Learning in same-age peer groups is unique to schools. It happens at no other time in our lives and, arguably, sets up antagonisms between pupils and teachers that would not and do not exist in learning groups of mixed ages.

Lack of curiosity and inability to concentrate
When education is curriculum-led, then curiosity inevitably comes a poor second to the task, for the child, of 'being taught'; and for the teacher, of delivering the material. Add to this that the national curriculum in the United Kingdom has been designed by outside experts, then 'what you need to learn' is even more removed from the pupil's experience and organismic needs. The current curriculum for maths, for example, was designed by university professors without reference to the expertise of the classroom teacher, educational or child psychologist, and certainly not to any children themselves. Add to this what we know about intelligence, learning styles and attention spans (which are shorter than the average lesson), and compare this with the reality of many schools and, despite the best efforts of committed and skilled teachers, it is no wonder that children's curiosity is thwarted and stifled.

Concentration is highly individual. People have different learning rhythms, and a time of day at which they are most receptive to learning. Within the current schooling system neither content nor structure, nor the time or duration of the activity are negotiable, and the day is punctuated by bells signalling the time to change activity. We now know a great deal about different learning styles and multiple intelligences. Some of us need to hear before we understand, while others need to see a diagram or demonstration, and yet others need to get their hands dirty and to experience in order to learn. Despite all this, still almost all learning in schools requires listening, reading and writing. Many children, probably a majority of them boys, who dislike writing or find it difficult, are disadvantaged. It appears necessary to restrict teaching and learning to these media because to do anything else presents a management problem to the teacher. One of us, wanting to support her child's love of books, who refused to do more than gently encourage him to read after school when he was five years old, was told by his teacher: 'Well

he's got to get to grips with it soon. I've got thirty in my class.'
Compare the above with the following experience.

A boy, who is educated at home, is intensely interested in amphibians. He reads about them, reads novels featuring them, draws them, makes puppets of them, looks for them at every opportunity in local rivers, pet shops ands aquatic centres. At seven his knowledge is comprehensive and he can talk about his subject in a way which engages both adults and children who would otherwise not be interested in amphibians. This curriculum was pursued intermittently but regularly over twelve hours a day for several weeks. It included a study of pollution; anatomy and physiology; life cycles; navigation to find the pet shops; monetary calculations involving the comparative cost of amphibians and reptiles and looking after them; geography; design, including the properties of various craft materials; and all the time improving reading skills. This boy then had three weeks in which he read only comics and showed no abiding interest in anything much apart from his ongoing physical activities and playing with his friends. This was followed by a period of intense and studious interest in the Romans.

A poor sense of the future

Schools both influence and are influenced by the wider culture which values immediate material gratification and pleasure-giving experience above all else. Popular culture encourages children to live in a continuous present, moving from one pleasurable activity to the next without reflection. The tendency of schools, in cooperation with examination boards, towards the rigid division of knowledge into different subjects supports a dislocation of time, cause and effect. Such divisions are inconsistent and antithetical to the natural and social sciences, and to postmodern thinking and philosophy. Given the pace of modern life and the exponential changes and developments in new technology, many children being educated now will be working in jobs which have not yet been invented. In this context we need to be expanding rather than delineating children's thinking. Most educationalists also perpetuate what to many young people is patently a myth: that if they achieve well in examinations they are guaranteed a better life as an adult than the one they would have if they do not achieve well in this system.

No sense of the past
For Gatto (2002) the children he taught are 'ahistorical', that is: 'they have no sense of how the past has predestined their own present, limits their choice, shapes their values and lives' (p. 27). For children living in a continuous present, 'history' is a thing of the remote past. They have little or no sense of being joined up, of belonging or of context.

Numbness of moral facility
Whatever we are told, it is the actions of those around us and, most particularly as children, the actions of adults, which influence our beliefs about how we should treat others and ourselves.

> It is registration time for a class of five-year-olds. Outside the classroom a harassed parent can clearly be heard berating a child for her behaviour on the way to school. The child enters the room alone and sobbing audibly. The teacher pauses in the registration process, says in a firm voice: 'Hello Natasha. Sit down please' and continues with registration without offering her any other attention. The children also ignore Natasha. Another teacher in the same school, which has a 'good' reputation, routinely ignores boys who are crying having just been left by their parents during the first week of their school lives. What do the children see and what does it mean to them? Possibly: 'We don't show our feelings in school because they are not important here,' 'I am not important,' 'Ahmed, Michael and Delroy are not important,' perhaps even, 'I am a girl so I'm more important than the boys'; maybe: 'We don't help each other here,' and that's confusing because one of the school 'rules', written large in the school reception area is: 'Be kind and helpful to others.'

To criticise the individual teacher is only half the point. She has twenty four-and-a-half-year olds or thirty five-year-olds and detailed instructions about what must be covered during each day. She has no allocation of time to deal with separation anxiety, sadness or ambivalent feelings about school. The pressure accelerates early in a child's school career due to the need to meet targets, and many children we love have at times been ignored or shamed and humiliated by insensitive or persecutory teachers. The many warm, intuitive gifted teachers are just as subject to the demands of the state and, although some last a career, many leave the profession bitter and burned-out. Inter-school competition cannot but help produce inter-pupil competition and a situation which relies on losers. Home-educated children starting school in their teenage years report amazement and sadness at the levels of spitefulness, victimisation and cliquiness which characterise the relationships of many of their peers in school.

- *Unease with intimacy or candour*
Many of the structures of schools militate against intimacy, and emotional literacy, which is arguably more important than the '3Rs', and is not even on the curriculum. Most school children feel compelled to construct a self which fits in with prevailing cultural and school norms, by which they feel to some degree protected from the negative attention of their peers, and which can also be adapted to please teachers. This may make it harder to express or perhaps even to access other parts of their experience, and so the capacity or even the wish for intimacy is diminished.

- *Materialistic attitudes*
Gatto (2000) sees this as following the lead of teachers who, materialistically, grade everything. Again this is in the context in the West of highly materialistic societies in which everything can be bought.

- *Dependency, passivity and timidity in the face of new challenges*
'There is only one problem – they lack even the slightest spark of initiative or intellectual curiosity' (Conway, 2002, p. 22). How many of us have had the experience in social situations of using an unusual but apt word, revealing an interest or some fragment of knowledge and being rewarded by a joke, a raised eyebrow or an overt put-down? Where in public life do our trend-setters or policy-makers demonstrate philosophical thinking or principled argument? These questions interest us because the answers tell us something about current attitudes to education. It is not surprising that our young people fail to see the point of grappling with complex concepts or the intricacies of an informed argument. Children from homes with values differing from school, in which they are encouraged to question, to discuss and debate, where adults demonstrate regard for the child by allowing her time to gather her thoughts as she seeks to make her point, listening without interrupting, and are able to say: 'Yes I got that wrong' or 'Sorry' on occasion, sometimes have a tough choice at school. They can, if they are sophisticated and so-minded, 'play the game' in school and do well, or they can be categorised as 'know-it-all', as 'cheeky' or even as 'trouble-makers' by their teachers. Good children, like good adults, wait for the teachers, who are experts, to tell them when to act, what to do and when to do it.

We have already seen that the peer culture, fostered by school, prefers estrangement from adults. Often teachers simply do not have the time to listen to everyone's view. Although there have been some attempts at change, history and other books usually represent one uncritical, uncontested view of the truth. The modern curriculum still comprises mainly factual information, with little opportunity to learn how to think, to use philosophy or strategic thinking in a context which pupils find rewarding and relevant. We speculate that to do so might be to risk conflict about issues which really affect peoples' lives and which could in turn threaten the social control element of schooling. Thus energy which could be used creatively is often squandered on petty rivalries and comparisons in the school yard. Imagine the demand on teachers if all their pupils were really curious and wanted to learn for most of the day. We doubt that schools as currently conceived could meet that demand.

Given that the vast majority of children have no control over the timing, content, media, or structure of their schooling, their only choice is whether or not to do the work. The consequences of refusing can be so dire that many children steer a mid-way course, doing just enough to avoid an uncomfortable degree of negative attention, but lacking absorption in and commitment to the task, neither enjoying their work nor learning much. Articulating these points Gatto (2002) says that 'any reform that doesn't attack these specific pathologies will be nothing more than a façade' (pp. 26–7).

Some reforms

In the absence of the collective will to reform (let alone revolt), there are ideas, informed by a person-centred perspective, which could be pursued by education authorities, schools, individual teachers or small groups of teachers:

- In recognition of the fact that it is well nigh impossible to listen well to others if one is unheard oneself, and of the high expectations of teachers in the complexity and diversity of their roles, each teacher would have what in therapeutic circles would be called a supervisor, or in organisations a mentor or a coach (see Chapter 4). This person would not be their line manager or have any assessment role in relation to the teacher. They would be a trained facilitator, operating within an professional and ethical framework. They could be a professional colleague, working in a sphere separate from that of the teacher, with whom they may discuss confidentially any issues relating to their work, from class-room skills, to staffroom issues, from ethical dilemmas to balancing domestic responsibilities with professional duties. The service would be provided as a right, and teachers encouraged to take up the time which, at, say, an hour and a half a month, would be counted as part of their workload. (We know of at least one local authority which offers this and psychotherapy as part of its social services to foster parents.) At a time when there are serious shortfalls in school budgets, through no fault of the schools' administration, we recognise that this would require a cer-tain investment. At the same time, teachers are a finite resource, individ-ually and collectively. Unless their need to process and develop their experience and learning is met, the well of teacher's own finite resources will run dry. The wider issue is that we cannot expect young people to learn from what they are told if what they see are exhausted, harried and hurried teachers, reacting to pressures without the opportunity to reflect.

- Emphasis could be placed on taking responsibility for learning by asking the students what they need in order to learn and what they are pre-pared to offer to others. This might elicit undertakings such as 'I will ask for help when I need it' or 'I welcome questions in the classroom.' Pupils could discuss the kind of consideration they would like from oth-ers and whether they are prepared to offer the same. This might result in discussion of wider issues in the school community such as making sure that no-one is left out at playtime, or offering help to someone if a pupil thinks they are having difficulty. Both these examples entail dis-cussion of the balance between the interests of self and others.

- If a school does not offer a subject in which the pupil is interested, con-sideration could be given to allowing the pupil to visit another place in which to learn during the school day, or to the provision of a space in school for that purpose. Agreements would have to be reached between the young person, their parent or carer and the school regarding the safety of the young person and how and by whom the study will be facilitated or supported.

- Regular class meetings could discuss any problems or issues and may help pupils acquire the confidence to broach issues such as 'I am always the one to include Zena. Why is no-one else inviting her to play?' This might lead on to some reflection about why no-one does want to play with Zena, why people exclude other people, and why some people get excluded. Some may wonder what it's like to be Zena and, for her part, Zena might think about whether there's anything that she can do to become more popular.

■ Within the classroom, and arising from discussion, agreements can be made about the conduct of communication, for example, that no-one should be interrupted when they are speaking, and that name-calling or other humiliating treatment of anyone will not be tolerated by the group.

■ As our society becomes increasingly sensorily stimulating and speedy, the ability to find a spot of inner tranquility and stillness becomes a greater asset. To assist focus, attention to inner life in order to balance the attention paid to our outer lives, and to enhance the ability to concentrate, some form of meditation can be useful. Children as young as five can be taught to meditate (Fontana and Slack, 1997). Meditation can be taught formally and practiced routinely, say at the beginning and end of a lesson or a day. Children can become used to being asked to close their eyes and to visualise in silence, say, an animal, and being asked to focus on various details of it before writing or painting.

■ School rules could be reconsidered and agreed by a class or by the whole school. Consultation with everyone, including pupils and ancilliary staff could result in a code for which everyone feels some responsibility. Affirmative, rather than negative language – such as 'Walk in the corridor' rather than 'No running in the corridor' is specific about what is required and encourages cooperation.

■ When discussing consequences (as distinct from punishment) for ignoring any bilateral agreements, attempts can be made to choose a consequence which is relevant to the situation, and which is both agreed and sustainable.

All of these practical suggestions are based on principles of emotional literacy (Steiner, 1984, 1997; Growald, 1998; McCarthy, 1998) and the whole school approach of the health-promoting school (see Weare, 2000).

Life-long learning

If we can't take the child out of the adult, then we can't take the child's formal learning experiences out of the adult. Many of us therefore reach adulthood with some anxieties around learning, some fixed ideas about what we can and can't do that rarely match with our actual potential, and with a lack of awareness of or trust in our own learning processes.

We are fortunate to live at a time however when ongoing learning to compensate for lost opportunities, to empower communities, to help increase employability, or to ensure that workers keep up to date with the latest thinking, in a world increasingly rich in knowledge, has created increasing interest in how adults learn. New research into the structure and functioning of the brain has challenged traditional concepts of intelligence and the learning process. And perhaps the greatest myth of all has been successfully challenged: the adage that you can't teach old dogs new tricks has now been triumphantly disproved (Schore, 1994).

When Rogers was considering a revolutionary approach to learning, he was considering this within the context of formal educational establishments and qualification structures, and in these contexts his ideas were, and still are, challenging. How do we balance a belief in the value of self-validation, let alone an internal process of organismic valuing, with the need to indicate your level of competence to others who may wish to purchase your services? If I am selecting a counsellor, a trainer, a heart surgeon, what would I want to know about the skills and knowledge of the people providing these services? Would I feel confident enough to trust that if they thought they were competent, then they must be so, with no external validation? Where the only outcome I need to achieve is my own learning, then my own sense of satisfaction is the only validation tool I need. Where I need to indicate to others what level of competence I have attained however, the situation becomes more complex. There are now more stakeholders in my learning and I need to engage empathically with all their needs.

Training practitioners within the person-centred approach could be seen to offer a particular opportunity to meet this challenge. To what extent do training providers prescribe content and structure, and to what extent do they allow participants to design and develop their own structure and programme? Clearly, availability of resources such as specialist speakers, pre-prepared handouts and training rooms, can influence the degree to which pre-planning is necessary in designing a programme. There is also the question of how participants know what they don't know. Is there a minimum level of input required before participants are able to design their own learning? And is there an assumption that, as participants, left to our own devices, we will naturally create an effective learning programme for ourselves: that learning design skills are endemic? Or is it more likely that, in a novel situation, we are more likely to import previously experienced models of learning, even though we may not have experienced these as helpful? An example of this was the experience of one of us (JV) of a self-managed approach to learning on a Masters degree programme.

One option is to consider the facilitation of such events. A higher degree of structuring could be offered to participants who are new to the approach early on in the programme with a view to encouraging participants to exercise greater choice and autonomy as their confidence, understanding and

Intended to be an empowering model which encouraged participants to reflect on how they might learn together, the vacuum was quickly filled by those participants who had experienced other (quite different) Masters degree programmes. I wrote at the time: 'I am not looking for a positivist heaven of single reality certainty. I am trying to work out what the rules are around here, and I don't think I've grasped them; and I find this disempowering' (Lloyd, 1996). It was only at the point of completing my dissertation that I felt that, through reading, dialogue and experience, I had acquired sufficient understanding of the field of learning to be able to operate effectively within it.

insight develop. In this sense there is a significant difference between structuring and non-directiveness (see Coghlan and McIlduff, 1990).

The training programmes at Temenos, through the experience of the tutors and facilitators and the Course Meeting, are constantly holding and acknowledging the tensions that these issues raise. How do we offer an open and creative environment with freedom to learn and be in the world of certificates, diplomas, accreditation and regulation? So far this mediation between the two has been balanced by offering students freedom to choose at which level they wish to learn and what outcome they desire for themselves. Our courses offer an opportunity to participate at three levels: one of attendance only; one of 'professional' qualification, which requires a component of written work based around understanding practice and a demonstration of readiness to practise; and one of 'academic' qualification, which carries a further written component. The latter two require students to present themselves and their work at a final panel which comprises practitioners, tutors and an external representative. This, we feel, offers students an opportunity to own and celebrate the commitment they have given to getting this far in the learning process, and also reflects our passion that we should all be able to articulate the ways in which we work to a wide audience and make ourselves understood.

As preparation for this final process students present themselves, their work and their understanding of the subject matter during the training. This offers a consistent process through the training and does not 'ambush' students in an end process the likes of which they have not encountered before. The presentations that students deliver during the training group *are* the curriculum and in this respect each cohort creates its own learning and each year is different. Assessment is threefold: by self, peer and facilitator, matched against agreed learning outcomes that relate to person-centred theory and philosophy. There is no formal didactic teaching. The training consists of facilitation of the group process, student presentations and practice counselling sessions. During the practice time we have moved away from the usual routine of feedback and promote the process of facilitation. In this respect, students don't have to contend with externally located opinions or judgements about their performance, but are allowed to explore for themselves the impact of the work on their client and themselves and to identify any areas of learning (see Chapter 4).

What follows from this is the thorny question of how skill, knowledge and competence are assessed. To what extent are trainers seen as experts, who make the ultimate decision, and to what extent are participants involved in self- and peer assessment? There have been interesting experiments in this area. Silverstone (1997) shared the academic requirements of the local awarding body with her students and invited them to create their own process for demonstrating how these had been achieved. This acknowledges the needs of the awarding body and invites participants to take full responsibility for their learning process and validation. It does, of course, require the cooperation of that awarding body to offer a flexible accreditation process. For Natiello (1998/2001), the autocratic culture of the university within which she worked led her to offer a non-accredited programme rather than compromise the integrity of the approach. Instead, her team negotiated with a local Department of Education for the potential accreditation of the programme which was then sought individually by participants if desired. Clearly this has implications for individual funding support and for recognition by professional bodies of the investment made by individuals. At Temenos we have, to date, made a similar decision as an organisation to remain outside of accrediting and validating bodies, at the same time designing courses that meet external requirements and supporting those individual graduates who wish to seek relevant individual accreditation and/or registration.

Natiello (1998/2001) identifies two distinct groups of participants on her programmes: those who were seeking professional accreditation and therefore needed to evidence their learning in documented format, and those participants who already held qualifications and were more interested in the skills development and experience per se. The programme was therefore designed to accommodate both sets of participants and Natiello discovered that the more experienced participants were able to contribute a maturity and intellectual rigour to the theory inputs and provide peer supervision, moving away from reliance on the formal facilitation team. This seems consistent with Rogers' preferred approach, but there are potential problems of power imbalance here. Reflecting back on her experience of the self-managed Masters degree, Lloyd (1996) comments:

> What I have learned here is that, where I have a perceived gap in my own knowledge base that appears not to be shared by those around me, I seem also to suspend my confidence in my own critical thinking skills and judgement, and deny the validity of the knowledge and skills that I do possess.

We are also left with a question about how a participant with low insight is to be assessed. If their own assessment is at odds with that of their fellow participants and facilitators, how is this to be addressed? Where a group has developed close personal bonds, and where acknowledging the lack of insight perceived might result in the loss of the participant from the group, will a peer group articulate their concerns? What might the implications of their not doing so be for that participant's potential clients, and through them, for the reputation of the training body? There are no simple answers to these questions, although House and Totton (1997) address them in relation to counselling and psychotherapy. Even for those of us consciously working within the person-centred approach, Rogers' challenge was, and still is, a radical one.

Even where learning is apparently undertaken for its own sake, the needs of funding bodies to ensure that they are getting value for money establishes a need to demonstrate the value of the learning beyond the satisfaction of the learner. We see this in the work of Department for Education and Skills (DfES) in their provision of 'lifelong learning opportunities'. One of their key priorities is the engagement of socially disadvantaged people in learning by 'removing the artificial divide between formal and informal learning and allowing community based learning to flourish' (DfES, 2003). In a statement that appears to owe much to the legacy of Freire and Rogers, the DfES (2001, website) has declared its vision, to:

> support the development of stronger communities who are better able to maintain momentum in neighbourhood renewal, and to facilitate the development of a wider range of learning opportunities, including skills development for individuals. A broader range of support can enable individuals and groups to become more actively involved in self-help activity, neighbourhood management, asset-building and community enterprise. There is also value in training courses for community leaders.

An example of this is the Pennywell Community Business in Sunderland. This small, community owned organisation provides learning programmes for local residents on two Sunderland council estates. The 1950s and 1960s housing stock on the estates is of mixed condition, with no aspirational housing for those who want to improve their accommodation, leading to loss of skills and resources from the estates. Unemployment is significantly higher than the national average. In June 2000, 47 per cent of the adults had been unemployed for more than 12 months, 39 per cent for more than two years. Some 65 per cent have no qualifications, 30 per cent poor literacy skills, and only 18 per cent saw a relationship between education and enhanced employment opportunities (DfES, 2003). All residents are members of the company, and are actively involved in planning, designing and delivering programmes. The centre has created new jobs on the estate, largely part-time, and largely filled by local residents. Learning programmes tend to focus on job-seeking, information technology and electronic communications skills, basic skills, and family learning. Call centre training is offered in response to the growth of these centres in the area, and 'teledemocracy' courses enable local people to understand and access local council services and hold teleconferences with appropriate council officers to discuss issues of personal importance. Learning through recreational skills is also encouraged. All residents are given an email address and encouraged to use the internet and chat rooms. A pigeon club encourages transgenerational learning as older residents are able to pass on their enthusiasm and skills to youngsters, and there is a well equipped music studio. The sense of shared ownership is evident in the climate of trust that is established. Examples of this are the loan of computers to residents to use at home, and the handling of unruly behaviour by quietly speaking to informal leaders within the community.

Clearly funding bodies need to see quantifiable evidence to justify their financial support, and here again, John Tulip and Michelle Burlinson from the Pennywell Community Business have begun to develop an approach that is sensitive to the needs of their disenfranchised and often underconfident residents, and to the needs of their funders. Recognising that many of their residents are not yet empowered to achieve even basic level qualifications, they propose using a gentle and playful approach to personal development planning which allows learners to establish their own interests through experimentation and at their own pace, and works with them to review and achieve their own identified learning goals. The process enables the development worker to gather evidence of both time and resources utilised and 'soft' outcomes achieved for the funding bodies, without daunting the clients with unnecessary bureaucracy. This approach is, in effect, empathic to all stakeholders.

Perhaps the clearest example of a person-centred approach to learning is the University of the Third Age, affectionately known as U3A. Launched at a summer school in France in 1972, the British expression of this movement, Third Age Trust, was established as a registered charity in 1982 and, as at December 2002, had 122,556 members in 510 groups. Its purpose is to promote active learning, research and community service amongst those who have retired from their paid employment, and now entered their 'third age'. Learning resources and materials, including on-line courses, are provided centrally but the core of the organisation is the groups of members who self-organise for the purpose of learning. As they learn for pleasure, no qualifications are sought or received, and one of the founder members is quoted as declaring that: 'Those who teach shall also learn, and those who learn shall also teach' (University of the Third Age, 2003).

It seems to us that whilst not all identified as person-centred theoreticians or practitioners, the educational theorists we have cited are grappling with ideas and values central to the approach. What are the conditions in which people learn? Are some forms of learning and knowledge seen as more valid than others and by whom, and for what purpose? How can education address the global forces, some would say global crisis, of inequality between groups and nations? What would education which included conservation and enhancement of the environment look like? What would the implications be for the way people in the West expect to consume? These questions take us to the implications of the approach for wider considerations beyond the person which we discuss in the next chapter and in Part IV.

SUMMARY

- A person-centred approach to education privileges the needs and interests of the students, as they perceive them, as distinct from those of the teacher, the curriculum, the government or other external interests such as those of employers.
- Rogers emphasises the creation and offering of certain conditions for learning, and suggests that in such conditions there is a movement away from rigidity and the passive consumption of knowledge, towards creativity and active participation in the learning process.
- With Rogers, both Freire and Robinson criticise the 'banking system' of education; Freire argues that education can be freeing only when there is a seamless contribution of knowledge and ideas from both facilitator and student; Robinson argues that the banking system cannot work in the 21st century.

SUMMARY (contd)

- Gardner suggests criteria for specific intelligences and identifies eight types of intelligence to which he accords equal value. This concept allows for the multifaceted nature of the human organism.
- Current educational trends emphasise measurable learning outcomes, leave children overexamined and teachers overstretched and under-resourced.
- Adults carry memories of their own schooling, and this influences how they learn in later life.
- Person-centred principles of education sit uneasily with the demands of external validating and accrediting bodies; nevertheless, some educationalists and trainers have begun to negotiate this tension.

The Person of Today – and Tomorrow

> I believe that in our decaying culture we see the dim outlines of new growth, of a new revolution, of a culture of a sharply different sort. I see that revolution as coming not in some great organised movement, nor in a gun-carrying army with banners, not in manifestos and declarations, but through the emergence of a new kind of person.
>
> (Rogers, 1978c, p. 262)

In this chapter, we consider the implications of a person-centred approach for relationships in the wider world. We consider the qualities of what Rogers (1980c) describes as 'the person of tomorrow' as an introduction to three discussions on citizenship, justice and peace. Whilst we appreciate the aspirational tone and forward-looking focus of 'tomorrow', we question the implicit procrastination in the word and hence our use of the present 'today'.

The person of tomorrow – and today

Rogers (1978) talks about 'a new political figure' gaining influence and fostering an 'emerging culture'. He uses a number of terms, almost synonymously, to describe this figure: the fully functioning person (Rogers, 1957/1967, 1959) (see Chapter 3), the emerging person (Rogers, 1974/1980), the political person (Rogers, 1978b), and the person of tomorrow (Rogers, 1980c). All in some way describe a person:

▪ Who is in contact with herself, others and her environment.

- Who is able to be intimate and engaged, rather than withdrawn, passive and 'bystanding' (see Clarkson, 1996).
- Who is congruent, authentic, integrated and whole, open to new experiences and experiencing, to new ways of being and seeing.
- Who has a certain inner authority and is able to stand up for herself and others (see Natiello, 1987 and Chapter 7).
- Who is at ease with herself, caring and acceptant, rather than alienated (see Tudor, 1997) and
- Who is understanding and empathic.

This is a free-flowing and processing person who tends to actualise, not the finished article implied by Maslow's (1954) view of the self-actualised person.

In addition to the above qualities, Rogers (1980c) describes the person of tomorrow as sceptical of science and technology, anti-institutional, and indifferent to material things.

- *Scepticism regarding science and technology* – Rogers suggests that this person has a deep distrust of any science or technology 'that is used to conquer the world of nature and to control the world's people' (p. 350). Equally, Rogers suggests that this sceptical person supports scientific and technological initiatives which enhance self-awareness and which are controlled by the person. This second, criterial point is crucial as, otherwise, the person of tomorrow can appear anti-scientific, resistant to new technology, anachronistic and naïve.

- *Anti-institutional* – Rogers (1980c) describes this person as having 'an antipathy for any highly structured, inflexible, bureaucratic institution' (p. 351). The word 'antipathy' is an interesting one. It carries a sense of passive resentment and little or no sense of activity or engagement. In his analysis of Rogers' own self-concept, Holland (1977) echoes this point. Through a reading of Rogers' biography, Holland concludes that Rogers himself tended to retreat and withdraw when faced with conflict. Nevertheless, Rogers' scepticism argues for flexible, even fluid, structures which are *person*-centred and, necessarily given that they are based on relationship and communication, probably small-scale. We all have personal and professional experience of the joys and anxieties of a flexible and fluid structure at Temenos, where students and staff alike are often stimulated and frustrated by the changes we ourselves initiate!

- *Indifference to material things* – Rogers clearly places the qualities and attitudes of the person of tomorrow above materialism. This is particularly challenging for people living in materialistic, market societies in advanced economies in which implicit and explicit league tables regarding schools, toys, clothes, holidays, and earnings encourage us to want more and to compete to get more. In this Rogers almost seems to be prefiguring more recent ideas and practice about sustainable development and downsizing (see Chapter 17).

Citizenship

In Britain there has been a recent resurgence of interest in citizenship and in the contribution of education and psychotherapy to citizenship. The British government's Advisory Group on Citizenship (1998) considers that: 'citizenship and the teaching of democracy … is so important both for schools and the life of the nation that there must be a statutory requirement on schools to ensure that it is part of the entitlement of all pupils' (p. 7). Whilst supporting the notion of citizenship, Flew (2000) is particularly critical and sceptical of the government's fear of life without state intervention, of the imposition of citizenship as part of the national curriculum, and of the view that such government intervention will necessarily be efficacious in creating effective citizens. Referring to the potential contribution of psychotherapy to citizenship, Bellah *et al.* (1991) argue that 'the goal must be nothing less than a shift from radical individualism to a notion of citizenship based on a more complex understanding of individual and social happiness' (p. 107).

Being a citizen

Of course, *being* a citizen depends on legal status as much as if not more than having a felt or existential sense of citizenship. Historically and currently, some have had more status than others: property owners, men, adults, and people in the community have had more status than workers, women, children, detained patients and prisoners. A person cannot *be* a citizen if she or he *is* not a citizen, and in Britain we are still subjects rather than citizens. Citizenship is generally defined in relation to rights: to hold a passport, to residence, to vote, to pay tax and to receive benefits. These human rights are particularly pressing issues at present given the politics and economics of migration, immigration, and asylum. The psychology of these issues is often framed in a dynamic of inclusion or exclusion: 'Whom do we "let in"?,' 'We shouldn't be a "soft touch",' 'They get "special treatment",'

'They don't care,' 'This is the mother country. I thought it was a tolerant society.' Tudor and Hargaden (2002) discuss these dynamics in relation to admission and membership to citizenship as well as the pluralism of citizenship.

Belonging as a citizen

Despite *being* citizens in terms of status and rights, some people do not have a sense of *belonging*:

- Women who, as 54 per cent of the world's 6.2 billion people, hold up half the sky, do not hold anywhere near half the political power. In Britain, for instance, only 18 per cent of Members of Parliament are women.
- Older people, despite their life experience and increasing longevity, are generally marginalised by societies which deify youth and devalue the experience of the elderly, a theme W. Berry (1999) takes up in his proposal for the creation of sustainable local communities. The increase in the abuse of elders – the National Center on Elder Abuse (www.elderabusecenter.org) in the United States estimates between one and two million elders are abused each year, abuse which encompasses neglect, physical abuse, financial and material exploitation, emotional and sexual abuse – illustrates most starkly the lack of equal consideration for them as citizens.
- Children in many countries, including the UK, are still subject to corporal punishment.
- Disabled people are marginalised and excluded by a largely inaccessible environment.

Ultimately, belonging as citizen is about status, security and accessibility as much as it is concerned with experience and perception; and is dependent on an ongoing and proactive process of *becoming* through active participation in intersubjective relationships with other citizens.

Becoming a citizen

If we assume the status of citizen, we also face the question of the extent to which people participate as citizens, or not. Perhaps significantly, the word 'idiot' originally meant someone who took no part in the life of the state. Rogers' (1980c) vision of the 'person of tomorrow' provides us with some ideas about the qualities of an active, reflective, critical and involved fully functioning citizen.

One of the problems with the person-centred theory of the organism is that it can appear that the organism is the passive recipient of environmental influences: it moves towards positively valued experiences and away from negatively valued ones. If I meet with hostility I may well move away from the source of it. If I experience an inflexible, even oppressive institution, I may be antipathetic to it, stay and succumb or simply go elsewhere. If I see injustice I may cross over and walk by on the other side of the road. Martin Niemöller puts this well:

> *First They Came for the Jews*
> First they came for the Jews
> and I did not speak out
> because I was not a Jew.
> Then they came for the Communists
> and I did not speak out
> because I was not a Communist.
> Then they came for the trade unionists
> and I did not speak out
> because I was not a trade unionist.
> Then they came for me
> and there was no one left
> to speak out for me.
> Martin Niemöller

However, the pro-social tendency of the organism leads us to a more active view of the organism as 'a purposeful, open system, in particularly active interchange with its environment' (Barrett-Lennard, 1998, p. 75), and of the organism as a fully functioning person or citizen in an 'integrated process of changingness' (Rogers, 1958/1967, p. 158). In this sense, passing by, standing by (or bystanding) and turning a 'blind eye' are all examples which involve some denial of our own experience and some distortion of our sense of ourselves. This offers an understanding of passivity ('You can't change things'), discounting ('What can I do?'), disengagement ('It's not my problem') and fear ('If I do something I'll get into trouble'). The comic and radical Michael Moore questions his participation as an American citizen because he hasn't been arrested – yet! (see Moore, 2002). Conversely, a congruent, integrated organism in context will manifest as a person who takes active responsibility for herself, her relationships, her local environment, and the wider world. As the anthropologist Margaret Mead is said to have put it: 'Never doubt that a small group of thoughtful, committed citizens can change the world; indeed it's the only thing that ever does.'

Elaborating this, Tudor and Hargaden (2002) describe a movement from subject (as in British *subjects*) to subjectivity, and from subjectivity to intersubjectivity, a movement which is necessary before people can become fully functioning citizens. They state their concern with and interest in 'the *process* of citizenship (personally, psychologically and politically) and the ability (or otherwise) of people being, becoming and belonging as active citizens' (p. 157), and go on to quote Habermas (1994): 'The nation of citizens does not derive its identity from common ethnic and cultural properties but rather from the praxis of citizens who actively exercise their civil rights' (p. 23).

Citizenship brings with it both rights and responsibilities. Interestingly the *right* to vote is, with few exceptions, not matched by a *duty* to vote: in only 33 countries in the world is voting compulsory, with only nine of these strictly enforcing this law and duty. This is on the basis that compulsory voting is or may be viewed as an infringement of the freedom of expression. Another right and responsibility in many countries is the right to trial by jury, a right which, in Britain, dates back to the Magna Carta (1215) and is currently under threat from the present British government. This right is complemented by the responsibility of the citizen to serve on juries and thereby to be involved in the system of criminal justice.

Justice

In traditional judicial systems, the focus is on proving that an individual has broken a law, for which a penalty is imposed by a judge or magistrate, based on tariff and/or precedent. The emphasis here is on the relationship between the law, crime, and a finding of guilt and punishment. The victim of any crime becomes incidental to this system, except as providing the evidence of guilt; the offender is seen as an offender against the law, rather than against a particular person or community. This leaves the victims of crime and their families as passive bystanders or, fuelled by an often righteous media, an angry lynch mob. However, in recent years there has been increasing interest in the victims of crime and, importantly for our current interest, in the relationship between victim and offender, society and the law (the latter often summarised as 'community'). In this part of the chapter we consider the principles and practice of 'restorative justice' and draw the links between this and the person-centred approach.

Restorative justice

In contrast to the traditional system, the concept and practice of 'restorative justice' is often viewed as a 'victim-centred' response to crime, one:

> that provides opportunities for those most directly affected by the crime – the victim, the offender, their families, and representatives of the community – to be directly involved in responding to the harm caused by the crime. [It] is based upon values which emphasize the importance of providing opportunities for more active involvement in the process of: offering support and assistance to crime victims; holding offenders directly accountable to the people and communities they have violated; restoring the emotional and material losses of victims (to the degree possible); providing a range of opportunities for dialogue and problem solving among interested crime victims, offenders, families, and other support persons; offering offenders opportunities for competency development and reintegration into productive community life; and strengthening public safety through community building. (Umbreit, 2000, p. 1)

However, restorative justice does more than simply refocus justice to centre on the victim. It is also about *engagement*: engaging the victims, offenders and the community in a process of addressing the harm done by crime. In other words, approaches based on restorative justice are concerned with the restoration of relationships and the healing of pain caused by the offending behaviour and, in endeavouring to understand the cause of the behaviour, to prevent any further recurrence: 'Restorative justice views crime primarily as injury (rather than lawbreaking) and the purpose of justice as healing (rather than punishment alone)' (Newell, 2000, p. 44). As Sharpe (1998) puts it in her book on the subject: 'Justice, in any kind of system, should be the highest possible expression of accountability balanced with care.'

Newell identifies programmes which draw on this approach to justice as belonging to one of two categories: those that provide restorative *processes*, and those that provide restorative *outcomes*. Restorative *processes* include:

- Victim/offender mediation and reconciliation – where offenders and their victims are offered the opportunity to come together in a controlled setting which allows the victim to share the pain that has been caused, and the offender to answer questions about why and how they committed the offence.
- Family group conferences, used in care and protection cases, or situations in which a young offender is being dealt with within the youth

justice system – which enables the family of the offender to discuss how they can be brought to understand the impact of their behaviour.

- Victim/offender panels, developed originally as a means of giving convicted drunk drivers an appreciation of the human impact of their behaviour on victims and survivors, these provide the opportunity for an indirect constructive encounter (see Chapter 14) between the offender and victims of similar crimes where the offender or victim are unable or unwilling to meet directly. It can create closure for the victim and increase awareness for the offender.
- Sentencing circles, whereby a judge facilitates a conference, sets out the tariff for an offence, and leads participants in a discussion about the appropriate sentence.
- Community crime prevention.

Restorative *outcomes* include: restitution, community service, victim support service, victim compensation, and rehabilitation programmes for offenders. A fully restorative justice system would incorporate both restorative processes and restorative outcomes.

The processes can be invoked at any point in the formal judicial process. For example, Newell (*ibid.*) tells the story of a group of young men who had taken to hanging about in an underpass in an urban area, causing distress and inconvenience to local residents by their use of foul language, commission of minor thefts and criminal damage, and urinating. Finally, one of the local residents came out to remonstrate with the young men, an argument ensued and two of the young men assaulted the resident. When arrested and interviewed, the young men expressed their remorse and shame. They had not appreciated the impact of their behaviour. A pre-court mediation session was therefore held with the victim of the assault, who accepted that he had also become angry; the offenders' apologies were duly accepted and a full discussion took place, following which the underpass was cleared, with the offenders explaining the problem to their peers. The offenders received a caution, there was no recurrence of the problem, and the assault victim was satisfied.

Mediation can also occur after a sentence has been served. In another example quoted by Newell, a woman and her young son were the victims of an aggravated burglary in which they were terrorised by the burglar. The young boy suffered persistent nightmares, and as the burglar's prison term drew to a close, the woman became concerned that he might return. After approaching her local Citizen's Advice Bureau, she was offered mediation and a meeting was arranged with the newly released offender who was upset to hear how concerned the victim was, apologised in full, and reassured her that he had no intention of returning. The victim accepted the apology and reassurance, found the meeting helpful, and was in turn able to reassure her son whose nightmares stopped shortly after.

Even where it is not possible for a victim and offender to speak directly, this system allows for reparation. Newell cites another example of a woman who had been suffering nightmares since a burglary for which the offender had not been caught. She was offered the opportunity to meet with another burglar who was able to answer her questions to her satisfaction, releasing her from the fear she had been carrying, and allowing him the opportunity to apologise for his crimes and misdemeanours.

The principles of restorative justice are becoming increasingly evident in the United Kingdom's legal systems. Building on the experience in the Scottish youth justice system, the Crime and Disorder Act 1998 attempts to introduce the principles of restorative justice into the youth justice system in England and Wales. This piece of legislation and its associated guidance, together with the Youth Justice and Criminal Evidence Act 1999, suggest that restorative approaches to justice be mainstreamed.

Circles of support and accountability

The principles of restorative justice are also being brought to bear in the highly contentious area of dealing with sex offenders. Learning from experiences in Canada where 'circles of support and accountability' (COSA) are used to provide social support to high-risk sex offenders on release from prison, three pilot projects are now being established by the UK's Home Office Dangerous Offenders Unit in partnership with local police and probation services, and local communities, including faith groups such as the Quakers (Society of Friends) (see www.restorativejustice.org.uk). The COSA consist of six volunteers who meet with the core member/offender to provide them with support and friendship, initially intensively and then, as the person builds their own networks of friendship, less frequently. The COSA helps the person to articulate and to respond to fears and obstacles, hopes and aspirations, and to enable them to build a new life, with the overall aim being to ensure that the person does not offend again:

> Many sex offenders are lonely and isolated before offending, and even more leave prison or treatment having lost whatever small circle of social contacts

they had before. Since social isolation is a factor which can contribute to sex offending, the Circle seeks to provide a 'mini community' to which the offender, the 'Core Member', can relate and where he can be accepted and grow in self esteem, something which is necessary if the treatment he has received is to be of maximum benefit. (Foot, undated)

A circle is only set up at the core member's request and to meet their individual needs. They are fully involved, and it is unusual for the circle to meet without the core member being present. All members of the circle make a written commitment to the aims of the circle, which includes no re-offending, so everyone, including the core member is accountable for their actions to the others. The circle also helps with practical issues such as housing and benefits, and liaises with statutory bodies such as police and probation services, which are responsible for the supervision of the core member. For their part, volunteers are selected, vetted, trained and supported by project staff, who occasionally attend circle meetings and are therefore also known to the core member (see Heise, Dyck and McWhinnie, 2002).

The COSA are a powerful example of person-centred principles in action, involving as they do:

- The engagement of a local community (*psychological contact*).
- Supporting someone whose behaviour has breached one of its greatest taboos, in a humane and constructive way, believing that change is possible (*actualising tendency*).
- Upholding the individual person with love (*unconditional positive regard*) and *empathy* and without judgement (*non-directiveness of experience*), but with a clear holding to account (the other side of *psychological contact*).

Other applications

These principles and practice of the circles of support and accountability are also in evidence outside the formal justice system. In some schools, for instance, an approach based on restorative justice has been used to help improve teacher and pupil satisfaction, improve communication and cooperation, and increase progress in academically able pupils. Instead of seeing rule-breaking as an offence against the school, with pupils not being invited to accept responsibility for their actions and punishments which do not provide a way forward in resolving those disputes, a restorative justice approach accepts conflict as part of life; allows young people to take responsibility for their feelings and behaviour; and empowers young people, teachers and parents to handle conflict in positive ways. As a whole-school approach, it typically employs whole-school conflict resolution programmes and peer mediation for pupils and teachers and may be viewed as part of a broader vision of a health-promoting school (see Weare, 2000). Circles of support are also increasingly used in supporting adults and children with learning difficulties and children with challenging behaviours, engaging the wider community in working with and supporting its most vulnerable members.

Justice and peace are inextricably linked as a society cannot achieve justice without peace, and there can be no real peace, especially between nations, without justice. At the time of writing, during the invasion of Iraq, this is a topical and pertinent issue, especially with the passing in the United States of America of the Patriot Act 2001.

> Beware the leader who bangs the drums of war in order to whip the citizenry into a patriotic fervour, for patriotism is indeed a double-edged sword. It both emboldens the blood, just as it narrows the mind. And when the drums of war have reached a fever pitch and the blood boils with hate and the mind has closed, the leader will have no need in seizing the rights of the citizenry. Rather, the citizenry, infused with fear and blinded by patriotism, will offer up all of their rights unto the leader and gladly so. How do I know? For this is what I have done. And I am Caesar. (attr. Julius Caesar)[1]

Peace

Rogers began development of the person-centred approach as a counsellor with servicemen returning home after the Second World War (Rogers and Wallen, 1946). He came full circle, and ended his career by developing the approach to work for conflict resolution and international community development. In 1984, with Gay Swenson, he founded the Carl Rogers Peace Project (later the Institute for Peace) in La Jolla, California. He was nominated for the Nobel Peace Prize shortly before his death (see Appendix), and news of this nomination came on the day of his death, 4 February 1987 (N. Rogers, 2002).

As early as 1952, Rogers was proposing an open, non-judgemental dialogue between a therapeutically oriented team and both Russian and US

---

[1] Although these words are attributed to Julius Caesar, there is some debate as to their origin. Some have suggested that they first appeared after 11 September 2001.

leaders with a view to identifying, articulating and publishing the genuine views, attitudes and feelings of each toward the other as a first step towards conflict resolution between the two nations (Rogers and Roethlisberger, 1952). As Barrett-Lennard (1998) points out, there is a sense in which Rogers' theory of personal-emotional distress is essentially a conflict-oriented model, as the individual person in a state of anxiety feels unable to express, or even acknowledge, unvalued feelings and experiences. The person-centred therapeutic approach can therefore be seen as an approach to conflict resolution, enabling the client, through feeling received by a congruent, acceptant and empathic listener, to re-contact and express the rejected parts of themselves.

Where conflict exists between two people, two groups or two nations, Rogers considered that the same dynamic applies: each group would accept its own experiences and believe themselves to be wholly right and good, and the other to be wholly wrong. As in the therapeutic relationship, Rogers believed that a person-centred facilitator could help reduce this tension by listening non-judgementally and empathically to each side, and thus empowering each individual person involved:

> to become ... more expressive, more open to feelings, good and bad. And it is out of that more complete and powerful humanness that person touches person, communication becomes real, tensions are reduced, and relationships become expressive and understanding, with an acceptance of the negative as well as the positive. (Rogers, 1978, pp. 138–9)

Rogers applied this approach in practice in a number of organisational, professional and community settings around the world, perhaps most famously in workshops held in South Africa with Black, coloured, and white participants exploring together the personal implications of apartheid (see Rogers, 1986); and in Belfast where participation from both sides of the conflict provided a very real challenge to the facilitation team, but resulted in a degree of understanding between participants that fully supported Rogers' belief in the potential of the approach. Some of the learning from this powerful event is recorded in a video *The Steel Shutter* (McGaw, 1973).

International relations

In 1960 Rogers wrote *A Therapist's view of Personal Goals*, published in a Quaker publication, in which he considered the application of the person-centred approach to conflict resolution from the perspective of international relations. Of statements on United States (US) foreign policy made by their leaders, he says:

> ... that our diplomacy is always based upon high moral purposes; that it is always consistent with the policies we have followed previously; that it involves no selfish desires; and that it has never been mistaken in its judgement and choices. (Rogers, 1960/1990, p. 436)

If such statements were being made by an individual, he suggests, then they would not be credible, but would be seen as a façade, and at best a partial truth. So he speculates on what a more congruent set of statements might be, and proposes, with chilling resonance in the light of today's international arena over 40 years on, the following:

> We as a nation are slowly realizing our enormous strength, and the power and responsibility which go with that strength. We are moving, somewhat ignorantly and clumsily, toward accepting a position of responsible world leadership. We make mistakes. We are often inconsistent ... We have some very selfish foreign interests, such as in the oil in the Middle East ... We have complex and contradictory feelings towards the freedom and independence and self-determination of individuals and countries ... We tend to value and respect the dignity and worth of each individual, yet when we are frightened, we move away from this direction. (Rogers, 1960/1990, p. 436)

Rogers then considers the potential impact that such statements might have on US international relations, which might then follow the path of an improving relationship (Rogers, 1959). He suggests that the US would feel more comfortable, having now nothing to hide, and released from the energy required to convince others that the policies of the US are wholly moral and consistent, they would be able to focus creatively on the problems at hand. Able to acknowledge their selfish interests openly, the US leadership would be more able to express their empathic concern for the needs and viewpoints of others, and without the need to uphold a rigid concept of identity, would be able to adjust their position responsively. Experienced as more congruent and open by other countries, the US would be less feared and distrusted, and their openness more likely to be reciprocated by other nations. This would enable world leaders to work out solutions to real problems and conflicts, without the distorting distraction of façades. This is particularly poignant as we finish writing this book against the background of the invasion and occupation of Iraq by US forces, supported by troops from the United Kingdom and number of other countries. One of the significant aspects in the build-up to the war was an apparent lack of empathy, particularly on the part of both US and UK governments, towards the needs and viewpoints of others. In the case of the US its traditional isolationism fuels its unilateralism.

The Rust workshop

A quarter of a century after the publication of his paper on international relations, Rogers had the opportunity to try out his ideas in this arena at what came to be known as the Rust workshop. This was a meeting comprising influential people and key decision-makers, who met together in the Austrian village of Rust in November 1985, to consider what might be done to reduce the growing tension in South America. This was a joint venture with Rodrigo Carazo, the former president of Costa Rica, and his associate, Murray Silberman, both from Costa Rica's University of Peace, who were responsible for inviting the delegates; and the Center for Studies of the Person at La Jolla, California, headed by Gay Swenson and Carl Rogers, who provided the administrative and facilitation support to the event. The purpose of the event was to create

> a gathering in which influential international figures could meet 'off the record', and talk, argue, shout, embrace in a situation in which the staff made it safe to do so, until they could come to know one another deeply, come to trust one another more fully, and work together for peaceful solutions. (Rogers, 1986/1990, p. 460)

About 50 participants, half from South America, met on Thursday night, and left between Monday lunchtime and evening. Rogers' day-by-day account of the event describes both the frustrations and the deepening of relationship.

There is little detail in his account that would allow a practitioner to identify what the facilitation team actually did during the event, and Rogers acknowledges that the facilitation was appropriately low key. These were sophisticated participants, able to facilitate themselves: 'It could be said that this was not a demonstration of person-centred procedures; it was a demonstration of a person-centred way of being' (Rogers, 1986/1990, p. 476). Rogers also acknowledges that the participants contributed to the creation of the climate of trust, with some bringing experience of other procedures to reduce tension and resolve conflict. He saw the freedom allowed within the team's approach to enable such modes and techniques to be used as one of the strengths of the event. Rogers reports that for most participants, it was a meaningful and useful experience, which moved substantially towards achieving the purposes that brought the workshop into being: reducing tension, opening channels of communication, and offering an interpersonal experience of peace.

Clearly, this was not the whole story. At least one person felt negatively about the event, and Rogers believed that others shared this dissatisfaction. He identifies several mistakes and disappointments, including the last minute withdrawal of key participants from the US administration, and the lack of effective communications between the co-sponsors. Whilst the geographical distance between them and the differences in culture and approach contributed to this, Rogers also acknowledges that each side underestimated the contribution that the other was making to the workshop.

His acknowledgement of a lack of cultural awareness between the facilitation team and participants is supported by Soloman (1987) who notes that there appeared to be 'general disappointment in the conference amongst the Latins', evidently the group accounting for most participants with roles in government, and those seeing least connection between the 'political and the personal' (p. 346). Another member of the facilitation team, John K. Wood, felt that the desire of the team to model a particular approach actually inhibited their full participation in this philosophy in the event. He also suggests, but does not elaborate, that the basic assumptions of the person-centred approach to conflict resolution were in fact too simplistic to be useful in this event (see Wood, 1994). In his review of Rogers' work in conflict resolution and peace processes, Barrett-Lennard (1998) also reviews the impact of this workshop.

Despite Rogers' evident commitment to this area of application, with the exception of Devonshire and Kremer (1980) there has been little written about the person-centred approach to conflict resolution, and specific references to the person-centred approach are not evident in the literature of peace-making. However, the influence of person-centred principles is pervasive, and it is useful to consider current approaches within the peace movement to see if we can identify any similarities in approach.

Social action

In her classic handbook for social action, Shields proposes a number of 'tools' which are compatible with a person-centred philosophy (Shields, 1991). Firstly, she identifies the power of deep, interested, non-judgemental, reflective listening in helping people to identify and express their doubts, confusions and half-formed ideas; in helping to break taboos on certain topics; and in beginning the process of conflict resolution.

Fran Peevey, an American peace and social action campaigner, became increasingly concerned about the nuclear weapons build-up around the world in the 1960s and 70s, but was aware that she knew few people outside her own country, or how they might view the subject (Peevey, 1986). She therefore began to travel around the world, setting up a seat in public places under a banner which identified her as an 'American willing to listen'. She acknowledged that some of what she heard was challenging, particularly the attacks on her country, but she simply observed her internal response and kept on listening and clarifying. The impact of this on her was that she found that she heard the news in a different way, seeing things from within a broader context, and holding herself accountable to the people she had met. This reverses the logic of megaphone diplomacy whereby the leader who thinks he 'knows best' shouts loudest to convince others of his truth, and backs up his argument with the instruments of economic and military war. The more radical solution is to understand, or to attempt to understand.

The impact on those who spoke to her is not known, but Peevey's approach has inspired many other peace and environmental campaigners around the world, and has transformed many demonstrations, where demonstrators actively seek opportunities to listen to those who might be seen to be in conflict with them. One example of this cited by Shields (1991) is of a demonstration held in Canberra, Australia, against French nuclear testing in the South Pacific. The organisers set up tables and chairs in French café style and offered French pastries to passers-by to enjoy, whilst giving their written comments on what they appreciated about the French and French culture, and what they did not appreciate about the way that the French government was acting. The low confrontational style of the demonstration encouraged the French ambassador to visit the café and share a bottle of French wine with the demonstrators whilst joining them *in dialogue*. This mirrors the approach advocated by Rogers and Roethlisberger in 1952.

Just as Rogers identified that empathic, non-judgemental listening enables the establishment of an effective relationship between two parties in a conflict, so Shields proposes the building of bridges with the opposition. She proposes that campaigners need to be soft on the person and hard on the issue. This requires collecting factual information so that the campaigner can congruently present their concerns in a well-supported way, but it also requires an attempt to understand how the opponent might be perceiving the issue and a seeking for common ground in which to establish relationship. One of us (JV) worked with a group of anti-road campaigners some years ago and her experience supports this.

During the campaign, considerable aggression was expressed towards the 'suits': the people in the construction industry who made their living by building roads and thereby destroying some natural habitats. My suggestion that the activists might consider how these people might actually be feeling, and that they might share a concern for the environment, but might also be concerned about their jobs and mortgages, was perceived by some of the participants at the time as lacking in integrity. They believed absolutely in the rightness of their position. I let the matter rest. Some months later, I received a letter from one of the workshop participants explaining that she had temporarily sought work as a nanny with a family whose main breadwinner was an executive in a construction company. As she had lived in the house with him and observed his concerns for his future job security, she had been reminded of our discussion, and had been able to approach him empathically with questions about his own feelings about the impact on the natural environment of his work. She was astonished to learn that he shared many of her concerns, but felt trapped by the need to support his family in a particular lifestyle in a period when alternative employment options seemed few.

The work of the prestigious Oxford Research Group bears striking similarities to the Rust workshop described earlier. An independent team of researchers and support staff, they were established in 1982 to carry out research into the structures and processes of nuclear weapon decision-making worldwide, and have conducted studies for, amongst others, the United Nations University, the United States Institute for Peace, and the European Parliament. As part of their research, they arrange 'consultations between groups of policy makers and independent experts to discuss the priority issues of nuclear disarmament ... We foster dialogue between those who hold differing views on nuclear issues – always with a view to building bridges of understanding' (Oxford Research Group, undated). Such consultations are held away from the public eye and are professionally facilitated.

In their short publication *Everyone's Guide to Achieving Change*, the Oxford Research Group outline a step-by-step approach to dialogue with decision-makers which echoes, and might usefully have informed, the Rust experience.

Firstly, they propose three underpinning principles:

- Change happens at the level of the individual. This would support Rogers' view that conflict, and its resolution, essentially happens between individual human beings.
- Recognise the difference between dialogue and lobbying. Dialogue is a two-way process and involves listening. This echoes Rogers' (1959) descriptions of a process for an improving relationship.
- Get beyond the way of thinking that caused the problem in the first place. When the feedback changes, so does the system. When we really open ourselves in relationship to listen to another, we take the risk that our own views may be changed as a result: we move from the 'I am wholly right and you are wholly wrong' stance that Rogers identified at the root of many conflicts, to a more congruent expression of our own position and an empathic understanding of the other.

The second step is to identify the key decision-makers. This was one of the failings of the Rust workshop. Clearly the US administration were key parties to the conflict in South America, and were initially invited to attend, but withdrew shortly before the event. You can only dialogue with people who are there. A later step in the process advocated by the Oxford Research Group offers suggestions for handling decision-makers who are reluctant to engage. Spending more time on this, either before or during the Rust workshop, might have proved helpful.

The next steps are concerned with preparing for dialogue by identifying assumptions that each party may hold about the beliefs of the other; and planning a first contact which demonstrates your knowledge of the decision-maker's area of responsibility, and which is non-aggressive. Here we have four principles of effective person-centred communication: making (psychological) contact; congruent self-expression; a withholding of judgement (albeit potentially temporarily); and empathic listening with a view to understanding.

To support this, potential change-makers are advised to take care of their own anger, and there is a strong emphasis on non-confrontational communications. Tudor and Worrall (1994) identify the difference between congruent self-awareness and communicating our awareness to another, the latter being informed in therapeutic encounters by the evolution of coherent and ethical criteria. It can similarly be argued in the Oxford Research Group's approach to dialogue with decision-makers that the change agent may need to consider whether the expression of their feelings is likely to enhance the probability and quality of such dialogue. Thich Nhat Hanh's

(1987) proposition that in order to work for peace, one must first *be peace* has echoes of Rogers' *being process* and is a powerful argument for congruence, and one that has had a significant impact within the peace movement.

In considering preparations for a first meeting, the Oxford Research Group (undated) suggests a series of fairly straightforward questions about the intended outcomes of any encounter, and about the environment in which the meeting will take place. This echoes Worrall's (1997, p. 71) description of contracting within person-centred counselling: 'In a spirit of congruence or honesty I want to acknowledge, at least to myself and if necessary to my client, what my needs and expectations are in this relationship.' So the facilitator of change needs to be clear, at least within herself, about what she wants to achieve from the meeting, and to acknowledge that the decision-maker too will have her own needs and interests. From a practical perspective, Rogers (1986/1990) acknowledged the importance of creating an appropriate environment for the Rust workshop. He included the hotel staff in the team of people whose efforts he believed had created a safe and permissive climate for the event. In this he acknowledges that empathy and respect are also created in the environments we create, and not just in the verbal components of our relationships.

Considering follow-up and evaluation of an encounter, the Oxford Research Group considers how the facilitator of change can build sustainable relationships with decision-makers. This places relationship at the heart of change and takes place within a larger context. They recommend a clear strategy in relation to the press that will support change without endangering the relationship established. Again, this mirrors Rogers' experience at the Rust workshop where the needs of the press intruded into the workshop and, in an era before media 'spin', the content of press releases was not fully agreed with participants in advance.

Finally, the Oxford Research Group (undated, p. 13) reinforces the need to remember that change is possible:

> When faced with world problems – like hunger, over-population, nuclear weapons, the arms trade – you may be among those who are feeling overwhelmed by a feeling of 'Help! What on earth can I, just one person, do about this?' Take heart. That is a sane response. It's the basis of a whole new attitude to world problems, where change at the level of the individual is more and more recognised as essential to change in huge world systems.

The Research Group goes on to quote Mary Clarke, a biologist, as saying: 'To the extent that our future survival is due to our own behaviour – our own adaptiveness ... we have the option to rethink our ideas about what kinds of human behaviour and human cultural institutions are adaptive.' This links directly to Rogers' principle of the actualising tendency and to his theory of personality and behaviour (Rogers, 1951).

Finally, we come back full circle to the relationship between therapy and peace work. In Nicaragua, former soldiers from the Sandinista and the resistance armies, who had previously fought each other, now work together using their military skills in the reconstruction of their country. The Education and Action for Peace Programme offers training in non-violent conflict resolution and peace-building using a participatory training methodology that includes, that involves therapy and self-therapy, 'based on empathy, including personal and collective psychological rehabilitation' (Bendana, 1999, p. 371). This work, which began in 1991, has had encouraging results:

> Few images can be more depolarising than that of joint enemies working and caring together ... Demobilised soldiers from all sides of the conflict are communicating, building relationships of trust, and beyond that tackling common problems in a unitary fashion. Not that they have been converted, reneged on their past or abandoned old political allegiances, but rather they have established new working frameworks of reconciliation in a framework of tolerance and mutual respect. (p. 372)

SUMMARY

- Rogers describes the characteristics of the emerging 'person of tomorrow'. This prefigures contemporary notions of citizenship.
- Being and belonging as a citizen derive from status, security, and access; becoming a citizen involves the organism/person in particularly active interchange with its environment, including an involvement with the system of justice.
- The concept and practice of restorative justice concerns itself with the restoration of relationships and the healing of the pain caused by offence; and with processes, such as mediation between victim and offender, rather than outcomes, such as community service.
- Rogers contributed actively to the field of international conflict resolution and peace.
- The person-centred approach has views about engagement in social action.

Beyond the Individual, Beyond Therapy

IV

> Probably no-one who has tried consistently to carry on individual psychotherapy with an orientation that is essentially client-centred has failed to think about the possibility of applying this philosophy to group leadership and organizational administration.
>
> (Gordon, 1951, p. 320)

> Since its beginnings, client-centered therapy has also sought wider spheres of influence, beyond the individual, both in attempting to explore the relevance of its ideas in contexts broader than traditional dyadic therapy and in seeking to apply its approach to wider social milieus.
>
> (Wexler and Rice, 1974, p. 313)

In Part III we explored certain implications and applications of the person-centred approach. In doing so we focused primarily on the individual, albeit in their immediate relational, family, environmental and social contexts. In this part, we change the focal point from the individual person to couples, groups and organisations, and to the wider environment itself (echoing a similar structure in Wexler and Rice's 1974 volume). In doing so, the person-centred approach takes a systems perspective on these entities or organisms. According to Angyal (1941), what makes a system is the fluidity of the relationship between the discrete elements that make up the system. When we talk about a couple or a group, for instance, as a system, we're recognising that the relationship between the partners or members changes over time, and that different aspects of the relationship become more or less significant at different times. It's in this sense that change to any element in a system affects the whole system: if one member of the group changes, her relationship with everyone else in the system is necessarily different because

211

she's different. This description of a system informs much of what we have to say in this part of the book.

In three of the first four chapters – on couples, groups, and organisation – we also consider the implications of a study of these systems for the approach itself and the role of the person-centred practitioner as a facilitator of the process of these systems. In this sense, a subheading of this part might be: 'Encountering the system'. Thus, in the chapter on groups we discuss facilitation and leadership. In the person-centred approach these two words are used synonymously, at least theoretically. In the world of work and organisation, however, 'leadership' is used more widely and we explore the impact of person-centred 'facilitation' on notions of leadership. Four of the five chapters contain short case studies which show the application of person-centred principles in the arena under discussion. The final chapter, on the environment, applies the principles of the person-centred approach to our human understanding of the ecosystem.

Couple

We've discussed the significance of relationship and relationships between adults in Chapter 9, and between parent and child in Chapter 10. In this chapter we consider the contribution of the person-centred approach to our understanding of the couple in relationship and to our work as therapists with couples. Rogers (1973) wrote about marriage and its alternatives and we've referred to this in Chapter 9. 'Couples counselling' or therapy generally refers to work with an identified couple, whilst the broader term 'relational counselling' or 'relationship enhancement therapy' (see Guerney, 1984) refers both to therapeutic work with any dyad or pair, such as a parent and child or colleagues at work, as well as to couples counselling and family therapy. It's also possible to see family therapy or therapy with couples as examples of group therapy (see Chapter 14). The key to all of these therapeutic forms is that both therapists and clients understand relationships as *systems*, and that the therapist or facilitator applies the principles of the approach to their own relationship *with* the system, as well as to relationships *within* the system, that is, between partners, or group members.

The couple and the system

In addition to being two individuals, a couple create their own unique relational system which gives birth, often tangibly, to another entity: two become three. Traditionally, the couples therapist focuses on this relationship, on the space *in between* the individuals, rather than on the individuals themselves. Within the person-centred approach Barrett-Lennard (1984), Levant (1984) and Natiello (1991/2001) have explored this transition from person to system; and Barrett-Lennard (1998) reviews the history of the impact of Rogers' theory on the practice of marital counselling and couple therapy. We consider a systems approach to be entirely compatible with person-centred thinking, since, as we've shown in Chapters 2 and 3, we see the human organism itself as a complex system. O'Leary (1999) identifies a number of useful ideas about systems thinking which are useful for the systems therapist or facilitator:

- *The whole is greater than the sum of its parts*
  This is certainly consistent with an holistic view of the human organism, although a whole family, for instance, may also have to cope with one member wanting to differentiate herself in some way. From a person-centred perspective we need to acknowledge *both* the tendency to differentiate *and* the tendency to integrate. This tension is is often a key dynamic in a couple's relationship.
- *Any change in one part of a system affects the whole system*
  This helps both therapist and client to look at all parts, and not just at the 'presenting problem' or a particular identified person, in order to make and effect change. Some parents seek help, perhaps therapy, for a child. In our view it is incumbent on the therapist to ask whether the child is the client or, drawing on a systems perspective, whether it would be more effective for the family and less pathologising of the child to see either the parents on their own or, indeed, the whole family. As we discussed in Chapter 9 some therapists work only with parents who are legally, practically and psychologically reponsible for caring for their children. Any change in the parent/s will inevitably affect the children. Similarly if one partner in a relationship goes into therapy (or, for that matter, trains as a therapist), this will often have a profound effect on the relationship.
- *Individual reality is co-created*
  From this perspective there is no 'sick role', only a relational system which is in some way incongruent, and whose vulnerability or anxiety is being expressed by certain people in the system. Hence the importance of a systemic assessment for all individuals and systems.
- *Causality is circular, not linear*
  This helps us move away from linear causal thinking and blaming. Taking the complaint: 'I can't be myself because you're so dominating,' it may be equally 'true' that one person is so dominating because another is not being himself. Faced with disagreement, dispute or a row, the couples therapist, rather than taking sides or even trying to 'sort it out', attempts to understand both parties and, perhaps most importantly, to see how they *both* create, co-create and re-create this

particular pattern and way of relating. Berne refers to this pattern of creating and re-creating repetitive patterns of social behaviour as a 'psychological game' (Berne, 1968).

Natiello (1991/2001) similarly discusses a number of principles of systems theory and their relevance for groups as living systems (see Chapter 14).

Whilst it is useful to identify these ideas and their implications for practice, we do not wish to restrict their application to therapy with more than one person. They are perhaps more obvious and more obviously relevant in the context of couples therapy, but they are not unique to it. O'Leary (1999) points out that they may also be applied to the systems *within* the individual, whether that is understood within the person-centred approach as 'configurations of self' (Mearns, 1999), as ego states within transactional analysis, or as subpersonalities (Rowan, 1990).

In terms of the development of the couple system, Rogers' model is based on an organismic process of differentiation and integration (see Chapter 5). This is similar to Bader and Pearson's (1988) process model of the couple's relationship which they based on Mahler, Pine and Bergman's (1975) process model of child development. They view differentiation developmentally as manifesting from five to nine months of age, in which total bodily dependence on mother begins to decrease. This involves a certain amount of pulling away from mother and checking back. Pleasure in the outside world 'is expressed in close proximity to mother' (Mahler, Pine and Bergman, p. 289). Based on the hypothesis of a process of necessary separation-individuation in normal development, Bader and Pearson propose a similar movement in the developing relationship of the couple from symbiosis *through differentiation*, practising and rapprochement, to mutual interdependence.

Couples therapy

> Person-centred couples counselling contains elements of curiosity, of a philosophy about relationships, of letting go, of confrontation at the same time as acceptance, of empathic understanding for each individual and of active facilitation of dialogue. (O'Leary, 1999, p. 122)

In terms of working with the system of the couple or dyad, the principles of the person-centred approach (see Chapter 1) apply equally to the couple and to the individuals comprising it. The approach:

1   Acknowledges the tendency of the couple to actualise their relationship, through seeking both integration and differentiation.

2 Makes this process – of the couple having different views – part of the relationship, and initially focuses on the contact between them (the first of the necessary and sufficient conditions for change), as well as their mutual respect and understanding. The relationship may be facilitated with reference to these conditions (Rogers, 1959), by the couple themselves (see Rogers, 1973) or as a result of individual therapy (Rogers, 1954/1967b).

3 Reflects a non-directive attitude on the part of the therapist, certainly as far as the content of the presented material is concerned (see, for instance, Cain, 1989c; O'Leary, 1999). In our experience, a common theme for couples who seek therapy is that one wants outside help, and the other doesn't; one says there's a problem, and the other says there isn't. In these situations, rather than getting into whose perception or experience is 'right', it is more effective and relevant for the therapist to reflect to the couple that there is a difference between them. The ensuing discussion then often focuses on how they feel about, understand and negotiate difference, and on their conceived values (see Chapter 8).

In addition to these principles, some person-centred practitioners working in the field of couples, family and group therapy have speculated about what they see as necessary amendments to person-centred theory and practice. O'Leary (1999), for example, cites approvingly the work of the family therapists Boszormenyi-Nagy and Ulrich (1981) and the translation or development of unconditional positive regard into 'multi-directional partiality' whereby the therapist is experienced as being on more than one side at once. O'Leary's advocacy of this partiality seems to be based on some assumptions about the classical person-centred therapist not being active enough or not taking enough initiative, and about unconditional positive regard being too passive a condition. We consider the first, precondition of *contact* as both necessary and sufficient to describe the active engagement of the therapist with all parties to the therapy. In our view this is a sufficient challenge to any tendency of the therapist to be partial, judgemental, disapproving or approving. O'Leary also makes the point that relational counsellors want to bypass the '*described*' spouse and to meet the '*real*' version. However, this seems to ignore the idea that an individual's *perception is* their reality (see Rogers, 1951), however distorted it seems to be, and however helpful it may seem to the therapist to see one person's perception in the context of another's reality. Although basing his work in the person-centred approach and, in some respects, closely so, O'Leary (1999) acknowledges his dialogue with it: 'For me, person-centred relational counselling is a dialogue between these principles and the challenges of facilitating a conversation between two intimates' (p. 9). Many writers on couples therapy from other theoretical perspectives advocate teaching the couple certain skills and techniques to improve communication. Whilst we don't view much of this as necessary, we echo Rogers' (1957) point about techniques, that while their use is generally problematical, they may also on occasion 'become a channel for communicating the essential conditions which have been formulated' (p. 103). O'Leary goes further than this, and advocates the teaching and modelling of specific skills. We view this as problematic for two reasons:

1   That the 'teaching' of 'skills' is often done without reference to the philosophy, principles, or theory of an approach, person-centred or otherwise, as if skills exist in some neutral zone, without a theoretical base and
2   That 'modelling' is a specific technique which has its origins in behaviourism and, as a form of operant conditioning, is antithetical to the person-centred approach (see Wood, 1995).

In terms of our dialogue between principles, theory and practice, we present now a case study of a piece of couples therapy, following which we reflect on the work in the light of Rogers' (1954/1967b) 'characteristics of a helping relationship'.

CASE STUDY: THE PROCESS OF AN IMPROVING RELATIONSHIP

Almost as soon as they met Adam and Evelyn fell in love. Within a month Adam had, to all intents and purposes, moved in with Evelyn. They spent all their spare time together and used to phone each other at work several times a day. Being busy with each other, they both cut off from their own friends. After a few months they had their first row. This was followed by a number of minor disagreements through which they discovered that they differed in some of their attitudes to friends, family and work. Over time, both found that they needed to 'come up for air': Adam spent some nights at his flat; sex, whilst still good, became less frequent; they stopped phoning each other at work; each began to re-establish contact with their friends; each resumed some of their independent interests. After six months, Adam raised the issue of buying a house together, to which Evelyn had a strong, negative reaction. She was happy with the current arrangements and felt Adam was being too demanding; Adam, for his part, felt he had said and done something terribly wrong and

(cont'd)

backed off. They became less intimate; their sexual relationship deteriorated. Minor miscommunications fuelled further rows and both felt misunderstood. At this point they sought help from a couples therapist.

In the initial session they reviewed what they described as their 'whirlwind romance'. It was apparent that, despite their differences, they were very much in love, and committed to each other and to their relationship. *In other words, they were in contact.* In the second session Evelyn talked more about her reaction to Adam's suggestion that they buy a house together and, in talking, realised how frightened she'd been. Adam looked puzzled and a little remote. Evelyn realised that it was one thing for Adam to move in to her house, but quite another for her to give up her independence and 'throw her lot in' with Adam. As she talked about this, she became quite distressed and got in touch with how much she had felt hurt and financially exploited in past relationships. She had trusted others, had been 'let down' and had worked hard to achieve financial and emotional independence. *Evelyn was developing congruence between her experience, awareness and communication.* As Evelyn talked, primarily to the therapist, Adam's face visibly 'melted'; he moved closer to Evelyn and put his arm around her shoulders. In the third session they came in to the consulting room looking much closer and happier. Adam spoke to Evelyn, telling her how much he'd been affected by what she'd said in the last session. *This is an example of reciprocal communication.* For his part, he'd also been frightened at her reaction to his suggestion. He felt he had spoilt something and recognised a pattern from his childhood of withdrawing in the face of actual or perceived disapproval. At this Evelyn smiled, recognising this as her experience of her 'weak' father and of other men she had known. They both recognised a sense of how their past experiences 'locked into' each other's and, in the rest of this and a further two sessions, made a series of connections – what they referred to as 'light bulbs coming on' – which illuminated both their individual and separate histories, as well their common present experiences and interactions. *Their understanding became mutually accurate.* In a sixth and final session they surfaced genuine differences and talked a lot about how they saw the future and what each wanted in terms of career, money, family, lifestyle and friends. Following this therapy, within six months they did buy a house together with separate space for each of them. Whilst maintaining their own friends, they also developed friendships as a couple. Feeling more independent, they actually became closer.

This case study reflects Rogers' law of interpersonal relationships, based on his theory of interpersonal relationships (Rogers, 1959):

> Assuming a minimal mutual willingness to be in contact and to receive communications, we may say that the greater the communicated congruence of experience, awareness and behavior on the part of one individual, the more the ensuing relationship will involve a tendency toward reciprocal communication with the same qualities, mutually accurate understanding of the communications, improved psychological adjustment and functioning in both parties, and mutual satisfaction in the relationship. (p. 240)

SUMMARY

- A couple are – and co-create – their own, unique relational system.
- Systems thinking is useful for the systems therapist/facilitator.
- The principles of the person-centred approach apply to working with a couple or particular dyad.
- Practitioners differ about whether or not person-centred principles are sufficient for work with couples.

Group

13

According to the *Shorter Oxford English Dictionary* a group is 'an assemblage of objects standing near together, and forming a collective unity; a knot (of people), a cluster (of things)...confused aggregation...a number of persons or things in a certain relation, or having a certain degree of similarity' (Onions, 1933/1973, p. 896). These definitions conjure up images of groups in everyday life:

- Young people standing together, 'hanging out' on a street corner, forming, however temporarily, a collective unity which defines its identity by who's 'in' and who's 'out'.
- A knot or tangle of friends, laughing and teasing each other, linking arms as they walk down the road, moving in and out of conversation with each other at a party.
- A confused aggregation of people gathering for a meeting or some event, uncertain of themselves or others.

All these examples show individuals coming together to form a group which then becomes something more than the sum of its component parts. Of course, one of the basic human groups is the family. As Barrett-Lennard (1998) points out: 'Historically, Rogers' professional involvement with families in difficulty preceded the emergence of his own therapeutic orientation, and could be said to have helped to give rise to it' (pp. 137–8). Families and family therapy have been studied from a person-centred perspective by Rogers (1961/1967c), Raskin and van der Veen (1970), Levant (1978, 1982), Barrett-Lennard (1984), Cain (1989a) and notably by Gaylin (1989, 1990, 1993).

If the organism is pro-social, then we are necessarily group animals. We are born into a family group, most of us learn in groups, we often work and socialise in groups, we govern and protest in groups, and we come together in various groups at various times for different purposes throughout our lives. Schmid (1996) makes the point that, in many ways, the group acts as the interface between person and society. For these reasons alone it is worth looking at the experience of being in groups. Furthermore, the person-centred approach has, since Rogers' own book on groups, *Carl Rogers on Encounter Groups* (Rogers, 1970/1973), a strong tradition of promoting the experience and study of groups, with regard to:

- Encounter – see Rogers (1970/1973), Bebout (1974), Beck (1974), Barrett-Lennard (1979) and Merry (1995).
- Cross-cultural communication – see Devonshire (1991), Coghlan and McIlduff (1991), McIlduff and Coghlan (1993a), Rogers (1991) and Wood (1999).
- Diversity – see Sanford (1999).
- Large groups and community – see Bozarth (1981), Wood (1984, 1999), Natiello (1991/2001) (and Chapter 15).
- Group facilitation – see Rogers (1978b).
- Training – see Cilliers (1996) and Mearns (1997).
- Research – see Dierick and Lietaer (1990), Marques-Teixeira *et al.* (1996), MacMillan and Lago (1996), Barrett-Lennard (1998) and Figge (1999).
- Systems theory – see Natiello (1991/2001).

Of these, in this chapter we comment briefly on encounter groups; we then consider one of the core concepts of the person-centred approach, that of the organism, as a useful metaphor for understanding groups; and discuss aspects of group facilitation. In these discussions we integrate the three core principles of the person-centred approach (see Chapter 2). We conclude the chapter with a brief case study of a work group.

Group encounter

The first mention of 'encounter' in the context of therapy dates back to 1914 and a series of poetic writings published by Moreno, the founder of psychodrama. Wibberley (1988) traces four influences on encounter:

1   The first from the 40s from Kurt Lewin (1890–1947) and the training groups at the National Training Laboratory in Bethel, Maine which, over time, became more concerned with personal growth than with organisational development.
2   A second from the more aggressive confrontational style of groups founded in 1958 and run originally in a residential therapeutic community for drug addicts called Synanon (see Yablonsky, 1965).
3   The third from William Schutz (1925–2002), who had a psychoanalytic background, joined the staff of the Esalen Institute in California in 1967, and developed what became referred to as an 'open encounter' model of group and groupwork (see Schutz, 1973) and
4   The fourth from Rogers who favoured a more participative approach on the part of the group facilitator.

Rogers' style of encounter was less structured than that of the other traditions, with more emphasis placed on communication between members of the group and on congruence and genuineness. In the later years of his life Rogers extended this form of group as he became more involved in conflict resolution, and peace initiatives in several of the world's 'hot spots' (see Chapter 12). This reflects the strong counter-cultural influence of encounter, which led at the time to it being viewed as an influential social experience. Rogers (1970/1973) even claimed that the encounter group was one of the most successful of modern social inventions:

> ... the trend towards the intensive group experience is related to deep and significant issues having to do with change ... in persons, in institutions, in our urban and cultural alienation, in racial tensions, in our international frictions ... it is a profoundly significant movement. (p. 169)

'Encounter' is related to the French word for 'meeting'. Schmid (1998) observes that the word also 'points to the "against", indicating *vis-à-vis*; as well as resistance' (p. 75). This is helpful in that it draws attention also to the possibility of conflict in encounter. Whilst a popular conception of encounter is that it involves high levels of confrontation, it is not a requirement. In his account of encounter, Bebout (1974) emphasises contact, intimacy, commonality and 'vicarious empathy'. Echoing Rogers' necessary precondition, he suggests that 'the first prerequisite for encounter between persons is *contact*' (p. 372). There are many forms of groups, natural or intentional; we consider the encounter group of community meetings and gatherings at person-centred conferences and events in Chapter 16. For further reading on encounter see Merry (1995) and Yalom (1995), and for further accounts of the history of groups see Shaffer and Galinsky (1974) and Tudor (1999).

Group as organism

Wilfred Bion (1897–1979), the 'father' of group dynamics theory, first regarded the group as an organism in its own right (Bion, 1961), a metaphor and theme which is common also in person-centred approaches to groups. Rogers (1970/1973) likens the group to an organism and talks about trusting the group 'to develop *its own potential* and that of its members ... [with] a sense of *its own direction*' (pp. 49–50, our emphasis). Wood (1982) takes this conceptualisation further and talks about the group *as* an organism. In this respect the person-centred and group analytic traditions are close (see Sturdevant, 1995). The philosopher Arthur Koestler (1905–83) uses the term 'holon' to describe the subsystem which is a whole in itself as well as a part of a larger system, and which has an integrative tendency to function as part of the larger whole (Koestler, 1978). A person in a group may therefore be viewed as a holon, within a larger organismic system. The implication of this understanding of groups is that we can draw on what we know about the organism (see Chapter 2) and apply it to groups:

■ *The group tends to actualise*

> The group as a whole can provide for itself better than can any single member of the group ... [and has a] fundamental right to self-direction and to self-actualization on its own terms. (Gordon, 1951, p. 338)

■ *We cannot understand the group without reference to its environmental field*
This is true both of informal groups and, more obviously of intentional groups. With regard to the immediate context of the group, for instance, we might ask where it meets, how or whether its meeting time is preserved and respected, and how it is viewed by others outside the group such as partners and friends. Natiello (1991/2001), Barrett-Lennard (in press) and Wood (2003b) all comment on the importance of the environment for the sustenance and development of the group. Wood cites Barker (1968) in finding that particular settings have been shown to affect consciousness and human behaviour.

The group behaves as an organised whole
This is so especially if it is regarded and understood as an organised whole, for instance, by a facilitator or consultant. In an early contribution on 'group-centred psychotherapy', Hobbs (1951) makes the point that *'group therapy*, and not individual therapy in a group, is the goal' (p. 305). However, whilst advocating the primacy of the group (see below), Schmid (1996) argues that the person-centred approach is 'person-centred' and not 'group-centred' and that 'it does not allow the individual to disappear in the collective. It maintains the delicate balance or tension between the individualistic and the relational' (p. 622). Natiello (1991/2001) emphasises the importance of the interrelatedness of the group and cites the physicist Fritjof Capra's (b. 1939) view that 'systems are integrated wholes that derive their essential properties from their interrelations rather than from the properties of their parts' (Capra, 1982, p. 239).

The group interacts with reality in the service of the actualising tendency
We can see this in the reaction of some groups who draw closer together to face a hostile 'outer' reality: unity in the face of adversity. In terms of the group's 'inner' reality, the person-centred approach maintains that, over time, the group will take care of its individual members and work towards a mutually satisfying and unified outcome. This is based on Rogers' (1951) view of the organism, that 'rather than many needs and motives, it seems entirely possible that all organic and psychological needs may be described as partial aspects of this one fundamental need' (pp. 487–8). The group expresses its needs as the needs *of the group* and not as a set of aggregated individual needs.

The group develops an organismic valuing process
Given facilitative conditions, the group will discover for itself what kinds of attitudes and behaviours it's willing and able to accommodate. It will set its own boundaries and can be trusted to negotiate a *modus vivendi* which satisfies the group as a whole and the individuals within. Often this shows in a *contract* which is generated by the group, multilateral, and group-centred, as distinct from a unilateral *rule* imposed by the group therapist. For further discussion of the distinction between contracts and rules, see Tudor (1999). Given this, the imposition of any group *rules*, which are by definition unilateral, non-negotiable and external, is anti-organismic. This is a particularly pertinent issue for learning groups which often have to contend with externally imposed

standards in the form of curricula, assessment, monitoring and validation (see Chapters 4 and 10).

- *The group is always in motion*
  This is captured by Rogers' (1970/1973) description of a group in the early stages of its life 'milling around'. Rogers himself noted 15 'patterns' in the process of groups which Barrett-Lennard (1979) suggests may be summarised as three phases: engagement, trust and process development, and encounter and change. Such patterns or phases are essentially descriptive, and most person-centred practitioners prefer to conceptualise 'group development' in terms of this organismic movement. This constitutes a person-centred alternative to Tuckman's (1965) famous and prescriptive sequence: 'forming, storming, norming and performing', to which he and a colleague later added a fifth 'adjourning' stage (Tuckman and Jenson, 1977).

In the later years of his working life, Rogers became interested in working across cultural and political divides, a practice which we explored in Chapter 12. Working with oppressed groups or groups of oppressed people, Rogers (1978) suggests, in his familiar 'if-then' formulation, that *if* a person with facilitative attitudes gains entry to the group, *then* a process will result which, in effect, is anti-oppressive and enhancing of personal power. It is characterised by:

- The expression of long-suppressed, mostly negative, hostile and bitter feelings.
- Recognition of the individual's uniqueness and strengths and the development of mutual trust.
- The diffusion of the most irrational feelings and the clarification and strengthening of feelings based on experiences common to the group.
- The growth of self and group confidence.
- The movement towards innovative, responsible, even revolutionary steps, taken in an atmosphere of realism and
- Shared leadership in constructive action, and individuals feeling supported to take action even when action involves risk.

This brings us on to the theory and practice of group facilitation.

Group facilitation

If we assume that a group is, like any other organism, capable of self-regulating, then there is inevitably a question as to the role of or even need for, a designated facilitator. Gordon suggests that 'the very existence of a group leader, either real or perceived, may be a deterrent to the distribution of leadership throughout the group' (Gordon, 1986). In this he is supported by Bozarth (1992/1995/1998) who argues that it is ideal not to have facilitators, but that 'if there are designated facilitators, they shouldn't do very much except be themselves' (p. 154). In response, Newton (1996, 1997) contests that in order for the potential of the group to be realised, the right conditions have to be present. Depending on the nature of the group and the expertise within the group to create these conditions, a designated facilitator with specific skills might offer essential support to the group's development. Gordon (1986) also acknowledges that responses made by groups to 'dis-equilibrium', that is, any change to the way that the group or its members have done things in the past or events which do not match their expectations, may be non- or only partially adjustive. Gordon illustrates this by describing the response of an individual who finds himself in a conflict which upsets his personal equilibrium. His response will depend on many things, including his insight into and understanding of the nature and cause of the conflict, and his skill in handling conflict and solving problems. As he becomes tense and uncomfortable, he may seek relief, for example, in alcohol, even though such a response may give, at best, only temporary relief, and may indeed make the situation worse. Groups behave in similar ways, and may respond to the potential conflict created by any change with behaviours that give only temporary and partial relief, such as scapegoating, withdrawing, blaming external forces, or regressing to overdependence on a leader. In such cases, he proposes that the most effective facilitator is one who can create the conditions for the leadership to revert back to the group. In other words, the role of the person-centred facilitator is to create the conditions which will maximise the group's potential to adjust to the disequilibrium experienced, and in doing so, to transfer that expertise to the group so that they can develop more fully their own adjustive capabilities.

This approach acknowledges the difference between offering expertise to a group and taking an expert role, the former being a resource for the group, whilst the latter is a differential power position. It also acknowledges the value for some groups of a temporary period of dependence or reliance upon a designated facilitator. It should be apparent from this however that facilitation should always be *offered* to the group, as it is from the group that the person-centred facilitator draws the legitimacy of her authority.

Tudor and Merry (2002) summarise some of the characteristics of an effective facilitator: '...in terms of attitude, being genuinely free of a desire to control the outcome; in terms of belief, respecting the capacity of the group to deal with its own problems; and, in terms of skills, skills in releasing individual expression' (p. 55) (see Rogers, 1978). Rogers (1983) describes the best facilitator in the words of the Chinese philosopher Lao Tse:

> A leader is best
> When people barely know he exists,
> Not so good when people obey and acclaim him,
> Worst when they despise him.
> But of a good leader, who talks little,
> When his work is done, his aim fulfilled,
> They will say 'We did this ourselves'.[1]

Having established the role of the person-centred facilitator, there is still considerable debate as to how it should be fulfilled. Given the core principle and attitude of non-directiveness, there is a particular debate about the efficacy and validity of using structure and activity in person-centred groups. This is especially important as research quoted by Sturdevant (1996) demonstrates that people with a high external locus of control gain more benefit from structured groups. Our various experiences of working with groups within organisational settings also supports the view that it appears necessary at times to provide a high degree of structure. Coghlan and McIlduff (1990) offer a useful resolution by distinguishing between behaviours which are directive and those which facilitate structure, arguing that intervention and structure do not necessarily equate with direction. Consequently, they propose that it is legitimate and congruent within the approach for a facilitator to offer low directivity with a high degree of structure to a given group.

Finally, the question of whether a facilitator is *person*-centred or *group*-centred will inevitably arise at some point. Does a facilitator ignore the needs of an individual to follow the predominant flow of the group, or give attention to individual needs at a cost to the rest of the group? This dilemma only arises if facilitators see themselves as the centre of the network of relationships, relating primarily *either* to individual *or* to group. The way out of this potential impasse is to support the group to identify and meet the needs of all its members. This does presuppose that the group feels some sense of responsibility to individual members, and that members necessarily feel a sense of belonging to the group. Where relationships between group members have broken down, it may be more useful for the facilitator

---

[1] It is not clear which translation of Lao Tse's *Tao Te Ching* Rogers was citing; see Lao Tse (1973) for an available translation.

to offer to work with individuals initially on a one-to-one basis. This echoes the point made in the previous section of this chapter about the desirability of systemic assessment of a group such as a family. As an example of this, one of the authors (JV) was invited to work with a clinical team who were in conflict with their manager. Only after several separate meetings between the facilitator and team representatives, and between the facilitator and the service manager, to clarify what each wanted from a joint event; to identify and address concerns; and to agree a purpose and structure for the day with all concerned, did the group finally come together, the team having established *via the facilitator* a sufficient working relationships to begin working together.

CASE STUDY: AFRAID OF THE DARK, SURPRISED AT THE LIGHT (JV)

I was invited by their manager to work with a team who had been identified as dysfunctional. A history of fraudulent behaviour by one team leader, followed by the implementation of strict autocratic discipline by the next, had left the team resentful and unsure about appropriate behaviour in the team. Clients who were cared for by the team offering a rehabilitation service were not improving, and visiting families were making negative comments about the atmosphere in the rehabilitation centre.

Engaging with the team in this environment was problematic. Nevertheless, I visited their workplace twice, attending two separate team meetings to discuss their interest in and needs from a team day, and corresponded with them individually with a summary of what I had heard from them and a proposed structure for our time together. With so little trust in each other and therefore in themselves as team members, the level of anxiety was high, and I therefore worked extremely slowly, checking out carefully at every point what we might do and that they were happy with every suggestion before we moved on. I offered a high degree of structure in order to give participants a high degree of predictability to the day, whilst continually checking that this still met with their agreement, so that they were slowly invited to check what they themselves needed and to acknowledge the possibility of choice. This included an agreement about what could be discussed by team members over the lunch break, as they were afraid of what might be said about their disclosures, and about the process outside the relative safety of the room, in other words when the facilitator was not present. It later emerged that my willingness to take seriously and act on these concerns was a crucial part of the process. Equally, the willingness of the team to express their concerns was indicative of the relationship that had begun to be established in the two preliminary visits and through our correspondence.

The other significant turning point for the team came in an exercise in which they were invited in small groups to identify and write down the things that they enjoyed about their jobs. As the focus of every discussion within the team over the previous two years had been on what was wrong – with the service, the team, and with each other – this was a radical question for them. Working in small groups with colleagues they chose allowed them some degree of safety in identifying their responses. However, it was when they came together in the full team group to share their answers, as they listened to each other, that their faces lit up with wonder. Suddenly they saw themselves, each other, and their team in a different light and the potential of how they might work together differently was revealed. It was a deeply moving moment, and one which saw the beginning of the rediscovery of the team's constructive tendency to actualise, a process that was measured in the healing of the clients they cared for. This was evidenced by the movement of clients through the rehabilitation centre and into community settings. Before, these clients had been stuck in the service, demonstrating insufficient improvement in their mental health to enable them to move on to more independent living arrangements.

SUMMARY

- Humans are essentially and socially group animals.
- Groups act as and represent the interface between the person and society.
- The person-centred approach has a long and strong history in promoting the experience and study of groups, and represents one of four traditions of encounter.
- One way of looking at a group is to see it as an organism.
- A person-centred facilitator can be useful in groups, especially where they are experiencing change or conflict which has upset their usual functioning.
- A person-centred facilitator aims to be non-directive, and may offer a high degree of structure to a group.

Community 14

Experiencing community is a logical extension of experiencing group. Just as the person-centred approach has made a significant contribution to our understanding of group and groups (as we explored in the previous chapter), so too it has a 'track record' in the promotion, creation, experiencing and study of intentional communities, communities that are established temporarily either for their own sake or as part of a conference. Reports and reflections on such experiences can be found in Rogers (1978a, 1991), O'Hara and Wood (1983), Wood (1984, 1994, 1997, 1999, 2003b), McIlduff and Coghlan (1991a, 1993b), Devonshire (1991), MacMillan and Lago (1993), Barrett-Lennard (1994, 1998, 2003), Merry (1995) and in Lago and MacMillan (1999). In this chapter we explore the elements of these communities for learning, and relate this phenomenon to Scott Peck's (1987) ideas of 'community-building'. In this context we also refer to the antagonisms which exist both within and between communities and cultures. Following this we briefly consider the person-centred approach to residential therapeutic communities, and conclude with some discussion of the far-reaching implications of creating community as a sustainable way of being.

The concept and meaning of community has been extensively studied, debated and reviewed, especially from sociological perspectives. In a major review article written nearly 50 years ago Hillery (1955) identified 94 different sociological definitions of community!

From a person-centred perspective, 'community' refers both to an environment and to relationships, as in 'community *as* relationship' (Barrett-Lennard, 2003). Barrett-Lennard sees community as a 'zone' lying somewhere beyond the family but 'as a closer, more personal context of activity and configured meaning than the pluralist nation state or other big systems in the modern world'. Community is in effect defined by a 'felt sense': 'a quality of bonding and felt commonality'. He goes on to define a number of characteristics:

- A strong sense of commonality.
- A common language.
- An interdependence in the relation of members.
- A code of conduct, or other generally understood and sanctioned norms of behaviour.
- A sense of community – this is similar to what Alfred Adler (1870–1937) referred to as *Gemeinschaftsgefühl* or 'community feeling'.
- Smallness – Barrett-Lennard cites Redfield's (1960) work on *The Little Community* in support of this, to which we would add Schumacher's (1973) contribution *Small is Beautiful*, and Rogers' (1974/1980) support of 'human sized groupings'. In effect: small is sustainable (see Chapter 16).

Within particular person-centred organisations or organisations of people – gatherings, events, conferences, training organisations, even national and international associations – 'community' is the forum in which person-centred principles are put into action in a larger context. 'Community' has become a person-centred tradition, often reflected at professional gatherings or conferences, where delegates meet and 'commune'; and also in the forum of encounter groups, in numbers from tens to hundreds, which meet together for an agreed period of time.

Communities for learning

Such meetings create opportunities for people to 'encounter' one another and to create community for a specific, short period of time. They are generally not sustained after the end of the fixed or agreed time, and participants return to their individual lives. Over the past 30 years many such opportunities have been created, some as a 'learning laboratory'. One of the earliest was a residential workshop which took place in 1975, lasting two weeks and comprising 136 participants. Rogers organised and facilitated the workshop, together with a number of colleagues, and wrote up his account of the experience (Rogers, 1978). Wood (1984) and Barrett-Lennard (1994, 2003) have also published accounts of the same event. The workshop was set up and advertised purposefully:

> The aim will be to build a workshop around an approach to human relationships and human growth which recognizes that the potential to learn and the power to act lie within the person – rather than in an expert dealing with him or her, or in a system controlling him or her.
>
> The workshop will provide a place where people who believe in the worth and dignity of the individual and in each person's capacity for self-direction can come together to create a community. The workshop values what each participant has to offer … We trust the workshop will demonstrate the psychological climate which we know can evoke self-understanding and self-directed behavior. It is hoped that the experience will not only lead to inner personal growth but to an increased understanding of one's responsibility in the world, and how one can act on that sense of responsibility. (Rogers, 1978, pp. 151–2)

Rogers himself acknowledges that this was not only an announcement of a workshop: 'It is a significant political statement, and was intended as such.' The brochure also laid out ideas for the format/structure and suggested a fee scale based on income. More recently Wood (2003b) offers a checklist for organisers of such large group experiences:

- Necessity: is there a need?
- Time and place: what organisational structure will most likely facilitate significant dialogue?
- People: invite people for diversity but with shared intention.
- Active involvement in the meetings as participants. (p. 12)

Barrett-Lennard (1994) describes his own experience of this group as 'kaleidoscopic, agonizing, exhilarating, frustrating, enlightening, unpredictable, and absorbing' (p. 71). From further research, which comprised participant observation and questionnaires, as well as his own reflections, he has developed a theory of community, based on process principles and consisting of nine general propositions:

1 *A human community is an affiliated collective of persons and relationships in a larger whole of recognized composition that is drawn together by common circumstance, mutual need, shared interests, experience and/or beliefs, and capacity for member communication.*

In his earlier formulation (Barrett-Lennard, 1994), he talks about an 'inside view' of community being derived from empathic contact with a cross-section of members who are absorbed in expressive engagement in their world.

2 *The members of a community are mutually aware and interconnected.*
Again in his earlier formulation Barrett-Lennard (1994) refers to the significance of the reciprocal valuing of members and suggests that the more that 'linkages' evolve, the stronger and more fully formed the community tends to be.

3 *The qualitative development of the community tends to build on itself.*

4 *Formed communities tend to maintain if not also to enhance themselves; to have a distinctive identity interwoven with the personal and subsystem relations and self-definition of members; and to satisfy human needs for affiliated belonging and presence with others.*
In his research into the large group experience held in 1975, Barrett-Lennard (2003) found that 'the importance members attached to their small groups and one-to-one encounters strongly accords with the idea that a communal experience and level of relationship hinges in crucial part on networks of more personal relationships among the members.' He concludes from this, importantly in our view, that 'workshops where many are strangers at the start, but which proceed directly to intensive big-groups sessions, are effectively short-circuiting steps in the building of relationship in a community', a conclusion which is supported by other reports such as Coghlan and McIlduff (1991).

5 *A well-functioning community is an open system in interface with other systems, living, natural and constructed. It is responsive to new external data and to fresh information and initiatives from within, and is thus in dynamic motion.*
This echoes some facets of Rogers' descriptions of the organism.

6 *When communities satisfy growth needs of constituents, beyond a period of initial development, they tend to behave in constructively responsive ways in relation to other communities, organisations and individuals.*

7 *A poorly functioning or severely threatened community may seek to isolate itself, or engage in power-manipulation or conflict in relation to other human collectives. Its members may not be openly present with one another, and subgroups tend to compete for control. The self-maintaining tendency leads to rigidity, not growth and personally and communally self-limiting patterns of association develop.*

8a Most *actual communities, localised or dispersed, live within the bounds and legal jurisdiction of a large 'host' society* ... [this] *relationship can be lethal, relatively 'distant' or benign, or supportively enriching.*

8b The *well-being of a community depends not only on inward processes but also on informed awareness of its milieu; and the life quality of a society depends, in significant part, on its recognition of and response to communities within it.*

This is supported by much of the literature on 'quality of life' and the significance of supportive communities in maintaining and promoting people's mental health and well-being (see Tudor, 1996; Raeburn and Rootman, 1998).

9 *A community is an emergent whole with a life of its own which normally it seeks to maintain. As a life form, it should not lightly be conceived, subverted or destroyed* (Barrett-Lennard, 1994, 2003).

Whilst this research and theory are based on the study of temporary, intentional communities, often set up as a 'learning laboratory' expressly for the purposes of research, these propositions are also applicable to many forms of community and communal experience both within and beyond the person-centred approach. Even in recent times, there is a long, international tradition of communal and collective living (see Bunker *et al.*, 1999); and Stockwell (1984) describes an attempt at community living informed by person-centred principles.

The person-centred approach has undoubtedly made a substantial contribution to our understanding of intentional large groups which strive to create and operate as communities, although interest and practice can become reified. Whilst we acknowledge the contribution of the person-centred approach to community and to community encounter, we think that particular gatherings of person-centred practitioners, such as conferences, can sometimes overemphasise community to the exclusion or detriment of other activities. This is based on a confusion of purpose between community-building on the one hand, and *conferring* with colleagues on the other. Reflecting on his experience of a particular conference, Pratt (2003) comments:

> The community meeting appears to be held in very high regard if not as an essential part of conference programmes ... therein lies a dangerous assumption: that this is the only conference activity that one could justify as communal ... some participants argued strongly for the importance of the community meeting above all other conference activities or events. Indeed, at one point all the other workshops and exploratory sessions were branded as a form of unworthy consumerism in comparison to the community meeting [which] ... appeared to be almost a form of sacred dogma that was not to be questioned. (p. 3)

Arguably, the genuine conferring or conferencing between colleagues through the exchange of experiences and ideas, through presentations, papers, discussion, dialogue, debate and informal means, has a communal benefit equal to or greater than the constant re-experiencing and reification of the process of community. In an article on the effect of group, dialogue and learning, Wood (2003b) reflects on the advice carved on the Temple of Wisdom at Delphi – *Gnothi seauton* (Know thyself) and *Meden agan* (Nothing in excess). He considers 'the achievement of these two pieces of advice to be the desirable attitude of participants entering a person-centred large group experience' and adds that 'one should also become familiar with the roller coaster ride of chaotic emotions and imaginings in group encounters' (p. 2).

In the next part of the chapter we compare some of the above ideas with those of Scott Peck.

Community-building

'Community-building' is a term used by and based on the work of Scott Peck (1987, 1990) and refers to the building of intentional communities. This work is, in many respects, similar to the temporary communities created, developed and studied within the person-centred approach. Peck (1990) believes in fostering the development of communities based on the belief that the mutual caring and creativity engendered within them can help ameliorate some of the conflicts in the world:

> If we are going to use the word [community] meaningfully we must restrict it to a group of individuals who have learned how to communicate honestly with each other, whose relationships go deeper than their masks of composure ... and [learn] to delight in each other [and] make others' conditions our own. (p. 59)

Peck captures here something of the quality of community that he believes is necessary for the healthy survival of the human race. We can define these qualities as reflected in the principles and conditions of the person-centred approach:

- A belief in people's constructive endeavour.
- Our ability to make and maintain contact with each other.
- Honest and real communication.
- A willingness to be transparent.

- A prizing of each other.
- An ability to understand the other empathically.
- A willingness to be *in* rather than to direct process.

Although Peck does not specifically refer to Rogers' work, these attitudes and qualities are similar to some of the directional trends which Rogers (1974/1980) sees that 'emerging persons' would reclaim, thereby fostering a culture and community in which members tend to actualise and move:

- Towards a non defensive openness in all interpersonal relationships.
- Towards the exploration of the total self.
- Towards the prizing of individuals.
- Towards human sized groupings.
- Towards leadership as temporary.
- Towards a more genuine and caring concern for those who need help.

Peck (1987) proposes four stages of community-building which groups experience: pseudocommunity, chaos, emptiness and, finally, community. These compare with Mearns' (1997) identification of a sequence of stages within the development of the larger group in a learning context: polite tolerance, confusion and disorientation, glimpsing the potential and valuing and working in the open process (see also Rogers, 1970/1973; Barrett-Lennard, 1979; and Chapter 13). In her systems analysis of groups (see Chapter 14), Natiello (1991/2001) links the principle of 'integrated wholes' (Capra, 1982) to Peck's concept of pseudocommunity, a term which he uses to describe the stage or moments when members are trying to 'fake' community by being artificially friendly and non-confrontational. In these situations or exchanges 'there are some parts of the whole system whose interrelatedness is diminished, and consequently, not contributing fully to the exchange and intensity of energy' (Natiello, 1991/2001, p. 127). In Peck's (1987) developmental schema, the concept of emptiness lies at the heart of building community: 'There are only two ways out of chaos ... one is into organization – but organization is never community ... the only way from chaos to community is into and through emptiness' (p. 94). This has echoes of the Buddhist view that confusion is the stage before enlightenment. Sometimes we simply have to sit with our anxiety, our unknowing and our anxiety about not knowing, before we can, perhaps, emerge into clarity.

Community, networks and networking

As we and others have acknowledged, there's no such thing as a community in isolation (see Barrett-Lennard's proposition 8a above). Communities, as all organisms, are in particularly active interchange with their environment, whether positive or antagonistic. Furthermore, there are historical, societal and political trends which affect community and community-building. As Furedi (1997) points out: 'There is little doubt that the 1980s saw an acceleration in the disintegration of social solidarity and of communities. During this period, virtually all forms of collective institutions became weakened' (p. 185). At the same time, there was an explosion of interest in 'networks', enabled by new technology. At best, networks can form an extended group matrix or web, connecting people with people and ideas all over the world. The world wide web (www) is an example of this. In many ways the challenge of our postmodern times and the information technology we have literally at our fingertips is to use this to build communities which have and sustain what Barrett-Lennard summarises as 'a quality of bonding and felt commonality'.

Networks have, however, led to 'networking', which Peck (1990) regards as largely having replaced community. Networking to get a job, to meet people, to expand business opportunities, or to gain something we need, quashes the creation of more permanent or more satisfying experiences of community. Networking creates temporary structures for particular purposes or tasks. These temporary structures replicate a sense of community, but ultimately offer little satisfaction beyond the immediate 'buzz', and offer no sustainability as actual communities. They are *virtual* and that's both their strength and their weakness. Networking is a creative solution which in many ways (through use of the internet, email, mobile phones and texting), matches the speed of modern life. However, it's a less personal process, and in such impersonal transactions we lose personal encounter. The common assertion that email *itself* promotes quick, short and *therefore* curt communication, discounts the humans in charge of the keyboard. In networking, there is a clear and present danger that people relinquish personal responsibility: 'This problem was caused me by other people, or by social circumstances beyond my control, and therefore it is up to other people or society to solve this problem for me. It is not really my personal problem' (Peck, 1990, p. 32). Taking responsibility for our problems and our relationship with them both counteracts this trend of isolated networking and is consistent with Rogers' concept of the fully functioning person (1958/1967) and stages of process (1958/1967) (see Chapter 3).

Networking doesn't require us to be whole, integrated, aware and responsible beings, and in some senses it encourages or perpetuates fragmentation and distortion of ourselves and our lives. It tends to be task- or goal-driven and does not offer us a nurturing environment: 'The fragmentation caused by excessive networking', says Gatto (2002), 'creates diminished humanity, a sense that our lives are out of control – because they are' (p. 48). Networking goes hand in hand with hot desking, power lunches and power dressing. Margaret Thatcher's now infamous statement that 'there's no such thing as society' reflected perhaps her own contempt for community and at the same time promoted her particular brand of market-driven individualism: networking to 'get on' and 'get one up', rather than building community for mutual interest and care.

Community as therapeutic

We know from studies in the field that community is a crucial variable in the maintenance and promotion of mental health. Good neighbours, good friends and good social networks (in the positive sense of the word) are important for positive mental health (see Parry, 1988).

In a time of increasing global conflict, the idea and reality of sustainable and sustaining communities appear even more necessary and urgent. It appears that communities are more frequently destroyed than supported. Many developed countries, such as the USA and Australia, were built on the back of the destruction of indigenous communities, and their beliefs, values and ways of being. Barrett-Lennard (1979) coins the term 'communicide' to describe this. The widely perceived demise of community has social and personal consequences: an increasing number of people live alone, and families are becoming almost universally nuclear, with fewer children and less opportunity, and maybe even less desire, for contact with extended family. People, therefore, no longer have the same opportunities to learn about birth, death and dying, child development (Chapter 5) or creative parenting (Chapter 9), simply by watching how those around them go about it. Children become private property rather than a collective asset and a shared responsibility. Like many people who have travelled, some of us have been struck by the welcome and the loving attention given to all, including visiting children, in smaller communities in other cultures and countries, where everyone is known to everyone else, and there are few or no strangers. Members of these communities tend to take collective responsibility, and children straying into danger or transgressing social rules are helped without fear. We don't wish to reify or romanticise this. The private abuse of children within families may be as common in such countries as it is in Britain. Equally, there are examples of genuine community care in this country, although they often stand out as such. One of our children visited a café in which he is known with a family friend who wasn't known. The café owner asked him: 'Who are you with to-day?', which gave him the opportunity to indicate if anything was amiss.

In his essay on *Conserving Communities*, W. Berry (1999) proposes a number of suggestions for sustaining the well-being of local communities. These include raising the following questions or implied questions:

1   Asking of any proposed change or innovation: What will this do to our community? How will this affect our common wealth? This has echoes of the notion that, in relation to any proposal that affects the earth, we should think about the consequences for the next seven generations. Bowers (2001), for instance, argues that the materialism of the current generation is eroding the earth's resources, and compromising the right of future generations to inherit an environment that has been wisely maintained.
2   Asking how local needs might be supplied from local sources, including the mutual help of neighbours, and producing as much of the community's own energy as possible. This reflects the slogan of the ecology movement: 'Act local, think global.'
3   Understanding the ultimate unsoundness of the industrial doctrine of 'labour-saving', if that implies poor work, unemployment, or any kind of pollution or contamination.
4   Striving to increase earnings (in whatever form) within the community for as long as possible before they are paid out, making sure that money paid into the local economy circulates within the community; and decreasing expenditure outside the community.
5   Making the community able to invest in itself by maintaining its properties, keeping itself clean (without passing on its dirt and waste to some other place), caring for its old people and teaching its children. Berry (1996) makes the point that old and young take care of one another and that the young must learn from the elders and not necessarily and not always in school: the community knows and remembers itself by the association of old and young.

All of this implies a community and an economy based on cooperation rather than competition, and we know that much of the world lives in societies governed by market economies, based on competition.

Genuinely cooperative community requires a commitment that goes beyond individual relating, one which moves us into the realms of 'us and us' relating in which we can hold, contemplate and consider the whole. In a rare contribution, De Marignac (1984) describes experimenting with the person-centred approach in her neighbourhood in a local reading group, a church group and in her family. The 'whole' includes people; social, cultural, political and ecological systems; nations; the natural and built environments; as well as plants and creatures who also inhabit the earth (see Chapter 16). As we move further from the implications of individual *human* relating, we can consider community as a microcosm of society and, indeed, of the cosmos.

Such ideas have implications for the person-centred practitioner's engagement with and activity in the community:

- *Psychopolitical activity* – Since Freud first used the term 'psychotherapy' in 1895, psychotherapists across all theoretical orientations have been involved in various forms of psychopolitical activity: Alfred Adler was a socialist; Wilhelm Reich was Marxist and advocated free contraception in Germany in the 1930s; Jacob Moreno's psychodrama and sociodrama inspired the theatre of the oppressed (Boal, 1979). More recently, a number of projects have had an integrated strategy of intervention which is both political and therapeutic (for details of some of these, see Tudor, 1997).

- *Endogamous community* – Castel, Castel and Lovell (1982) talk about therapists and clients forming an 'endogamous' or tight-knit community, in which 'the boundaries between personal problems and social problems vanish and therapy can deal with the whole spectrum by working to transform the individual and his surroundings at the same time' (p. 161).

- *Conscientizaçao* – inspired by Freire (see Chapter 10); O'Hara (1989) describes the need for *conscientizacao* or social consciousness-raising.

- *Sharing life therapy* – as described by Stamatiadis (1990) (see Chapter 3).

- *Therapists as citizens* – Samuels (2001) develops the notion of 'citizens-as-therapists', which Tudor and Hargaden (2002) take up. They describe a communitarian view of therapists as citizens, a view which emphasises the citizen as a member of the community. Hoffman (1999) describes her facilitation of a citizens' jury (whereby people explore contentious social issues) based on person-centred principles of empowerment and the valuing of each member of the group.

When we promote and participate in genuine community, whether through formal community-building events, in intentional groups, or in day-to-day interactions, we challenge individualism, unilateralism and isolationism. In doing so we are applying notions of psychological community to the realisation of actual community in the geographical, social and ecological structures within which we live.

In the final two chapters of this book we apply person-centred principles to the system of organisation and to the ecosystem of the environment itself and, in doing so, examine to what extent the approach is itself in 'rhythm' with these wider milieux.

SUMMARY

- From a person-centred perspective community refers both to an environment and to relationship.
- Community may be defined as a quality of bonding and felt commonality.
- Within the approach, there is a tradition of establishing temporary communities for learning. These can be seen as expressions of 'community-building'.
- Networks are forms of community and are distinct from networking.
- Community is a crucial variable in the promotion and maintenance of positive mental health.
- The concept of community challenges the person-centred practitioner to be active in the world.

Organisation 15

> It is not the *rules of the arena* that guide our way of using ourselves, but rather our commitment to *a way of being* in the world based on certain beliefs about human beings, responsibility, openness, and mutuality. If we can bring to our workplace a trust in the actualising tendency; a willingness to give up institutional power and control; an offering of congruence, empathy and unconditional positive regard to others, and the courage to stand firmly in our beliefs, we have the opportunity to contribute to radical changes that can help move us into a more creative future. (Natiello, 1990/2001, p. 85)

On average, those of us who have jobs spend more time at work and travelling to work than at home. This alone makes work and the workplace an important subject of enquiry. Rogers developed his original theoretical constructs largely out of his experiences in therapy with individual clients. He later developed an interest in the therapeutic potential of groups, developing the encounter group, initially as a training vehicle for counsellors, but then in larger groups for community development and conflict resolution. Describing his beliefs about how groups operate, he suggested that they are:

> like an organism, having a sense of their own direction even though it could not define that direction intellectually … Similarly … a group recognises unhealthy elements in its processes, focuses on them, clears them up or eliminates them, and moves on towards becoming a healthier group. This is my way of saying that I have seen the 'wisdom of the organism' exhibited at every level from cell to group. (Rogers, 1970/1973, p. 50)

Rogers describes this 'wisdom of the organism' more fully when he writes about the actualising tendency, which he considered to be universally present in all organic matter, and which is essentially positive, forward moving, constructive, realistic and trustworthy. Given favourable environmental conditions, he posited that the organism will naturally grow to express all of its potential (Merry, 1995). He held this to be equally true whether the organism in question was a human being or a group of human beings. We could therefore legitimately extend this to include organisations.

Organism and organisation

A key question arises from this theory concerning the nature of the environmental conditions considered to be necessary for optimum growth. Thinking about an individual human being, Rogers suggested a set of conditions which he believed to be necessary and sufficient for psychological growth and development (see especially Chapters 3 and 5). He believed that his approach to working with groups was essentially the same as his approach to work with individual clients. This move from a theory of individual human development to a theory of groups and organisations and their development, necessitates a leap from the biological to the metaphorical.

Perhaps we need to consider first those underlying principles of person-centred philosophy which are readily transferable to organisations. The revolution in scientific thinking which informed Rogers' theoretical development has also been reflected in much organisational writing over the last 25 years. Rogers learned from quantum physics. We warm to the picture of him sitting on a beach in California, watching the stars and imagining the earth spinning, the universe exploding, the earth shrugging its shoulders, and the atoms in his pen whizzing round in their own ecstatic dance (Rogers, 1990). After his reading of quantum physics he could no longer subscribe to the concept of a single external reality (Rogers, 1978/1980). Therapeutically, this meant that Rogers met each client, each encounter, as a unique experience about which he could know only what that person expressed in their shared relationship. He took into the encounter no diagnostic framework, no presuppositions outside his general philosophy, and no specific objective other than the general one of wanting to support the client's own growth (Merry, 1995). Wheatley (1994) offers a direct correlation in current organisational thinking:

> I no longer believe that organisations can be changed by imposing a model developed elsewhere ... There are no recipes or formulae, no checklists or advice that describe 'reality'. There is only what we create through our engagement with others and with events. Nothing really transfers; everything is always new and different and unique to each of us. (p. 7)

Not only that, but the quantum nature of the universe is such that it is bristling with potentialities. Each attempt to formalise a single reality, a single interpretation of what is happening, closes down hundreds of thousands of other unexplored options, losing richness from the organisation and the opportunity for more creative choices: 'There is no such thing as the survival of the fittest, only the survival of the fit. This means that there is no one answer that is right, but many answers that might work ... nature encourages wild self expression' (Wheatley and Kellner-Rogers, 1996, p. 16).

What of the concept of organisation as organism? In the earlier quote, Rogers described a group as '*like* an organism' (our emphasis), and organisations are still largely thus described in the literature. Wheatley and Kellner-Rogers (1996) have no such doubts however, and assert that: 'organisations *are* living systems. They too are intelligent, creative, adaptive, self-organising, meaning-seeking' (p. 3, our emphasis). Battram (1998) defines them as 'complex adaptive systems' which are both self-organising and learning. Pratt, Gordon and Plamping (1999) define them metaphorically as living or ecosystems, in which individuals and teams can be seen as purposeful, interdependent entities who can interact intelligently, autonomously, and through a process of constantly adapting to each other. The question here is not what organisations really are. If we accept a world of multiple realities, they are many things to many people. The question rather is how the assumptions we make about them change our behaviour in relation to them: 'If you think of organisations as a living system, you pay attention to certain features such as connections, relationships, and meaning. If you think of mechanical systems you pay attention to design, control mechanisms etc.' (Pratt, Gordon and Plamping, 1999, p. 19). If our concepts define our behaviours, so in a quantum world, do we create the conditions for the response we expect. The concept of organisation as organism, whether literal or metaphorical, is now well documented in the literature of organisational development (OD).

Organisational development: a person-centred perspective

> What might be the effect upon an industrial organization if a consultant hired by management acted on the conviction that his role was to get the organization to learn to solve its own problems with the resources within the organization itself? (Gordon, 1951, pp. 320–1)

A literature review indicates a number of specific psychological approaches to OD including psychoanalytic (DeBoard, 1978), gestalt (Merry and

Brown, 1987), and Jungian (Stein and Hollwitz, 1992). Despite Rogers' evident early interest in this area, as discussed in his work on encounter groups, for example (Rogers, 1970/1973), we have yet to identify a body of work dedicated to a person-centred approach to OD. Plas' (1996) work is a step in this direction, but concerns the development of a person-centred approach to leading individuals at work, rather than to the organisation as a whole.

This absence seems particularly striking when, in French and Bell's (1999) standard text on OD, *Client-Centered Therapy* (Rogers, 1951) is listed in the 'Chronology of events in management and organisation thought' (p. 64), and Rogers is further cited as a key contributor to the 'Applied Behavioural Scientific Basis' of the discipline (p. 99). Rothwell, Sullivan and McLean (1995) see Rogers' 'championing of a new view of people and change' (p. 18) as a key philosophical influence in the evolution of OD.

We hope here to begin to bridge this gap in the literature of both OD and the person-centred approach. Perhaps a useful place to start is in defining terms. OD emerged as a specialist field in the late 1950s and early 1960s, and there are probably as many definitions as there are writers about it. Rogers' own experience of it was within the context of 'organisational development groups' for managers whose primary aim he describes as 'the growth in skill as a leader of persons' (Rogers, 1970/1973, p. 13). As the study and practice of OD has grown over the last 30 years, this is probably too limited a definition to be of value. We turn instead to French and Bell's (1999) ten primary distinguishing characteristics of OD. These appear to underpin the range and variety of individual definitions:

- OD focuses on culture and processes.
- Specifically, OD encourages collaboration between the leaders of organisations and their members in managing culture and processes.
- Teams of all kinds are particularly important for accomplishing tasks and are targets for OD activities.
- OD focuses on the human and social side of the organisation, and in so doing, also intervenes in the structure and technical side.
- OD is characterized by participation and involvement in problem-solving and decision-making by all levels of the organisation.
- OD focuses on total system change, and views organisations as complex social systems.
- OD practitioners are facilitators, collaborators and co-learners with the client system.

▪ An overarching goal is to enable the client system to solve its own problems by teaching the skills and knowledge of continuous learning through self-analytical methods. OD views organisational improvement as an ongoing process in a constantly changing environment.

▪ OD relies on an action research model with extensive participation by client system members and, finally,

▪ OD takes a developmental view that seeks the betterment of both individuals and the organisation. Attempting to create 'win-win' solutions is standard practice in OD programmes.

There are some obvious connections with person-centred theory here: the maximising of participation of all members; the holistic nature of the approach; the collaborative role of the facilitator; the support of the organisation's own developmental and problem-solving processes; the philosophy of optimism, and the action research base. These clearly presuppose a positive, societal movement towards greater complexity, growth and fulfilment of potentiality, and concern for other people and the larger environment. These are key features of Rogers' actualising tendency (Bozarth, 1998). Senge (1990) supports this in his argument that 'the entire global business community is learning to learn together, becoming a learning community' (p. 4). It is perhaps therefore worth clarifying the extent to which we can identify a person-centred approach to organisations in the current literature.

In his classic text *The Fifth Discipline*, which revolutionised organisational thinking in the West, Senge (1990) describes the emergent organisation as a 'learning organisation' which strives for continuous learning and growth, in order to renew and transform itself continuously in a changing environment. It does this, he suggests, through the development of five disciplines:

▪ Personal mastery – which involves individual learning and skill development.

▪ Mental models – which involve the development of new ways of looking at the world, and which correspond to Rogers' (1951) idea of a loosening of constructs or fixed ideas.

▪ Systems thinking – which identifies the organisation as being in process and in relationship with its environment.

▪ Group learning.

▪ Shared vision – which emphasises the need for every member of the organisation to be involved in creating its future direction; this is a direct analogy to Gordon's (1951) proposition that 'a group's adjustive behavior will be most appropriate when the group utilises the maximum resources of its total membership. This means maximum participation of all group members, each making his most effective contribution' (p. 325).

Rogers proposes that an individual's inherent actualising tendency leads to ongoing fulfilment of his potential as an optimally functioning person. He also recognises that this process is vulnerable to environmental impact (see Chapters 2, 3 and 7). Organisations too are vulnerable, and exist within a complex relational context. Commercial organisations need to be highly sensitive to market and technological changes. Public sector organisations are similarly sensitive to public opinion, and are vulnerable to the political needs of local and national government. Parallel to an individual's conditions of worth, an organisation may see its survival as being dependent upon its ability to please its paymasters, and may consequently suppress or ignore information about its experience which threatens its ability to do so. Indeed, Senge (1990) proposes that most organisations today suffer from severe 'learning disabilities'. He defines seven clear types, all of which are examples of an organisation failing to represent its experiences accurately in the here-and-now, as they try to operate within unhelpful, inaccurate and archaic paradigms or concepts of how things should work. Rogers' organismic valuing process, by which an organism moves towards positively valued experiences and away from negatively valued ones, is also mirrored in Senge's (1990) proposition that 'there are two fundamental sources of energy that can motivate organisations: "fear and aspiration"' (p. 225). He proposes that fear motivates reaction or adaptation in a continued attempt to please the other whilst aspiration is the source of invention, the energy of hope.

As we have seen, based on clinical practice, Rogers identified six conditions which, he argued, were necessary and sufficient for therapeutic change. Given the parallels between individual therapy and organisational theory outlined above, here we apply the conditions to organisational change.

1 *Two persons are in psychological contact*
   A key question here is which two persons? Who can be seen to represent the organisation? We have already drawn parallels between Gordon's (1951) proposal that groups' performances are optimised when they are able to maximise the contribution of all members, and Senge's (1990) emphasis on the need for all staff to be involved in creating a shared vision. From a quantum perspective, Wheatley (1994) argues that 'the more participants we engage in this participative

universe, the more we can access its potentials and the wiser we can become' (p. 65). The challenge to OD consultants is, therefore, to find ways to work with as many of the organisation's stakeholders as possible, and that may include customers, suppliers, politicians and local communities. A reframing of this condition might therefore be: 'All interested persons are engaged.'

2   *The first, whom we shall term the client, is in a state of incongruence, being vulnerable or anxious*
Here again, the question of how many and which people in an organisation need to be in a state of anxiety arises. For many organisations, the problem is always seen as elsewhere: 'the enemy', says Senge (1990), 'is out there' (p. 19).

In traditional OD work, commitment for any development work has to be obtained at board level. This recognises the traditional power structures within the organisation. Incongruence experienced elsewhere cannot be worked through unless the senior management team acknowledges its existence and validity. If senior management does not acknowledge the need for development and change, this can be disempowering, especially for an internal OD consultant. However, taking a quantum view, Wheatley (1994) offers a way out of this impasse:

> Acting locally is a sound strategy for changing large systems ... We are more likely to become synchronised with that small system, and thus to have an impact. These changes in small places, however, create large systems change, not because they build one upon the other, but because they share in the unbroken wholeness that has united them all along ... There is value in working with the system any place it manifests because unseen connections will create effects at a distance, in places we never thought. (p. 42)

So, we reframe this condition as: 'Some part of the organisation is experiencing a state of incongruence, feeling vulnerable or anxious.'

3   *The second person, whom we shall term the consultant, is congruent or integrated in the relationship*
According to French and Bell (1999), the OD consultant needs to be fully in touch with her own feelings in order to allow for maximum spontaneity and choice in interventions, and should ensure, in the interests of clear communications, that her words and apparent feelings are congruent. In order to be effective, she must strive continually to develop and model the effective behaviours that she desires for her client. This will help each individual member of the organisation

maximise his contribution, and is key to supporting the emergence of another potentiality within the organisation: 'the strange attractor'. From complexity theory we understand that, under certain conditions, when the system is far from equilibrium, creative individuals can have an enormous impact, as the effect of a lone fluctuation gets amplified (Wheatley, 1994). By being congruent and integrated in relationship, the OD consultant can serve as an amplifier for others.

4   *The consultant experiences unconditional positive regard for the client*
In 1987, Harrison published a radical and shocking pamphlet which introduced the concept of love into the workplace as part of the drive for business excellence and quality of service (Harrison, 1987/1995). He argued that excellent service quality was not just the result of aligned processes and vision, but also of *attunement*, or the creation of harmony and resonance between parts of the organisation through the development of a support culture. Some years later Wheatley (1994) proposed that 'those who are open to others and who see others in their fullness create positive energy. Love in organisations, then, is the most potent source of power we have available' (p. 39). At a philosophical, rather than a functional level, a humanistic value system that incorporates a belief in the importance and dignity of individuals within organisations and the democratic process in all economic activities is central to OD (Lippitt and Lippitt, 1986; Rothwell, Sullivan and McLean, 1995; French and Bell, 1999).

5   *The consultant experiences an empathic understanding of the client's internal frame of reference and endeavours to communicate this to the client*
For a number of authors in this field, empathic listening is a core competence for the OD consultant (Lippitt and Lippitt, 1986; Rothwell, Sullivan and McLean, 1995; French and Bell, 1999). The OD consultant is not an expert on substantive content, but aims to engage with the client in a collaborative, developmental approach to improving organisational processes, and as such, needs to work within the client's frame of reference (French and Bell, 1999). Although some OD consultants will then attempt to diagnose their client, this should be done openly and should be offered to the client following a shared process of data collection and interpretation.

6   *The communication to the client of the counsellor's empathic understanding and unconditional positive regard is to a minimal degree achieved*
An OD consultant's survival depends upon them being experienced as helpful by the organisation. It is clear from this that there is a

relationship between person-centred thinking about this 'assumed condition' (Rogers, 1958/1967) and OD.

There is clearly a case for proposing that Rogers' six conditions for therapeutic change also necessarily apply to and within organisations, though whether they are sufficient is more difficult to prove from the literature. Rothwell, Sullivan and McLean (1995) list no fewer than 187 essential competencies for OD consultants, and French and Bell (1999) support them in requiring from an OD consultant an in-depth knowledge of management and organisation theory, as well as a range of systems and analysis tools. Evidence from action research is needed to demonstrate whether Rogers' six conditions are sufficient to facilitate organisational change.

We began with a question about the degree to which a philosophy developed from individual psychotherapy could be relevant to organisations. To what extent should the OD consultant be working with individuals within the organisation, and to what extent can she work effectively with a group or whole system? 'It depends', says Wheatley (1994):

> This is not an either/or question. There is no need to decide between the two. What is critical is the relationship created between the person and the setting. That relationship will always be different, will always evoke different potentialities. It all depends on the players and the moment. (p. 34)

Organisational culture and relationships

Whilst considering the organisation as organism, we still need to consider the relationship between the organisation and its constituent members. Such relationships exist within and are mediated by the values and behaviours enacted within an organisation which collectively make up its particular culture or cultures. Schein (1985) defines culture as:

> a pattern of basic assumptions – invented, discovered, or developed by a given group as it learns to cope with its problems of external adaptation and internal integration – that has worked well enough to be considered valid and therefore, to be taught to new members as the correct way to perceive, think and feel in relation to those problems. (p. 9)

Such behaviours and values are codified in the policies and procedures that an organisation espouses, as well as in the physical environment created and the way that work is structured and managed. Schein proposes that such artefacts are the visible indicators of underlying beliefs about the nature of human beings, their relationships and their activity. An illustration of this is in the work of Ricardo Semler (b. 1959).

In 1993, Semler, the head of one of South America's fastest growing companies, with a waiting list of thousands hoping to join it, published his revolutionary business biography. This sent shock waves through the business and management community. Having failed to get into a traditional business school, Semler had not learned 'the way business is done'. He used a form of action learning to establish what was working, what was not working, and what needed to be changed. He noticed, for example, huge files of policies and procedures which were too unwieldy for anyone to read. Having confirmed by experiment that even the management team had not read them, he threw them out, and replaced them with a 20-page 'survival manual' for new staff. This consisted largely of cartoons illustrating statements such as the following:

▪ *Hiring*

> Before people are hired or promoted, the others in that unit have the opportunity to interview and evaluate the candidates. (Semler, 1993, p. 256)

This challenges the more traditional idea that only managers, as representatives of the employer, can select new organisation members, but assumes instead that team members are more likely to understand the requirements of the work, and the specific skill set, including team skills, needed for the optimum performance of their team. Increasingly within the National Health Service (NHS) in the UK, clinical teams are including patient representatives on selection panels.

▪ *Working hours*

> Semco has flexible working hours, and the responsibility for setting and keeping track of them rests with each employee. People work at different speeds and differ in their performance depending on the time of day. Semco does its best to adapt to each person's desires and needs. (Semler, 1993, p. 257)

This challenges the traditional concept that people need to work in the same way and at the same speed, and that employees can't be trusted to manage and monitor their own input. It recognises individual difference and the trustworthiness of employees.

Working environment

> We want all our people to feel free to change and adapt their working area
> as they please. Painting walls or machines, adding plants, or decorating the
> space around you is up to you ... change the area around you according to
> your tastes and desires and those of the people who work with you.
> (Semler, 1993, p. 258)

This gives employees the power over their work environment and
enables them to create a working space that is best for them as individuals. The final sentence builds in the assumption that they will be able
to work out with colleagues any differing needs.

Unions and strikes

> Unions are an important part of worker protection. At Semco, workers
> are free to unionise and the persecution of those connected with unions
> is absolutely forbidden. Unions and the company don't always agree or
> even get along, but we insist on mutual respect and dialogue ... Strikes are
> considered normal. They are part and parcel of democracy. (Semler,
> 1993, pp. 261–2)

This gives a clear statement of support to unions, and a congruent
statement about the probability of conflict and how this will be resolved.
The underlying principle is that conflict is normal and that it can be
resolved respectfully.

Participation

> Don't settle down. Give opinions, seek opportunities and advancement
> and always say what you think ... your opinion is always interesting, even if
> no-one asked you for it ... make your voice count. (Semler, 1993, p. 264)

Here responsibility for participation is placed clearly with the employee,
with an underlying commitment on the part of the employer to welcome
such participation.

Evaluation by subordinates

> Twice a year you will receive a questionnaire to fill in that enables you to
> say what you think of your boss. Be frank and honest, not just on the form
> but in the discussion that follows. (Semler, 1993, p. 266)

The practice of upward and peer appraisal is now becoming more
common. This makes a clear statement about the role of the leader in
supporting the staff as well as the management team.

Semco Woman

> Women in Brazil have fewer employment, promotion and financial oppor-
> tunities than men. At Semco we have various programmes run by women
> to seek to reduce this discrimination … if you are a woman, participate. If
> you aren't, don't feel threatened and don't fight against this effort. Try
> to understand and respect it. (Semler, 1993, p. 270)

Again, this recognises inherent inequalities, both existing in the
workforce, but also in the attempts to address these. It acknowledges
openly that some staff members might feel threatened by the anti-
discriminatory programmes.

Having all spent a considerable part of our working lives in public and
private sector bureaucracies, we are all struck by the open communication
and exquisite simplicity of Semler's approach. One of us (JV) spent some
months recently as part of a small team trying to write and negotiate
the encyclopaedic volumes of policies for a new NHS organisation, and then
faced the challenge of communicating and implementing them, with the
almost certain knowledge that they will never be read by most staff members. It is interesting to consider the implications of these two contrasting
approaches and what they imply about the basic beliefs and values of the
two organisations in question. Semler's approach seems predicated on the
belief that people are essentially trustworthy, able to self-regulate in
response to work, able to work well as a team, negotiating to resolve any
conflicts; that conflict is natural and resolvable in a climate of mutual
respect. The relationship here between employer and employee is essentially
an adult one. Valued staff who are unable to meet their career aspirations
within the company are encouraged to leave and develop their skills elsewhere, and are welcomed back when a suitable career opportunity arises
within the company again. There is no sense of betrayal or dependence.

Whilst formal policies and processes can communicate an organisation's
culture and values, Schein (1985) believes that the creation and management of a healthy culture is the essential task of leadership; indeed it is 'the
only thing of real importance that leaders do' (p. 2). If leaders do indeed
create the culture of an organisation, how might a person-centred leader
behave?

Having reviewed some key principles of the person-centred approach
with regard to the organisation and its development, we now turn to issues
of facilitation and the facilitator as leader.

Facilitation and leadership

> What would be the effect upon a group if its supervisor tried consciously to create an accepting atmosphere in which its members could work? Can you be 'therapeutic' in your relations with those for whom you are a boss, leader, administrator? (Gordon, 1951, p. 320)

At the time these were revolutionary questions, to which Gordon responded first by developing a set of propositions about the nature of groups (see Chapter 13) and, from these, proposing a 'non-leading' or 'group-centred' leadership role which he describes thus:

> The group-centered leader believes in the worth of the members of the group and respects them as individuals different from himself. They are not persons to be used, influenced or directed in order to accomplish the leader's aims. They are not people to be 'led' by someone who has 'superior' qualities or more important values. The group-centered leader sees the group as existing for the individuals who compose it. It is the vehicle for the expression of their personalities and the satisfaction of their needs. He believes that the group as a whole can provide for itself better than can any single member of the group. He believes in the group's fundamental right to self-direction and to self-actualization on its own terms. (Gordon, 1951, p. 338)

Current leadership thinking reflects a number of these statements. Workers, for instance, are recognised as individuals of intrinsic worth, who bring diverse and valid gifts to the enterprise, and who are capable of a large degree of self-regulation. We can also see that Gordon's description of a person-centred model of leadership was still located within the therapeutic context: a therapy group exists for the individuals who compose it. In the world of work, however, a person is paid to be there in return for the provision of certain services. The people who provide that funding, whether as customers, shareholders or taxpayers, also have a right to have their needs represented in the thinking and activities of the group and organisation. In his later thinking, Gordon (1980) built on the research into leadership behaviours by Myers to identify task specialist and human relations specialist skills as equally significant in effective leadership behaviour. The former, which he defines as 'production-centred' (p. 6), are required to meet organisational needs; and the latter, which he subtitles 'person-centred' (p. 6), are required to meet employee needs in what Schein (1985) identified as the psychological contract. Although specifically espousing a person-centred philosophy, Gordon still presents a paternalistic model of leadership: 'Leader effectiveness requires treating people decently whilst at the same time successfully motivating them toward high performance' (p. 6). The programme he describes however is more democratic, in that it emphasises the responsibilities of team members in a participative approach, and encourages significantly greater involvement in performance appraisal than was traditional at that time.

Rogers was intrigued with the possibility that person-centred philosophy might have an application in the world of work. He quotes research by Cherry (1975) on the relationship between his own definition of the fully functioning person, Maslow's definition of the self-actualising person, and qualities viewed as desirable in a senior manager. Rogers (1978b) delights in the findings that 'warmth, capacity for close interpersonal relationships, compassion and considerateness correlated very significantly with the qualities of productivity, creativity, co-operativeness and job satisfaction' (p. 100). He quotes the experience of a colleague in a large but anonymous company who demonstrated the increased profitability that could be obtained from a person-centred approach to management (Rogers, 1978b). Sadly, we are given few specifics about the nature of this approach beyond greater trust in and less close supervision of employees; good horizontal and vertical two way communication; and a dispersion of responsibility, choice and decision-making. However, whilst Rogers was interested in the potential application of person-centred approaches to leadership and management, his own experimentation with this was flawed by his lack of attention to the differences between the therapeutic and the organisational context. The greatest support for his philosophy in a work context comes from people who are themselves embedded in the organisational world.

Perhaps the most significant of these is Robert Greenleaf, a management consultant with 40 years' experience as a management researcher and developer at The American Telephone and Telegraph Company (AT&T), and founder in 1964 of the Center for Applied Ethics. During the late 1960s and early 1970s, he was trying to help university leaders deal with the student unrest they were then experiencing. In order to understand the causes of the unrest, Greenleaf began to study what the students were themselves interested in, and in the process re-read Hermann Hesse's (1932/1995) *Journey to the East*. As a lifelong student of how to get things done in organisations, Greenleaf recognised a prophetic message in Hesse's story of a group of men setting out on a mythical journey:

> The central figure of the story is Leo, who accompanies the party as the servant who does their menial chores, but who also sustains them with his sprit

and song. He is a person of extraordinary presence. All goes well until Leo disappears. Then the group falls into disarray and the journey is abandoned. They cannot make it without the servant Leo. The narrator, one of the party, after some years of wandering, finds Leo and is taken to the Order that had sponsored the journey. There he discovers that Leo, whom he had known first as servant, was in fact the titular head of the Order, its guiding spirit, a great and noble leader. (Greenleaf, 1970/2002, p. 19)

Inspired by this story, in 1970 Greenleaf wrote and published his seminal paper *The Servant as Leader* which has had a major impact on the development of leadership theory over the last 30 years. Servant leadership begins, not from an aspiration for greater power and influence, but from a real motivation to serve others. The difference between servant and traditional leadership

> manifests itself in the care taken by the servant first to make sure that other people's highest priority needs are being served. The best test, and the most difficult to administer, is this: Do those served grow as persons? Do they, while being served, become healthier, wiser, freer, more autonomous, more likely themselves to become servants? And what is the effect on the least privileged in society; will they benefit, or at least, not be further deprived? (Greenleaf, 2002, p. 24)

Here we have a definition that we think Rogers would have recognised, as he would the extraordinary quality of presence that Greenleaf identifies in his description of Leo's relationship, but one which puts the role into a wider context. The idea of service has a history in person-centred thinking, too. Taft, whose influence on Rogers he acknowledged, gives the following etymology:

> The word 'therapy' has no verb in English, for which I am grateful; it cannot do anything to anybody, hence can better represent a process going on, observed perhaps, understood perhaps, assisted perhaps, but not applied. The Greek noun from which therapy is derived means 'a servant', the verb means 'to wait'. (Taft, 1933, p. 3)

Spears and Lawrence (2002) identify the following characteristics as central to the development of servant leaders:

- *Listening deeply to others* – both individuals and groups, and to one's own inner voice.

- *Empathy* – striving to understand, accept and recognise co-workers for their special and unique spirits; and the assumption of good intentions.
- *Healing* – oneself and others; understanding that the search for wholeness is shared by servant and served.
- *Awareness* – especially self-awareness; understanding of the ethical dimension; able to view most situations from a more integrated holistic position.
- *Persuasion* – as opposed to coercion or manipulation; the willingness to influence from one's own congruent self-expression.
- *Conceptualisation* – the ability to dream great dreams; to see beyond the day to day realities of the present.
- *Foresight* – linked to intuition and wisdom, this enables the servant leader to learn from the past, see the realities of the present, and anticipate possible consequences in the future.
- *Stewardship* – an idea refined by Block in *Stewardship* (1993) and defined as 'holding something in trust for another'.
- *Commitment to the growth of people* – the recognition that people have intrinsic value beyond their current role, and the key role of the servant leader in nurturing the personal, professional and spiritual growth of employees. This includes allocation of resources such as time and money for personal and professional development; encouraging and attending to staff ideas; encouraging team involvement in decision-making; and actively assisting displaced staff to find alternative satisfying employment.
- *Building community* – recognising that, for many people in the West, large organisations have replaced traditional communities (see Chapter 14).

The first four of these, together with the commitment to the growth of people, seem to fit well with Gordon's ideas about group-centred leadership.

However, where Gordon sees the leader as either essentially without an agenda (1951), or later as having a specific responsibility for task accomplishment (1977), Greenleaf recognises that, as a member of the organisation, the leader may and should bring their own passion and ideas into the group, but must do so as an equal, without seeking to coerce others into agreeing with them. The concept of community-building is strongly implied both in Gordon's work, and in Rogers' descriptions of the team at the University of Chicago Counselling Centre team (see Kirschenbaum, 1979). Greenleaf also adds the strategic skills of conceptualisation and foresight, together with the responsibility of stewardship, which extends the attention of the leader into the wider community. We imagine that Rogers would have argued that these roles and responsibilities should be distributed throughout the work group, and this is more consistent with current thinking about leadership as a widely distributed, emergent property of a work group, rather than a specific organisational role (National College for School Leadership, 2003). Nevertheless, we agree that anyone aspiring to servant leadership must possess these skills or attitudes, and, as one of the tests of servant leadership is the ability to inspire and to help others develop into this role, there is no philosophical conflict between this kind of leadership and the person-centred approach.

Person-centred leadership challenges the leader, the wider organisation and every individual member of the work group. Many people, perhaps most, will gladly take on the added responsibility in exchange for greater freedom and job satisfaction. However, there are some people who have less energy available to bring to their workplace; who do not see themselves as doing the work they would want ideally to do; who are dealing with profound challenges in other parts of their lives, and who simply want to come to work, do a competent job with minimal energetic engagement, and go home again. One of us (JV) brought in this style of leadership to a team in an engineering company.

Most of the team members immediately embraced the opportunity for greater creativity and decision-making in their work, and I was humbled to see how much of their potential my previous leadership style had been suppressing. But one team member was completely lost in the new culture, and unable to adapt. As his work behaviour became increasingly dysfunctional, I sat down and listened to him, and agreed that the style of leadership that was congruent for me, and welcomed by the rest of the team, was not helpful for him. Luckily, he was able to identify another department where his considerable knowledge and skills could be employed, and where a more traditional form of leadership provided him with a greater sense of safety and structure. I approached the manager concerned and agreed to second the team member to that department for six months on my budget, as an opportunity for both of them to see how it worked. At the end of six months, the manager was delighted to find a permanent job for the team member who was making a major contribution to his new environment.

CASE STUDY: PURPLE CHAIRS AND LARGE SCREENS (JV)

Managing the conflict between the needs and preferences of different stake-holders is a key task for organisational leaders and for OD consultants. An example of this was in my work as an OD consultant in a project team tasked with the creation of one of two new Shared Services Centres which was to take over the provision of financial services to 25 member organisations from their current in-house provision. The benefits were significant. Standardisation of processes was to enable all the organisations to benefit from the best practice of individual members, and investment in the latest technology was to enable a faster and more efficient service. Professional staff and managers would then be released from the day-to-day transactional work to consider ways of improving services. The cost of the improved services to the member organisations, and ultimately their clients, was the transfer, change and reduction in current finance jobs.

There has been much written on the nature of managing change in organisations and in particular about how to best manage staff resistance to it. As a person-centred practitioner, it is important to me that I respect other people sufficiently to be honest and open about what I am doing, and the possible consequences of this, and to allow other people their congruent responses. Having your job changed and transplanted to a new organisation 30 miles away with limited public transport links is not an opportunity for most people. If you are disabled and have no personal transport, it comes close to being a disaster. If you are nevertheless willing to transfer and then find that there are no suitable jobs for you, then you face some very difficult decisions and no little sense of loss and rejection, and you are likely to be very angry. From a management perspective, listening empathically to righteous anger and hurt resulting from your decisions, or decisions of a team you are part of, can be difficult, and the willingness and ability to do so with honesty, respect and compassion is a core principle of person-centred organisational work, whether management or consultancy.

Maximising the involvement of as many people as possible in the project was considered crucial. Finance Directors were represented on a local project board which made some of the strategic decisions about the new organisation, including where it would be based. Each member organisation was invited to nominate team members to the project team, both full- and part-time, to design the new processes and to implement them. It was interesting to note that, in the area where the local project board was most demanding and challenging during the planning process, the

(cont'd)

Centre opened on time and with the greatest local support. Getting conflict into the open and willingly sharing power can be demanding, frustrating and time-consuming, but ultimately seems to have paid off. Trade union consultation meetings were set up locally and nationally to ensure that the people who would be supporting staff on the ground were fully briefed. Early meetings established a climate of honesty and trust on both sides: the project team were open about the worst case on job losses, despite some management concerns about our sharing this; the trade unions were equally open about their political opposition; and principles for working together were established. The concern of senior management that early announcements of potential job losses would result in good staff leaving at a crucial time was heard, considered and responded to with guidance on staff retention, and early workshops for staff in which we endeavoured to engage them in thinking about the potential benefits of the new organisation as well as the more obvious costs to them. As well as being offered the opportunity to express concerns openly, and told how the process of staff selection and redeployment was to be handled, they were also invited to input their ideas and preferences for what the new workplace might look like and how it might be managed. These ideas were then fed into the commissioning plans for the new building, implementation plans and management training programmes.

A site visit by staff enabled us to involve them in decision-making about preferred furniture and IT hardware, and left us with some difficult decisions as staff preferences for the more expensive purple furniture conflicted with inevitable budget pressures. The commitment to keep staff engaged, however, allowed us to prioritise expenditure on items that were of importance to them and purple chairs and large flat screens were provided, much to the obvious delight of transferring staff.

The selection process also created its own conflicts. We decided in principle to endeavour to transfer any staff member to a similar job without interview unless there were more applicants than jobs. This caused some concerns for the new organisation's management team who were concerned about the calibre of staff they were going to be given. Again, it was important to listen seriously to their concerns and to maintain the commitments we had made to staff and trade unions. The result was a high investment in initial training for all staff and a development of a performance management process to identify and manage any performance problems early on.

(cont'd)

Staff not wishing to transfer were given access to independent career advisors and career planning and job search-related skills workshops. This is now standard good practice. More importantly for me, they were treated with respect and allowed to express their frustration and anger, which they did with varying degrees of congruent self-expression, and were consistently invited to engage in thinking about potential alternatives. Local trades union involvement was encouraged to ensure that individual staff members were enabled to represent themselves as fully as possible in any discussions. Some staff made major career changes and were delighted as a result. Others were simply disrupted and were less happy.

At the launch event for the new organisation, several of the new team members expressed their delight at how things had turned out. The senior managers were surprised how smoothly the process seemed to have been managed, and how well the new teams had responded: 'They couldn't believe that we actually gave them what we said we would – a nice building, up-to-the-minute technology for all of them, and a full programme of good quality training.' There are real conflicts between the needs of different stakeholders in an organisation, but there are also immense resources and creativity, and individuals are both sophisticated enough to understand the conflicts and resilient enough to manage them, especially if you help to maximise their choices. For me, the person-centred approach to organisational work comes down to respect for the conflicting needs *and* for the resources that exist; empathy, especially when someone's life gets disrupted through no fault of their own; speaking my truth; and acting with integrity. The reflection of these to the core conditions is obvious. For this particular team, 'being received' was epitomised by purple chairs and flat screens.

Having considered the application of person-centred principles and the approach to the systems of the couple, the group and the organisation, we turn our attention in the next and final chapter to its applications to still wider organisms and environments.

SUMMARY

- The move from a theory of individual human development to a theory of groups and organisations and their development, necessitates a leap from the biological to the metaphorical.
- Organisations cannot be changed by imposing a model developed elsewhere.
- Organisations are intelligent, creative, adaptive, self-organising and meaning-seeking.
- Organisational Development (OD) emerged as a specialist field in the late 1950s.
- OD focuses on total system change, and views organisations as complex social systems.
- The conditions which Rogers identified as necessary and sufficient for individual therapeutic change are relevant to organisational change.
- Some current thinking about leadership echoes the person-centred approach to facilitation.

Environment

16

Sometimes I look around me with a feeling of complete dismay. In the confusion that afflicts the world today, I see a disrespect for the very values of life. Beauty is all around us, but how many are blind to it! They look at the wonder of this earth and seem to see nothing.

(Pablo Casals)

We began this book by introducing the notion of the organism that lies at the heart of the person-centred approach. Throughout, we have emphasised the interplay between organism and environment. It is appropriate then to conclude this book by considering what the approach might have to say about the environment and environmental issues. In previous chapters we have developed a systems view of couples, groups, communities and organisations, and have considered them *as* organisms, especially the group *as* organism, and the organisation *as* organism. Viewing the earth as organism or mega-organism with its own tendency to actualise, we are drawing on ideas from Gaia theory (Lovelock, 1979/1987, 1988/1996, 1991) and deep ecology (Naess, 1989), both of which we view as entirely compatible with person-centred principles and practice. For Lovelock (1979/1987), it is clear that Gaia is a self-regulating system: 'It [is] not the biosphere alone that [does] the regulating but the whole thing, life, the air, the oceans, and the rocks. The entire surface of the Earth including life is a self-regulating entity' (p. ix). Given its interest in human values and the natural world, its questioning of a utilitarian perspective of nature, its cross-cultural perspective, its scepticism about some technological structures, its consideration of relationships between individuals, community and the wider world, its involvement in social justice, peace and non-violence, deep ecology could well be viewed as a person-centred eco-psychology. We also reflect on the necessary and sufficient conditions for growth, and ask which specifically are relevant for our relationship with the environment. Finally, we discuss the relevance of the non-directive attitude in this context.

The environment is different from the other client systems we have discussed in this part of the book, in that it is not a client, or at least is such only metaphorically. This is similar to Samuels' (2001) perspective in his 'political clinics', where he asks participants to choose a political theme and then to think about it 'as if' it were a client. He then asks them to say whatever comes into their minds, as a way of understanding their own process in relation to politics. This exercise explores what Samuels and others would call countertransferential responses or attitudes. If we were to follow Samuels' idea in an 'environmental clinic', we might ask therapists, facilitators or activists to think about the environment as if it were a client and as if they were in relationship with it. Samuels invites people to think about their own responses to the issue, and then to see them and think about them as countertransferential. We are more interested to explore the 'as if', empathic relationship, a perspective we develop later.

We emphasise the metaphorical here as we see a danger that some expressions of psychological interest in the environment and the ecological might both reify the subject, and ascribe human qualities and motivations to the natural world. Taking issue with this anthropomorphising of inanimate or even animate objects in Charles Kingsley's work, the poet and commentator John Ruskin says:

> The foam is not cruel, neither does it crawl. The state of mind which attributes to it these characters of a living creature is one in which the reason is unhinged by grief. All violent feelings have the same effect. They produce in us a falseness in all our impressions of external things, which I would generally characterize as the 'Pathetic Fallacy'. (Ruskin, 1856)

Ruskin also uses the term more widely to refer to an author's extreme emotion, which can distort the true view of the world. Whilst we take issue with the implication that there is one 'true' view of the world, we agree with his criticism of the pathetic fallacy.

From system to ecosystem

Throughout its history, psychotherapy has been criticised for being too individualistic. Within the person-centred approach both Holdstock (1993) and Brazier (1995) offer such critiques. Psychotherapy can both individualise distress and pathologise the individual (see Chapter 7). Even this, however, is still a critique at the level of the individual human being. More recently, Bowers (2001) has developed Ruskin's criticism of anthropomorphism to encompass what some view as 'anthropocentrism' or the undue human-centredness of many ideas. For him, this approach to theory and practice 'undermines cultures that have developed complex systems of interspecies communication and moral reciprocity with the natural world'. Implicit in Bowers' enquiry into the nature of eco-justice and the role of education, is the idea that we are all connected with our environment, no matter how estranged from it we may experience ourselves to be. Arguably, the more estranged or incongruent we feel, the more likely we are to consume and pollute. Unnecessary packaging, the amount of litter we produce, the impact of holiday travel, are all both personal and ecological issues. Bowers (2001) goes on to argue that even the social justice issues of class, race and gender focus on the emancipation of the *individual*, disregarding the wider context of the large-scale and economically driven plunder of the earth's resources. Of course, such spoiling and pollution affects individuals, from the air we breathe and the water we drink, to the fragmentation of communities, and the loss of jobs. Orr (1992), writing in a North American context, makes the link between this 'unsustainability' and the need to view things in their wholeness:

> To see things in their wholeness is politically threatening. To understand that our manner of living, so comfortable for some, is linked to cancer rates in migrant laborers in California, the dissappearance of tropical rain forests across the USA, and the depletion of the ozone layer is to see the need for change in our way of life. To see things whole is to see the wounds we have inflicted on ourselves and on our children for no good reason. (p. 88)

There is, therefore, an urgent need to consider the rights of *all* people on the planet to an adequate standard of living, without the majority having to adopt Western values, institutions and practices to ensure it. The pressure on people to adopt unsustainable materialism, explains, for instance, what is seen as the 'crisis' of immigration in Western Europe, and its economic, political and psychological consequences.

T. Berry (1999) argues that the movement we now need to make is from being human or person-centred, to being earth-centred. Echoing Rogers' questions concerning the whole organism, Berry believes that this requires us to think differently about the content, purpose and process of our education systems, and to move from the creation of productive units within an industrial society, to a self-educating earth community sensitised to 'those profound communications made by the universe about us, by the sun and moon and stars, the clouds and rain, the contours of the earth and all its living forms' (p. 64). He goes on to argue that we need to reinvent ourselves completely: to use our critical capabilities, our stories and dreams, to create a new species identity. He argues that, economically, we need to develop reciprocal relationships with other life forms in order to build a sustaining pattern of mutual support; and that, legally, we need to ensure that we acknowledge the rights of other species, seeking harmony with rather than domination over all living things. Here, Berry is, in effect, applying what Rogers refers to as the conditions of an improving relationship (1959) to our relationship with Gaia. Given the difficulties of applying Rogers' conditions to international relations (see Rogers, 1960/1990 and Chapter 11), this is an ambitious project.

Organism and tendencies

When we discussed conflict resolution (in Chapter 11), we included references to the conflict between environmental activists and developers. The environmental movement as we now recognise it can be traced back to the early 1960s, with the publication in 1962 of *Silent Spring*, Rachel Carson's powerful denunciation of the impact of agri-chemicals on the natural environment. Although writing at the same time, there is little evidence that Rogers specifically considered the growing environmental movement in the same way that he interested himself in international conflict resolution. Nevertheless, Rogers grew up on a farm and was passionate about moths in his adolescence. He placed the organism at the heart of person-centred thinking. Many of the images he uses to illustrate his ideas are drawn from the natural world: 'Whether we are speaking of a flower or an oak tree, of an earthworm or a beautiful bird, of an ape or a person, we will do well, I believe, to recognize that life is an active process, not a passive one' (Rogers, 1963/1978/1980, p. 118). In effect, his organic images bed his theory of human psychology in a wider ecological setting. Ellingham (1999) suggests that the difference between the psychodynamic paradigm and the humanistic one can be seen in the difference in their root metaphors: 'The former employs the machine as its root metaphor, the latter the living organism' (p. 121).

Rogers views the directional tendency towards greater complexity and growth (the *actualising tendency*) in human beings as an expression of a more universal *formative tendency* at work in the universe from micro-organisms through crystal and in stellar space:

> In humankind, this tendency exhibits itself as the individual moves from a single-cell origin to complex organic functioning, to knowing and sensing below the level of consciousness, to a conscious awareness of the organism and the external world, to a transcendent awareness of the harmony and unity of the cosmic system, including humankind. (Rogers, 1963/1978/1980, p. 133)

Rogers refers to the actualising tendency and the formative tendency, taken together, as 'the foundation blocks of the person-centered approach' (1963/1978/1980, p.114). He goes further in the same paper and suggests that the hypothesis of the formative tendency 'could be a base upon which we could begin to build a theory for humanistic psychology' (*ibid.*, p. 133).

Necessary and sufficient conditions for growth and change

Throughout the book we have referred to the core principles of the approach (Sanders, 2000) and looked at them as they seem relevant to the subject of each chapter. That the conditions are necessary and sufficient in one context is, for us, no guarantee that they are elsewhere. We've referred to Rogers (1980), who argues that different kinds of relationship demand different blends of congruence, empathic understanding and unconditional positive regard, and to Patterson (1989/2000), who suggests that the conditions are necessary but not sufficient in the context of education. We follow the same process here, and explore which of the conditions are necessary to our relationship with our environment, and whether the conditions are sufficient to enhance that relationship.

The theory of therapy (see Chapter 3) presupposes two people, in relationship and reciprocally aware of each other. When we talk about our relationship with the environment, we take the view that neither the awareness nor the relationship is reciprocal. We may have a relationship with our environment, but there's no evidence that the environment has a *conscious* relationship with us. Therefore, the first precondition of contact, or psychological contact, is not met.

Similarly, the environment is not conscious of its own incongruence. We may see it as distressed, vulnerable or anxious, but 'it' doesn't see itself in this way, or at all! Nevertheless the response of the environment may be viewed as an organismic expression of an incongruent relationship between humans and their total environment, including biosphere, atmosphere, oceans, rocks, flaura and forna.

The way we treat the environment is an expression of our congruence or a symptom of our incongruence. At best, we may have a relationship with our natural and built environments in which we are congruent and integrated. Rogers (1980c) identifies a benevolence towards nature as one of the characteristics he expected of people in the next generation: 'They feel a closeness to, and a caring for, elemental nature. They are ecologically minded, and they get their pleasure from an alliance with the forces of nature, rather than in the conquest of nature' (p. 351). A central element of congruence is awareness, and there are many examples in the literature on ecology of the developing awareness human beings have of the ecosystem, and the necessity and methodology of such awareness. As Naydler (1996) puts it: 'Contemplating the natural phenomena with alert senses and an open mind, is potentially a more powerful and exact instrument than any piece of specialized scientific equipment.' An example of trying to catch intuitively what Wood (2003a) refers to as the *genius loci* or the spirit of the place, is a project in Pishwanton Wood, Scotland. Colquhoun (1997) reports on the study of this specific piece of land, comprising 60 acres, by means of a particular assessment of the landscape. This involved:

1   The initial impressions of the researchers who walked the land and who each produced a 'mood map' of the place.
2   An inventory of its physical features, based on the memories of the initial walk.
3   Experiencing through investigation the changing nature and sense of the landscape.
4   Through further contemplation, finding 'the spirit of the place'.

Merry (2000a) argues that any conflict we experience may be a symptom of our collective or individual incongruence. He sees the person-centred approach, with its emphasis on human being as organism, interacting with its environment in order to fulfil its potential, as a biological, and possibly an ecological approach. He considers Rogers' concept of a fully functioning person being open to experience, and considers how this might exist on several dimensions: experience of ourselves as individual, fully functioning, independent, autonomous people (congruent self-awareness); experience of others as equally independent, autonomous and valued in their own right;

experience of ourselves as part of a larger human group, such as family or community; and experience of ourselves as part of a larger ecological whole:

> I believe there are moments, either fleeting or sustained, when individual people experience that they are part of something larger than themselves. When we are free of distortion and denial, we open up the possibility of experiencing ourselves both as discrete and separate individuals and as significant participants in the continuation of life itself. (pp. 34–5)

Rogers argues that we develop defences in response to unhelpful aspects of our environment, particularly during childhood; and that these defences lead us to behave in ways which are at odds with or incongruent with our natural tendency to actualise (see Chapters 5 and 6). Our destructive behaviours and our inability to respond openly to our natural environment, are signs of our incongruence on a larger scale. Just as in personal relationships we need to be internally congruent before we can experience empathic understanding or unconditional acceptance of another, so in this context, our incongruences leave us unable to respond empathically to the environment, and unable to respect it or value it appropriately. Examples of this include: the overuse and abuse of resources; the depredation of forests and green spaces; the use of animals purely as a service to human beings in the food chain; pollution (for example, that caused by cars); litter and unnecessary waste (such as non-disposable nappies). As Wood puts it (in a personal communication, 9 August 2003):

> Living well in a place involves nothing less than sustainabilty in its most inclusive sense. Preserving the ecosystem and its biodiversity, producing healthy natural food for local and regional needs ... actively participating in the community and fostering local values and stimulating the local economy are key features.

Joanna Macy (1983), an environmental activist and teacher, makes a further point. She believes that the current state of the natural world inevitably and naturally engenders widespread feelings of distress. Fear of pain, introjected social taboos against expressions of despair, and conflicting introjects about what is of value and importance, lead to the repression of such feelings. This repression engenders a sense of isolation and impotence. More information about the extent of the damage we are causing the planet tends to increase feelings of despair, and further deepens feelings of apathy and powerlessness. In a study on the psycho-spatial dimension of global environmental problems Uzzell (1999) found that people believe that environmental problems at the global level are more serious than those in their immediate locality. One result of this is a diminishing sense of responsibility as the focus of concern shifts from local to national, international and global levels. In a study of climate change and sustainable development at a local level, Lewin (2003) suggests that 'what becomes clear is that the message sent through the media and government is framing climate change as a global problem confined largely to the scientific and political domains' (p. 16). In order to counteract this abdication or denial of responsibility, Macy argues that we need to help each other express our emotional response to the damage we're doing to the planet, before we can begin to digest the information we need to help us begin to find solutions. Orr (1992) refers to this as a process of 'ecological literacy'.

This brings us to a point of choice. Swimme and Berry (1992) describe it in this way:

> ... the future of Earth's community rests in significant ways upon the decisions to be made by the humans who have inserted themselves so deeply into even the genetic codes of Earth's process. This future will be worked out in the tensions between those committed to the Technozoic, a future of increased exploitation of Earth as a resource, all for the benefit of humans, and those committed to the Ecozoic, a new mode of human-Earth relations, one where the well-being of the entire Earth community is the primary concern. (pp. 14–15)

For these authors this choice point is itself part of the unfolding process of human creativity. What's good for Gaia is good for us. We don't have to win what's 'good' for us as individuals at the expense of our partner, the group, the community or the organisation. Arne Naess (b. 1912), Norwegian philosopher and founder of deep ecology, comments:

> The extensive moralising within the ecological movement has given the public the false impression that they are being asked to make a sacrifice, to show more responsibility, more concern, and a nicer moral standard. But all of that would flow naturally and easily if the self were widened and deepened so that the protection of Nature was felt and perceived as protection of our very selves. (Naess, cited in Johnstone, 1994, p. 22)

James Lovelock (b. 1919), the originator of Gaia theory, makes a similar point: 'The most useful contribution from Gaia is in the public domain. Organisms, and this includes people, that improve their environment make it better for their progeny, whereas those that foul the environment worsen their chances' (2001, p. 9).

As we propose this contextual view of the conditions, we're drawing on Rogers' (1959) formulation of the theory, in which the therapist or facilitator meets the fourth and fifth conditions when he *experiences* unconditional positive regard and empathic understanding. This has two implications:

- If we are self-aware or congruent, integrated in our relationship with the environment, then we will behave with respect, and empathically.
- If we're empathic and unconditionally accepting of the environment, then we necessarily behave in ways which enhance our own future, and are congruent.

Finally, we question the necessity of the sixth condition in this context: that the environment 'perceives' our unconditional positive regard and empathic understanding. Our argument is the same as it is in relation to the first two conditions: that the environment is not conscious in any way that we understand that term, and that therefore this condition is not and cannot be met.

From this we conclude that the conditions which seem relevant in the environmental context are the core conditions, that is, the three conditions which the therapist, facilitator or activist has sole responsibility for. Whether they are both necessary and sufficient to effect change in this sphere is an open question.

A non-directive attitude

Within the ecological movement there is some debate about the extent to which it is desirable for humans to intervene in nature. Should we manage forests and woodland and, if we do, how do we value and allow wilderness (see Nash, 2003)? Taking a third way between these positions, Lovelock (2001) argues that 'the self-regulation of Gaia requires the existence of two firm constraints. This gives Gaia an ethical significance. We are truly accountable to the Earth' (p. 9). The non-directive attitude is not to be confused with passivity. As we have argued throughout the book (and specifically in Chapters 7 and 11), the logic of the person-centred approach is active, ecological citizenship. As Rene Dubos put it in the 1970s, in a phrase that has been taken up by the Green movement: 'Think globally, act locally.' This is particularly important in the light of people's diminishing sense of responsibility for ecological issues or accountability to the ecosystem. To given one example: greenhouse emissions are *local*, and in many places local government has authority over such emissions in the areas of transport, land use planning, energy consumption and waste management (see Lewin, 2003).

There are many inspiring stories of the improving relationship of human beings to their ecological environment, a good source of which are the magazines *Orion* (www.orionsociety.org) and *Resurgence* (www.resurgence.org). Here, as an example of the non-directive attitude to the environment, we present a 'case study' of the ecological work of Trees for Life. In citing this example we are aware both of the importance of the role of forests and of some of the controversies around this issue. Whilst deforestation contributes to atmospheric carbon dioxide, we can also see a concentration on the role of forests and land use as a distraction from reducing energy-related emissions (see Brown, 1998).

CASE STUDY: TREES FOR LIFE

Trees for Life is a Scottish charity established in 1993 by Alan Watson-Featherstone, a member of the Findhorn Community in Northern Scotland, a community known for its pioneering work in cooperation with nature. Watson-Featherstone's vision for Trees for Life is to regenerate and restore the native Caledonian Forest over a period of 200–300 years (Greenleaf, 1970/1982; Spears and Lawrence, 2002) to a large contiguous area in the Scottish Highlands, and eventually to reintroduce the missing species of wildlife which formerly lived in the old forest. In this the charity seeks not only to counteract the centuries of deforestation which have led to the almost complete loss of Scotland's native woodlands, but also to be pioneers in the newly emerging field of ecological restoration.

Most conservation campaigns today are focused on stopping the devastation of the world's forests, and there have been some successes to celebrate. But even if all the destruction currently taking place were miraculously to stop tomorrow, we would still be left with a world which is substantially degraded in terms of its ability to sustain life: human, animal and tree alike. Watson-Featherstone identifies a shift of consciousness as critical to achieving the changes needed, one which moves us individually and collectively away from the anthropocentric and parasitic relationship our culture presently has with the Earth. He writes: 'I sometimes think of our society's addiction to endless economic growth as making us like a giant mosquito, sucking the life force out of the planet and giving nothing back in return.' He goes on to quote Ishmael by Daniel Quinn who aptly describes this attribute of our culture by terming us as 'Takers' and contrasting us with the 'Leavers', the hunter-gatherer tribal peoples who, through the minimal impact of their lifestyles, leave their land and the world in essentially the same condition as they find it.

(contd.)

Watson-Featherstone believes that it is imperative that we develop a new role in our relationship with the Earth, that of 'Givers'. This 'non-directive' approach is mirrored in the work of Trees for Life in restoring a wild forest which is there for its own sake, rather than as a timber resource or visitor destination for people, as a home for wildlife, and to fulfil the ecological functions necessary for the well-being of the land itself.

The restoration work itself primarily comprises fencing that will keep out red deer and allow natural regeneration, the planting of native tree species and the cutting down of non-native commercially planted trees where they've been planted amongst Caledonian forest remnants and threaten its natural regeneration. The work is planned and organised by a team of largely office-based employees and carried out by volunteers on volunteer work weeks. This practical work provides the context for broader personal experiences available to the volunteers comprising several elements:

1   Personal empowerment – By providing volunteers with a direct, hands-on experience of doing something positive for the Caledonian Forest and for the planet, Trees for Life provides people with an opportunity to experience making a difference for the better in the world.
2   The development of meaningful connections – Through experiencing themselves as part of a group while living and working together for a week, volunteers can share their concerns and passion for nature and the planet and develop connections which last long beyond the actual week itself. In many cases, volunteers leave the weeks with a renewed sense of hope and inspiration for the future, which benefits them in their daily lives.
3   A sense of relationship with and learning from the environment – The people who undertake this work make a deeply personal, physical and psychological contact with wild nature. This enables many of them to experience the relationship between themselves and the earth as an organismic one. All of this practical work takes place in remote areas of the Highlands, amidst the mountains, lochs and remnants of the old forest. The quality of this environment often touches people profoundly, in an uplifting, healing and transformative way, and provides volunteers with a daily education that comes from work that's based on the principle that 'Nature knows best', the realisation of how much they can learn from their relationship with the environment, and the extent to which they are part of a larger ecological whole.

These experiences are consciously offered by Trees for Life and provide examples that correspond remarkably to T. Berry's (1999) conditions for an improving relationship with Gaia. (For further information about Trees for Life see www.treesforlife.org.uk.)

SUMMARY

- Although Rogers does not specifically consider environmental issues as such, the images he uses to illustrate his thinking embed his theory of human psychology as implicitly ecological.
- Rogers views the directional tendency towards greater complexity and growth (the *actualising tendency* in human beings) as an expression of a *formative tendency* at work in the universe.
- If we consider the Earth as organism, in the same way as other systems, then we can bring the principles of the person-centred approach to bear on our relationship with the environment.
- Environmental crises may be viewed as the result of incongruence in our human relationship to the natural world.
- As human beings we need both to differentiate and to integrate.

These reflections on the environment bear witness to the value, and values, of the person-centred approach. As we have attempted to show in this present work, its principles are applicable to a wide range of subjects and issues which, as human beings and persons, we face, in whatever situation and context, in this world.

Throughout this book we have developed the interplay between organism and environment and, in similar vein, have discussed the importance of differentiation and integration. Human beings are a miracle of differentiation, from the simple cell to a whole organism, distinct from other organisms. As human beings we have achieved incredible advances through differentiation. Because we can differentiate, we can split the atom, and map the human genome. Notwithstanding these advances, Csikszentmihalyi (1992) believes that integration is the next developmental stage for us as a species. As we have argued throughout, differentiation needs to be balanced with integration:

> The task of the next decades and centuries is to realise this under-developed component of the mind. Just as we have learned to separate ourselves from each other and from the environment, we now need to learn how to re-unite ourselves with other entities around us without losing our hard-won individuality. (Csikszentmihalyi, 1992, p. 240)

Appendix: Rogers' Nomination for the Nobel Peace Prize, 1987

Congress of the United States
House of Representatives
Washington, DC 20515

January 28, 1987

The Nobel Peace Committee
Drammensveien 19
Oslo 2
Norway

To the Nobel Committee

In February of 1984, I formed a Nobel Peace Nominating Commission in the forty-fourth Congressional District which I represent. The Nobel Peace Nominating Commission in San Diego, California is comprised of members of the community with various backgrounds and experience. Some of the members include former Nobel Peace Prize winner Dr. Jonas Salk,[1] Dr. Herbert York,[2] California State Senator Wadie Deddeh,[3] and Dr. Kimiko Fukada, Ed.D.

The process of nominating by the Commission is comprised of meeting and discussing potential nominees over a six month period, researching background information, and finalizing the decision in January 1987. This year was of particular excitement

---

[1] Scientist who identified the virus that causes polio.
[2] Chief Scientist of the Advanced Research Projects Agency who famously said that 'space is a place, not a program'.
[3] Served in the California State legislature (1966–82), and in the Senate (1982–93).

due to the close race for the finalist. Some of the contenders were: The Contadora Group,[4] Joan Kroc,[5] and President Corazón Aquino.[6]

This year, it is my pleasure and honor to nominate Carl Rogers for consideration by your committee for the 1987 Nobel Peace Prize. Mr. Rogers is a pioneer in the field of humanistic psychology and the founder of the Center for Studies of the Person in La Jolla, California. More specifically, he has been extremely involved in world peace efforts and group mediation in Northern Ireland, Central America, and South Africa. I have attached some background information on Carl Rogers with special emphasis on the Carl Rogers Peace Project. If there is any additional information needed please advise me.

Thank you for the opportunity to participate in this process.

Sincerely,

Jim Bates
Member of Congress

---

[4] An organisation of Latin American countries (Colombia, Mexico, Panama, Venezuela), formed in 1983 to encourage regional peace, especially in Central America, which, together with a support group, comprising Argentina, Brazil, Peru, and Uruguay (formed in 1985), signed the Caraballeda Declaration in 1986 to search for diplomatic means of solving conflicts, and which in 1987 submitted a regional peace treaty.

[5] A San Diego philanthropist who founded several local projects including a community centre and who, in 1998, founded the Joan B. Kroc Institute for Peace and Justice at the University of San Diego.

[6] President of the Philippines (1986–92).

Letter to Carl Rogers

Congress of the United States
House of Representatives
Washington, DC 20515

January 30, 1987

Dr. Carl Rogers
Center for Studies of the Person
1125 Torrey Pines Road
La Jolla, CA 92037

Dear Dr. Rogers

I am pleased to inform you that I have nominated you for consideration for the 1987 Nobel Peace Prize.

The nomination process, by which you were chosen, was the result of several weeks of work by distinguished members of our community including Dr. Jonas Salk, Betty Byrnes, Kimiko Fukada, Mary Jessop, Dr. Herbert York, Hamilton Marsten, Dr. William Hollingsworth, Senator Wadie Deddeh, Bill Claycomb, and General Ed Meyer.

In addition to my Commission's recommendation, several other nominations were considered including, The Contadora Group, Joan Kroc, President Corazón Aquino, and Freedom Foundation.

I would like to commend you and the Center's efforts toward peace and conflict resolution. In light of the potential nominees, your work in Central America, South Africa, Northern Ireland is truly deserving of consideration for the Nobel Peace Prize.

I support your efforts and hope for continued success toward reduction of psychological barriers which block us from global peace.

Sincerely,

Jim Bates
Member of Congress

References

Advisory Group on Citizenship. (1998) *Education for Citizenship and the Teaching of Democracy in Schools*. Sudbury: Qualifications and Curriculum Authority.

Allen, P. (2004) Interpersonal process recall in person-centred supervision. In K. Tudor and M. Worrall (eds) *Freedom to Practice: Person-Centred Approaches to Supervision*. Llangarron: PCCS Books.

American Psychiatric Association. (1994) *Diagnostic and Statistical Manual of Mental Disorders*, fourth edition. Washington, DC: APA.

Ames, E. W. (1997) *The Development of Romanian Orphanage Children Adopted to Canada*. Burnby, BC: Simon Fraser University.

Anderson, R. and Cissna, K. (1997) *The Martin Buber – Carl Rogers Dialogue: A New Transcript with Commentary*. Albany, NY: SUNY Press.

Angyal, A. (1941) *Foundations for a Science of Personality*. New York: Commonwealth Fund.

Aristotle. (1996) *Physics*. Oxford: Oxford World's Classics.

Association for the Development of the Person-Centered Approach. Website: www.adpca.org

Association of Humanistic Psychology Practitioners. Website: www.ahpp.org

Ayling, J. (1930) *The Retreat from Parenthood*. London: Kegan Paul, Trench, Trubner and Co.

Bader, E. and Pearson, P. T. (1988) *In Quest of The Mythical Mate: A Developmental Approach to Diagnosis and Treatment in Couples Therapy*. New York: Brunner/Mazel.

Barker, R. G. (1968) *Ecological Psychology*. Palo Alto, CA: Stanford University Press.

Barrett-Lennard, G. T. (1979) A new model of communicational-relational systems in intensive groups. *Human Relations, 32*, 841–9.

Barrett-Lennard, G. T. (1983) Understanding the person-centred approach to therapy: A reply to questions and misconceptions. In E. McIlduff and D. Coghlan (eds) *The Person-Centered Approach and Cross-Cultural Communication: An International Review, Volume II* (pp. 99–113). Dublin: Center for Cross-Cultural Communication.

Barrett-Lennard, G. T. (1984) The world of family relationships: A person-centred systems view. In R. Levant and J. Shlien (eds) *Client-Centered Therapy and the Person-Centered Approach: New Directions in Theory, Research and Practice* (pp. 222–42). New York: Praeger.

Barrett-Lennard, G. T. (1994) Toward a person-centered theory of community. *Journal of Humanistic Psychology, 34*(3), 62–86.

Barrett-Lennard, G. T. (1998) *Carl Rogers' Helping System: Journey and Substance*. London: Sage.

Barrett-Lennard, G. T. (2003) *Steps on a Mindful Journey: Person-Centred Expressions*. Llangarron: PCCS Books.

Barrineau, P. and Bozarth, J. D. (1989) A person-centered research model. *Person-Centered Review*, 4(4), 465–74.

Battram, A. (1998) *Navigating Complexity: The Essential Guide to Complexity in Business and Management*. London: The Industrial Society.

Bebout, J. (1974) It takes one to know one: Existential-Rogerian concepts in encounter groups. In D. A. Wexler and L. N. Rice (eds) *Innovations in Client-Centered Therapy* (pp. 367–420). New York: Wiley.

Beck, A. P. (1974) Phases in the development of structure in therapy and encounter groups. In D. A. Wexler and L. N. Rice (eds) *Innovations in Client-Centered Therapy* (pp. 421–63). New York: Wiley.

Bellah, R. N., Madsen, R., Sullivan, W. M., Swidler, A. and Tipton, S. M. (1981) *The Good Society*. New York: Knopf.

Bendana, A. (1999) Armies for peace in Nicaragua. In *People Building Peace*. Utrecht: European Centre for Conflict Prevention.

Bernard, J. (1976) *The Future of Marriage*. Harmondsworth: Penguin.

Berne, E. (1968) *Games People Play*. Harmondsworth: Penguin.

Berne, E. (1971) *A Layman's Guide to Psychiatry and Psychoanalysis*. Harmondsworth: Penguin. (Original work published 1947.)

Berry, T. (1999) *The Great Work*. New York: Bell Tower.

Berry, W. (1999) Conserving communities. In J. Mander and E. Goldsmith (eds) *The Case Against the Global Economy and for a Turn Towards the Local* (pp. 407–18). San Francisco, CA: Sierra Club Books.

Biermann-Ratjen, E-M. (1998) Incongruence and psychopathology. In B. Thorne and E. Lambers (eds) *Person-Centred Therapy: A European Perspective* (pp. 119–30). London: Sage.

Bion, W. (1961) *Experiences in Groups and Other Papers*. London: Tavistock.

Birch, L. (in preparation) *Learning the Core Conditions from Animals*. (Manuscript submitted for publication.)

Black, J. E. and Greenough, W. T. (1986) Induction of pattern in neural structure by experience: Implications for cognitive development. In M. E. Lamb, A. L. Brown and B. Rogoff (eds) *Advances in Developmental Psychology, Vol. 4* (pp. 1–50). Hillsdale, NJ: Lawrence Erlbaum Associates.

Block, P. (1993) *Stewardship: Choosing Service over Self Interest*. San Francisco, CA: Berrett Koehler.

Bloom, B. S., Engelhart, M. D., Furst, E. J., Hill, W. D. and Krathwohl, D. R. (1956) *Taxonomy of Educational Objectives. Handbook I: Cognitive Domain*. London: Longman.

Boal, A. (1979) *The Theatre of the Oppressed*. New York: Urizen Books.

Bohart, A. C. and Greenberg, L. S. (eds) (1997) *Empathy Reconsidered: New Directions in Psychotherapy*. Washington, DC: American Psychological Association.

Boszormenyi-Nagy, I. and Ulrich, D. (1981) Contextual family therapy. In A. S Gurman and D. P. Kniskern (eds) *Handbook of Family Therapy* (pp. 159–86). New York: Brunner/Mazel.

Boukydis, C. F. Z. (1990) Client-centered/experiential practice with parents and infants. In G. Lietaer, J. Rombauts and R. Van Balen (eds) *Client-Centered and Experiential Psychotherapy in the Nineties* (pp. 797–811). Leuven: Leuven University Press.

Bowers, C. A. (2001) *Educating for Eco-Justice and Community*. Athens, GA: University of Georgia.

Bowlby, J. (1971) *Attachment and Loss, Vol. I: Attachment*. Harmondsworth: Penguin. (Original work published 1969.)

Bowlby, J. (1973) *Attachment and Loss, Vol. II: Separation*. Harmondsworth: Penguin.

Bowlby, J. (1981) *Attachment and Loss, Vol. III: Loss: Sadness and Depression*. Harmondsworth: Penguin. (Original work published 1980.)

Boy, A. V. and Pine, G. P. (1995) *Child-Centered Counseling and Psychotherapy*. Springfield, IL: Charles C. Thomas.

Boy, A. V. and Pine, G. P. (1999) *A Person-Centered Foundation for Counseling and Psychotherapy*. Second edition. Springfield, IL: Charles C. Thomas.

Bozarth, J. (1981) The person-centered approach in the large community group. In G. Gazda (ed.) *Innovations to Group Psychotherapy*, second edition (pp. 36–42). Springfield, IL: Charles C. Thomas.

Bozarth, J. D. (1996) A theoretical reconceptualization of the necessary and sufficient conditions for therapeutic personality change. *The Person-Centered Journal*, 3(1), 44–51.

Bozarth, J. D. (1998) *Person-Centered Therapy: A Revolutionary Paradigm*. Llangarron: PCCS Books.

Bozarth, J. D. (1998c) The large community group. In *Person-Centered Therapy: A Revolutionary Paradigm* (pp. 149–59). Llangarron: PCCS Books. (Original work presented 1992 and 1995.)

Bozarth, J. D. (1998d) Unconditional positive regard in person-centred therapy. In *Person-Centered Therapy: A Revolutionary Paradigm* (pp. 83–8). Llangarron: PCCS Books.

Bozarth, J. D. and Wilkins, P. (eds) (2001) *Unconditional Positive Regard*. Llangarron: PCCS Books.

Brazier, D. (ed.) (1993) *Beyond Carl Rogers*. London: Constable.

Brazier, D. (1995) *Zen Therapy*. London: Constable.

British Association for Counselling. (1996) *Courses Recognition Booklet*. Rugby: BACP.

British Association for Counselling and Psychotherapy. (2002) *Ethical Framework for Good Practice in Counselling and Psychotherapy*. Rugby: BACP.

British Association for the Person-Centred Approach. Website: bapca.org.uk

Brodley, B. T. (2001) *Concerning 'transference', 'countertransference', and other psychoanalytically-developed concepts from a client/person-centered perspective*. Paper available on www.alllanturner.co.uk/papers/psyanaly.html

Brown, P. (1998) *Climate, Biodiversity and Forests – Issues and Opportunities Emerging from the Kyoto Protocol*. Washington, DC: World Resources Institute.

Buber, M. (1937) *I and Thou* (R. G. Smith, trans.). Edinburgh: T and T Clark.

Bunker, S., Coates, C., Hodgson, D. and How, J. (1999) *Diggers and Dreamers: The New Guide to Communal Living*. London: Diggers and Dreamers Publications.

Burke, B. and Dalrymple, J. (1995) *Anti-oppressive Practice – Social Care and the Law*. Buckingham: Open University Press.

Burnside, M. A. (1986) Fee practices of male and female therapists. In D. W. Krueger (ed.) *The Last Taboo* (pp. 48–54). New York: Brunner/Mazel.

Cain, D. (1989a) From the individual to the family. *Person-Centered Review, 4*, 248–55.

Cain, D. (ed.) (1989b) Psychodiagnosis [Special Issue] *Person-Centered Review, 4*(3).

Cain, D. (1989c) The paradox of nondirectiveness in the person-centered approach. *Person-Centered Review, 4*(2), 123–31.

Cain, D. (ed.) (2002) *Classics in the Person-Centered Approach*. Llangarron: PCCS Books.

Campion, M. J. (1995) *Who's Fit to be a Parent?* London: Routledge.

Capra, F. (1982) *The Turning Point*. New York: Bantam Books.

Carkhuff, R. R. (1969a) *Beyond Counseling and Therapy*. New York: Holt Rinehart and Winston.

Carkhuff, R. R. (1969b) *The Art of Helping*. Amherst, MA: Human Resources Development Press.

Carson, R. (1962) *Silent Spring*. Boston, MA: Houghton Mifflin.

Castel, R., Castel, F. and Lovell, A. (1982) *The Psychiatric Society*. New York: Columbia University Press.

Center for Policy Alternatives. (2003) *Equal Pay*. Website: http://www:cfpa.org

Centre for Public Law. (2002) Website: www.law.cam.ac.uk

Cherry, G. W. (1975) *The Serendipity of the Fully Functioning Manager*. Unpublished manuscript, Sloan School of Management, Massachusetts Institute of Technology.

Cilliers, F. (1996) Facilitator training in South Africa. In R. Hutterer, G. Powlowsky, P. F. Schmid and R. Stipsits (eds) *Client-Centered and Experiential Psychotherapy: A Paradigm in Motion* (pp. 547–55). Frankfurt am Main: Peter Lang.

Clarkson, P. (1992) *Transactional Analysis: An Integrated Approach*. London: Routledge.

Clarkson, P. (1996) *The Bystander*. London: Whurr.

Clarkson, P. and Fish, S. (1988) Systemic assessment and treatment considerations in TA child psychotherapy. *Transactional Analysis Journal, 18*, 123–32.

Coghlan, D. and McIlduff, E. (1990) Structuring and non directiveness in group facilitation. *Person-Centered Review, 5*, 13–19.

Coghlan, D. and McIlduff, E. (1991) Dublin 1985: Perceptions of a cross-cultural communication workshop. In E. McIlduff and D. Coghlan (eds) *The Person-Centered Approach and Cross-Cultural Communication: An International Review, Volume 1* (pp. 43–59). Dublin: Center for Cross-Cultural Communication.

Cohen, D. (1997) *Carl Rogers: A Critical Biography*. London: Constable.

Colquhoun, M. (1997) An exploration into the use of Goethean science as a methodology for landscape assessment: The Pishwanton project. *Agriculture, Ecosystems and Environment, 63*, 145–57.

Combs, A. (1989) *Being and Becoming*. New York: Springer.

Combs, A. W. (2000) Person-centered assumptions for counselor education. In D. J. Cain (ed.) *Classics in the Person-Centered Approach* (pp. 269–75). Llangarron: PCCS Books. (Original work published 1986.)

Conradi, P. (1999) Dreams, the unconscious and the person-centred approach: Re-visioning practice. *Person-Centred Practice*, 7(1), 12–26.

Conway, A. (2002) Teaching students not to think. *The Spectator*, 290 (No. 9096), 22–3.

Costello, J., Roy, B. and Steiner, C. (1988) Competition. In B. Roy and C. Steiner (eds) *Radical Psychiatry: The Second Decade* (pp. 55–67). Unpublished manuscript.

Coulson, A. (1995) The person-centred approach and the re-instatement of the unconscious. *Person-Centred Practice*, 3(2), 7–16.

Csikszentmihalyi, M. (1992) *Flow*. London: Rider.

De Board, R. (1978) *The Psychoanalysis of Organizations*. London: Tavistock.

De Carvalho, R. J. (1991) *The Growth Hypothesis in Psychology: The Humanistic Psychologies of Abraham Maslow and Carl Rogers*. Lampeter: Mellen.

De Marignac, D. (1984) Experimenting the person-centred approach in various groups of my close neighbourhood and aspects of my daily life. In A. Segrera (ed.) *Proceedings of the First International Forum on the Person-Centered Approach*. Oaxtepec, Morelos, Mexico: Universidad Iberoamericana.

Department for Education and Skills (DfES). (2001) *Skills for Social Inclusion and the Knowledge Economy: Towards a Shared Vision*. London: HMSO. Website: www.skills.org.uk

Department for Education and Skills (DfES). (2002) *Time for Standards*. London: HMSO.

Department for Education and Skills (DfES). (2003) *Lifelong Learning Opportunities*. Website: www.skills.org.uk

Devonshire, C. (1991) The person-centered approach and cross-cultural communication. In E. McIlduff and D. Coghlan (eds) *The Person-Centered Approach and Cross-Cultural Communication: An International Review, Volume 1* (pp. 15–42). Dublin: Center for Cross-Cultural Communication.

Devonshire, C. M. and Kremer, J. W. (1980) *Toward a Person-Centered Resolution of Intercultural Conflicts*. Dortmund: Pädagogische Arbeitsstelle.

Dierick, P. and Lietaer, G. (1990) Member and therapist perceptions of therapeutic factors in therapy and growth groups: Comments on a category system. In G. Lietaer, J. Rombauts and R. Van Balen (eds) *Client-Centered and Experiential Psychotherapy in the Nineties* (pp. 741–70). Leuven: Leuven University Press.

Duncan, B. L., Solovey, A. D. and Rusk, G. S. (1992) *Changing the Rules: A Client-Directed Approach to Therapy*. New York: Guilford Press.

Du Toit, D., Grobler, H. and Schenck, C. J. (eds) (1998) *Person-Centred Communication: Theory and Practice*. Oxford: Oxford University Press. (Original work published 1997.)

Dryden, W. (1990) *Rational-Emotive Counselling in Action*. London: Sage.

Eakins, B. W., and Eakins, R. G. (1978) *Sex Differences in Communication*. Boston, MA: Houghton Mifflin.

Edwards, P. (ed.) (1967) *Encyclopaedia of Philosophy*. New York: Macmillan (now Palgrave Macmillan).

Egan, G. (1997) *The Skilled Helper: A Systematic Approach to Effective Helping*, fourth edition. Pacific Grove, CA: Brooks/Cole.

Ellingham, I. (1995) Quest for a paradigm: Person-centred counselling/psychotherapy versus psychodynamic counselling and psychotherapy. *Counselling*, 6(4), 288–90.

Ellingham, I. (1997) On the quest for a person-centred paradigm. *Counselling*, 8(1), 52–5.

Ellingham, I. (1999) Carl Rogers' 'congruence' as an organismic, not a Freudian concept. *The Person-Centered Journal*, 6(2), 121–40.

Elliot, R., Mearns, D. and Schmid, P. F. (2002) Editorial. *Person-Centered and Experiential Psychotherapies*, 1(1 and 2), 1–3.

Embleton Tudor, L. and Tudor, K. (1996) Is the client always right? – A person-centred perspective. *Cahoots*, 55, 33, 43.

Embleton Tudor, L. and Tudor, K. (1997) *Sharing life therapy*. Presentation at Ten Years On: International Conference on the Person-Centred Approach, University of Sheffield, September 1997.

Embleton Tudor, L. and Tudor, K. (1999) The history of Temenos. *Self and Society*, 27(2), 28–31.

Engels, F. (1968) The origin of the family, private property and the state. In *Marx and Engels: Selected Works* (pp. 449–583). London: Lawrence and Wishart. (Original work published 1891.)

Equal Opportunities Commission. (1998) *New Earnings Survey*. London: EoC.

Erikson, E. (1965) *Childhood and Society*. Harmondsworth: Penguin. (Original work published 1951.)

Erikson, E. (1968) *Identity, Youth and Crisis*. New York: W. W. Norton.

Erskine, R. G. (1998) Attunement and involvement: Therapeutic responses to relational needs. *International Journal of Psychotherapy*, 3(3), 235–43.

Esser, U., Pabst, H. and Speierer, G-W. (eds) (1996) *The Power of the Person-Centered Approach: New Challenges, Perspectives, Answers*. Köln: Gesellschaft für Gesprächspsychotherapie.

Fairhurst, I. (ed.) (1999) *Women Writing in the Person-Centred Approach*. Llangarron: PCCS Books.

Farber, B. A., Brink, D. C. and Raskin, P. M. (eds) (1996) *The Psychotherapy of Carl Rogers*. New York: The Guilford Press.

Figge, P. (1999) Client-centred psychotherapy in groups: Understanding the influence of the client-therapist relationship on therapy outcome. In C. Lago and M. MacMillan (eds) *Experiences in Relatedness: Groupwork and the Person-Centred Approach* (pp. 95–105). Llangarron: PCCS Books.

Fischer, C. T. (1989) The life-centered approach to psychodiagnostics: Attending to life-world, ambiguity and possibility. *Person-Centered Review*, 4(2), 163–70.

Flew, A. (2000) *Education for Citizenship*. Studies in Education No. 10. London: Institute of Economic Affairs.

Fontana, D. and Slack, I. (1997) *Teaching Meditation to Children*. Shaftsbury: Element.

Foot, D. (undated) *Going Straight in Circles*. Document available online at: www.ccpas.co.uk/downloads/caring

Freire, P. (1972) *Pedagogy of the Oppressed*. Harmondsworth: Penguin.

Freire, P. (1976) *Education: The Practice of Freedom*. London: Writers and Readers Publishing Cooperative. (Original work published 1967.)

French, S. (1996) Simulation exercises in disability awareness training: A critique. In G. Hales (ed.) *Beyond Disability* (pp. 114–23). London: Sage.

French, W. L. and Bell, C. H. (1999) *Organization Development: Behavioral Science Interventions for Organization Improvement*, sixth edition. Upper Saddle River, NJ: Prentice-Hall.

Freud, A. (1966) *The Ego and Mechanisms of Defence* (C. Barnes, trans.). London: Hogarth. (Original work published 1936)

Freud, S. (1922) *Introductory Lectures on Psycho-Analysis* (J. Rivière, trans.). London: George Allen and Unwin.

Freud, S. (1962) *Two Short Accounts of Psycho-Analysis* (J. Strachey, trans. and ed.) (pp. 31–87). Harmondsworth: Penguin. (Original work published 1910.)

Freud, S. (1966) Project for a scientific psychology. In J. Strachey (ed. and trans.) *The Standard Edition of the Complete Psychological Works of Sigmund Freud*. London: Hogarth Press. (Original work published 1895.)

Freud, S. (1977) Three essays on the theory of sexuality. In J. Strachey, A. Tyson and A. Richards (eds) *The Pelican Freud Library, Vol. 7: On Sexuality* (A. and J. Strachey, trans.) (pp. 33–169). Harmondsworth: Penguin. (Original work published 1905.)

Freud, S. (1977) Analysis of a phobia in a five-year-old boy ('Little Hans') In J. Strachey, A. Tyson and A. Richards (eds) *The Pelican Freud Library, Vol. 8: Case Histories I 'Dora' and 'Little Hans'* (A. and J. Strachey, trans.) (pp. 167–305). Harmondsworth: Penguin. (Original work published 1909.)

Frick, W. B. (1971) *Humanistic Psychology: Interviews with Maslow, Murphy and Rogers*. Columbus, OH: Charles E. Merrill.

Furedi, F. (1997) *Culture of Fear: Risk-taking and the Morality of Low Expectation*. London: Cassell.

Furedi, F. (2001) *Paranoid Parenting: Abandon Your Anxieties and Become a Good Parent*. London: Allen Lane.

Fusek, L. (ed) (1991) *New Directions in Client-Centered Therapy: Practice with Difficult Client Populations. Monograph Series 1*. Chicago: Chicago Counseling and Psychotherapy Center.

Gardner, H. (1991) *The Unschooled Mind: How Children Think and How Schools Should Teach*. New York: Basic Books.

Gardner, H. (1993) *Frames of Mind: The Theory of Multiple Intelligences*, second edition. London: Fontana Press. (Original work published 1983.)

Gatto, J. T. (2002) *Dumbing Us Down: The Hidden Curriculum of Compulsory Schooling*. Gabriola Island, BC: New Society Publishers.

Gaylin, N. (1989) The necessary and sufficient conditions for change: Individual versus family therapy. *Person-Centered Review*, 4, 263–79.

Gaylin, N. (1990) Family-centered therapy. In G. Lietaer, J. Rombauts and R. Van Balen (eds) *Client-Centered and Experiential Psychotherapy in the Nineties* (pp. 813–28). Leuven: Leuven University Press.

Gaylin, N. (1993) Person-centred family therapy. In D. Brazier (ed.) *Beyond Carl Rogers* (pp. 181–200). London: Constable.

Gaylin, N. (2001) *Family, Self and Psychotherapy: A Person-Centred Perspective.* Llangarron: PCCS Books.

Gendlin, E. T. (1996) *Focusing-Oriented Psychotherapy: A Manual of the Experiential Method.* New York: Guilford Press.

Ginott, H. (1988) *Between Parent and Teenager.* New York: Avon. (Original work published 1972.)

Gordon, T. (1951) Group-centered leadership and administration. In C. R. Rogers (ed.) *Client-Centered Therapy* (pp. 320–83). London: Constable.

Gordon, T. (1975) *P.E.T. Parent Effectiveness Training.* New York: P. H. Wyden.

Gordon, T. (1980) *Leader Effectiveness Training. L.E.T.* New York: Wyden Books.

Gordon, T. (1997) *Credo for Relationships.* Document available on website: www.thomasgordon.com (Original work published 1972, 1978.)

Gordon, T. (2001) *Our Classroom Management Philosophy.* Document available on website: www.thomasgordon.com/schoolphilo.asp

Graham, K. M, Saunders, S. J., Flower, M. C., Timney, C. B., White-Campbell, M. and Pietropaolo, A. Z. (1995) *Addiction Treatment for Older Adults: Evaluation of an Innovative Client-Centered Approach.* New York: Haworth.

Grant, B. (1990) Principled and instrumental nondirectiveness in person-centered and client-centered therapy. *Person-Centered Review,* 5(1), 77–87.

Greenleaf, R. (1982) *The Servant as Leader.* Indianapolis, IN: The Robert K. Greenleaf Center. (Original work published 1970)

Greenleaf, R. (2002) Essentials of servant-leadership. In L. C. Spears and M. Lawrence (eds) *Focus on Leadership: Servant-Leadership for the 21st Century* (pp. 18–25). New York: John Wiley.

Grey, J. (1993) *Men are from Mars, Women are from Venus.* London: HarperCollins.

Growald, E. (1998) A case for emotional literacy. *Casel Collections, Vol. 1.* Chicago, IL: The Collaborative for the Advancement of Social and Emotional Learning.

Guerney, B. G. Jr. (1964) Filial therapy: Description and rationale. *Journal of Consulting Psychology,* 28(4), 303–10.

Guerney, B. G. Jr. (1984) Contributions of client-centered therapy to filial, marital, and family relationship enhancement therapies. In R. Levant and J. Shlien (eds) *Client-Centered Therapy and the Person-Centered Approach: New Directions in Theory, Research and Practice* (pp. 261–77). New York: Praeger.

Guerney, L. F. (1977) A description and evaluation of a life skills training program for foster parents. *American Journal of Community Psychology,* 5(3), 361–71.

Guerney, L. F. (1978) *Parenting: A Skills Training Manual.* Silver Spring, MD: IDEALS.

Guerney, B. and Guerney, L. (1989) Child relationship enhancement: Family therapy and parent education. *Person-Centered Review,* 4, 344–57.

Gurnah, A. (1984) The politics of racism awareness training. *Critical Social Policy*, *4*, 6–20.

Habermas, J. (1994) Citizenship and national identity. In. B. van Steenbergen (ed.) *The Condition of Citizenship* (pp. 20–35). London: Sage.

Hanh, T. N. (1987) *Being Peace.* Berkeley: CA: Parallax Press.

Harkness, M. (1998) The story of Percy the propositions prototype (or the Mini with motivation). *Person-Centred Practice*, *6*(2), 104–9.

Harrison, R. (1995) *The Collected Papers of Roger Harrison.* London: McGraw Hill. (First published 1987.)

Hatch, C. L. (1983) *Training Parents of Underachieving Black Elementary Students in Communication, Child Management Skills Utilizing Community Paraprofessionals.* Unpublished doctoral dissertation, The Pennsylvania State University.

Hathaway, S. R. and McKinley, J. C. (1970) *The Minnesota Multiphasic Personality Inventory Manual.* New York: Psychological Corporation. (Original work published 1940/1943.)

Haugh, S. (1998) Congruence: A confusion of language. *Person-Centred Practice*, *6*(1) 44–50.

Haugh, S. and Merry, T. (eds) (2001) *Empathy.* Llangarron: PCCS Books.

Heise, E., Dyck, D. and McWhinnie, A. (2002) *Circles of Support and Accountability: A Guide to Training Potential Volunteers. Training Manual.* Available online at www.arrowwebworks.ca

Heron, J. (1998) *Sacred Science: Person-Centred Inquiry into the Spiritual and the Subtle.* Llangarron: PCCS Books.

Hess, E. H. (1965) Attitude and pupil size. *Scientific American*, *212*, 46–54.

Hesse, H. (1995) *Journey to the East.* London: St Martin's Press. (Original work published 1932.)

Hillery, G. A. (1955) Definitions of community: Areas of agreement. *Rural Sociology*, *20*, 111–23.

Hillman, J. (1997) *The Soul's Code: In Search of Character and Calling.* London: Bantam Books.

Hirayama, E. (1998) *The Process of Personal Growth in Encounter Groups.* Tokyo: Fukumura Shuppan.

Hobbs, N. (1951) Group-centered psychotherapy. In C. R. Rogers (ed.) *Client-Centered Therapy* (pp. 278–319). London: Constable.

Hoffman, J. (1999) A person-centred approach to the facilitation of citizens juries: A recent development in public consultation. In C. Lago and M. MacMillan (eds) *Experiences in Relatedness: Groupwork and the Person-Centred Approach* (pp. 109–19). Llangarron: PCCS Books.

Holdstock, L. (1993) Can we afford not to revision the person-centred concept of self? In D. Brazier (ed.) *Beyond Carl Rogers* (pp. 229–52). London: Constable.

Holland, R. (1997) *Self and Social Context.* London: Macmillan (now Palgrave Macmillan).

Holt, J. (1967a) *How Children Fail.* Harmondsworth: Penguin.

Holt (1967b) *How Children Learn.* Harmondsworth: Penguin.

hooks, b. (1994) *Teaching to Transgress: Education as the Practice of Freedom*. London: Routledge.

Horney, K. (1939) *New Ways in Psychoanalysis*. New York: W. W. Norton.

Horsfield, D. (1999) My experience of Temenos and its counselling course. *Self and Society*, 27(2), 37–40.

House, R. (1997) Training: A guarantee of competence? In R. House and N. Totton (eds) *Implausible Professions: Arguments for Pluralism and Autonomy in Psychotherapy and Counselling* (pp. 99–108). Llangarron: PCCS Books.

House, R. and Totton, N. (eds) (1997) *Implausible Professions: Arguments for Pluralism and Autonomy in Psychotherapy and Counselling*. Llangarron: PCCS Books.

Hughes, R. and Buchanan, L. (2000) *Experiences of Person-Centred Counselling Training*. Llangarron: PCCS Books.

Hutterer, R., Pawlowsky, G., Schmid, P. F. and Stipsits, R. (eds) (1996) *Client-Centered and Experiential Psychotherapy*. Frankfurt am Main: Peter Lang.

Independent Practitioners Network. Website: www.lpiper.demon.co.uk

Jacobs, M. (1988) *Psychodynamic Counselling in Action*. London: Sage.

Janov, A. (1973) *The Feeling Child*. New York: Simon and Schuster.

Johnstone, C. (1994) *The Lens of Deep Ecology*. London: Institute for Deep Ecology Education UK.

Joubert, N. and Raeburn, J. (1998) Mental health promotion: People, power and passion. *International Journal of Mental Health Promotion*, 1, 15–22.

Jung, C. (1939) *The Integration of the Personality*. New York: Farrar and Rinehart.

Kahn, M. (1997) *Between Therapist and Client: The New Relationship*, second edition. New York: W. H. Freeman.

Kaplan-Solms, K. and Solms, M. (2000) *Clinical Studies in Neuro-Psychoanalysis*. London: Karnac Books.

Kaslow, F. W. (1982) Portrait of the healthy couple. *Psychiatric Clinics of North America*, 5(3) 519–27.

Keen, S. (1983) *The Passionate Life: Stages of Loving*. London: Gateway Books.

Keys, S. (2003) *Idiosyncratic Person-Centred Therapy: From the Personal to the Universal*. Llangarron: PCCS Books.

Kirschenbaum, H. (1979) *On Becoming Carl Rogers*. New York: Delacorte Press.

Kirschenbaum, H. and Henderson, V. L. (1990a) *Carl Rogers: Dialogues*. London: Constable.

Kirschenbaum, H. and Henderson, V. L. (1990b) *The Carl Rogers Reader*. London: Constable.

Klaus, M. H. and Kennell, J. H. (1976) *Maternal-Infant Bonding: The Impact of Early Separation and Loss on Family Development*. St. Louis, MO: C. V. Mosby.

Klein, M. (1952) Some theoretical conclusions regarding the emotional life of the infant. In M. Klein, P. Heimann, S. Isaacs and J. Rivière (eds) *Developments in Psycho-Analysis* (pp. 198–236). London: Hogarth.

Klein, M. (1975) *The Psycho-Analysis of Children*. London: Hogarth Press. (Original work published 1932.)

Koestler, A. (1978) *Janus*. London: Hutchinson.

Kohlberg, L. (1976) Moral stages and moralization: The cognitive-developmental approach. In T. Lickona (ed.) *Moral Development and Behavior: Theory, Research and Social Issues* (pp. 31–53). New York: Holt Rinehart and Winston.

Kohlberg, L. (1981) *Essays on Moral Development, Vol. 1*. New York: Harper and Row.

Kohut, H. (1971) *The Analysis of the Self*. New York: International Universities Press.

Kosko, B. (1994) *Fuzzy Thinking*. London: Flamingo.

Kurdek, L. A. (1991) Marital stability and changes in marital quality in newly wed couples: A test of the contextual model. *Journal of Social and Personal Relationships*, *9*, 125–42.

Lago, C. and MacMillan, M. (eds) (1999) *Experiences in Relatedness: Groupwork and the Person-Centred Approach*. Llangarron: PCCS Books.

Lago, C. and Smith, B. (eds) (2003) *Anti-Discriminatory Counselling Practice*. London: Sage.

Laing, R. D. (1986) *Wisdom, Madness and Folly: The Making of a Psychiatrist*. London: Papermac.

Lao Tse. (1973) *Tao Te Ching* (G-F. Feng and J. English, trans.). London: Wildwood House.

Lazear, D. (1992) *Teaching for Multiple Intelligences*. Bloomington, IN: Phi Delta Kappa Educational Foundation.

Levant, R. (1978) Family therapy: A client-centered perspective. *Journal of Marriage and Family Counseling*, *4*, 35–42.

Levant, R. (1982) Client-centered family therapy. *American Journal of Family Therapy*, *10*, 72–5.

Levant, R. (1984) From person to system: Two perspectives. In R. Levant and J. Shlien (eds) *Client-Centered Therapy and the Person-Centered Approach: New Directions in Theory, Research and Practice* (pp. 243–60). New York: Praeger.

Levant, R. and Shlien, J. (eds) (1984) *Client-Centered Therapy and the Person-Centered Approach: New Directions in Theory, Research and Practice*. New York: Praeger.

Lewin, P. (2003) *Climate Change and Sustainable Development*. Unpublished MSc dissertation, Institute of Energy and Sustainable Development, De Montfort University, Leicester.

Lewis, T., Amini, F. and Lannon, R. (2000) *A General Theory of Love*. New York: Vintage.

Lietaer, G. (1990) The client-centered approach after the Wisconsin project: A personal view on its evolution. In G. Lietaer, J. Rombauts and R. Van Balen (eds) *Client-Centered and Experiential Psychotherapy in the Nineties* (pp. 19–45). Leuven: Leuven University Press.

Lietaer, G. (1993) Authenticity, congruence and transparency. In D. Brazier (ed.) *Beyond Carl Rogers* (pp. 17–46). London: Constable.

Lietaer, G. (1998) From non-directive to experiential: A paradigm unfolding. In B. Thorne and E. Lambers (eds) *Person-Centred Therapy: A European Perspective* (pp. 62–73). London: Sage.

Lietaer, G., Rombauts, J. and Van Balen, R. (eds) (1990) *Client-Centered and Experiential Psychotherapy in the Nineties*. Leuven: Leuven University Press.

Lippitt, G. and Lippitt, R. (1986) *The Consulting Process in Action*, second edition. San Francisco, CA: Jossey Bass.

Lloyd, J. (1996) *On Not Being Able to Write a Dissertation*. Unpublished MA dissertation, Lancaster University School of Management, Lancaster.

Lovelock, J. (1987) *Gaia: A New Look at Life on Earth*, revised edition. Oxford: Oxford University Press. (Original work published 1979.)

Lovelock, J. (1991) *Gaia: The Practical Science of Planetary Medicine*. London: Gaia Books.

Lovelock, J. (1996) *The Ages of Gaia: A Biography of our Living Earth*. Oxford: Oxford University Press. (Original work published 1988.)

Lovelock, J. (2001) At the service of the Earth. *Resurgence, 206,* 7–9.

MacMillan, M. and Lago, C. (1993) Large groups: Critical reflections and some concerns. *The Person-Centred Approach and Cross-Cultural Communication, 2*(1), 35–53.

MacMillan, M. and Lago, C. (1996) The facilitation of large groups: Participants' experiences of facilitative moments. In R. Hutterer, G. Pawlowsky, P. F. Schmid and R. Stipsits (eds) *Client-Centered and Experiential Psychotherapy: A Paradigm in Motion* (pp. 599–609). Frankfurt am Main: Peter Lang.

Macpherson, W. (1999) *The Stephen Lawrence Inquiry*. London: HMSO.

Macy, J. (1983) *Despair and Personal Power in the Nuclear Age*. Gabriola Island, BC: New Society Publishers.

Mahler, M. (1968) *On Human Symbiosis and the Vicissitudes of Individuation, Vol. 1: Infantile Psychosis*. New York: International Universities Press.

Mahler, M., Pine, F., and Bergman, A. (1975) *The Psychological Birth of the Human Infant: Symbiosis and Individuation*. New York: Basic Books.

Marques-Teixeira, J. M., De Carvalho, M. M. P., Moreira, A. M. and Pinho, C. (1996) 'Group effect'? Implementation of the Portugese translation of the Barrett-Lennard inventory on five individual group types. In R. Hutterer, G. Pawlowsky, P. F. Schmid and R. Stipsits (eds) *Client-Centered and Experiential Psychotherapy: A Paradigm in Motion* (pp. 585–98). Frankfurt am Main: Peter Lang.

Marques-Teixeira, J. and Antones, S. (eds) (2000) *Client-Centered and Experiential Psychotherapy*. Linda a Velha, Portugal: Vale and Vale.

Maslow, A. (1954) *Motivation and Personality*. New York: Harper and Row.

Maurer, D. and Salapatek, P. (1976) Developmental changes in the scanning of faces by young infants. *Child Development, 47,* 523–7.

May, R. (ed.) (1961) *Existential Psychology*. New York: Random House.

McCarthy, K. (1998) *Learning by Heart: The Role of Emotional Education in Raising School Achievement*. Brighton: Re:membering Education.

McGaw, W. (Producer and Director) (1973) *The Steel Shutter* [Film]. La Jolla, CA: Center for Studies of the Person.

McIlduff, E. and Coghlan, D. (1991a) Dublin, 1985: Perceptions of a cross-cultural communication workshop. In *The Person-Centered Approach and Cross-Cultural Communication: An International Review, Vol. II* (pp. 21–34). Dublin: Centre for Cross-Cultural Communication.

McIlduff, E. and Coghlan, D. (eds) (1991b) *The Person-Centered Approach and Cross-Cultural Communication: An International Review, Volume I*. Dublin: Center for Cross-Cultural Communication.

McIlduff, E. and Coghlan, D. (1993a) The cross-cultural communication workshops in Europe – Reflections and review. In E. McIlduff and D. Coghlan (eds), *The Person-Centered Approach and Cross-Cultural Communication: An International Review, Volume II* (pp. 21–34). Dublin: Center for Cross-Cultural Communication.

McIlduff, E. and Coghlan, D. (eds) (1993b) *The Person-Centered Approach and Cross-Cultural Communication: An International Review, Volume II*. Dublin: Center for Cross-Cultural Communication.

Mearns, D. (1994) *Developing Person-Centred Counselling*. London: Sage.

Mearns, D. (1997) *Person-Centred Counselling Training*. London: Sage.

Mearns, D. (1999) Person-centred therapy with configurations of the self. *Counselling*, *10*(2), 125–30.

Mearns, D. and Dryden, W. (1990) *Experiences of Counselling in Action*. London: Sage.

Mearns, D. and Thorne, B. (1988) *Person-Centred Counselling In Action*. London: Sage.

Mearns, D. and Thorne, B. (1999) *Person-Centred Counselling In Action*, second edition. London: Sage.

Mearns, D. and Thorne, B. (2000) *Person-Centred Therapy Today: New Frontiers in Theory and Practice*. London: Sage.

Menahem, S. E. (1996) The case of 'Anger and Hurt': Rogers and the development of a spiritual psychotherapy. In. B. A. Farber, D. C. Brink and P. M. Raskin (eds) *The Psychotherapy of Carl Rogers* (pp. 322–33). New York: The Guilford Press.

Menaker, C. (1996) *Separation, Will and Creativity: The Wisdom of Otto Rank*. Northvale, NJ: Jason Aronson.

Merry, T. (1995) *An Invitation to Person-Centred Psychology*. London: Whurr.

Merry, T. (1999a) *Learning and Being in Person-Centred Counselling*. Llangarron: PCCS Books.

Merry, T. (ed.) (1999b) *The BAPCA Reader*. Llangarron: PCCS Books.

Merry, T. (2000a) On connectedness – A humanistic biological view. *Person-Centred Practice*, *8*, 28–36.

Merry, T. (ed.) (2000b) *Person-Centred Practice: The BAPCA Reader*. Llangarron: PCCS Books.

Merry, T. (2002) *Learning and Being in Person-Centred Counselling*, second edition. Llangarron: PCCS Books.

Merry, T. and Lusty, B. (1993) *What Is Person-Centred Therapy?* Loughton: Gale Centre Publications.

Merry, U. and Brown, G. I. (1987) *The Neurotic Behavior of Organizations*. New York: Gardner Press.

Miller, A. (1983) *For Your Own Good: Hidden Cruelty in Child-Rearing and the Roots of Violence*. New York: Farrar, Strauss and Giroux.

Minuchin, S. (1974) *Families and Family Therapy*. London: Tavistock.

Mitchell, J. (1975) *Psychoanalysis and Feminism*. Harmondsworth: Penguin.

Moodley, R. (2003) Double, triple, multiple jeopardy. In C. Lago and B. Smith (eds) *Anti-Discriminatory Counselling Practice* (pp. 120–34). London: Sage.

Moore, M. (2002) *Stupid White Men*. London: Penguin Books.

Morris, C. W. (1956) *Varieties of human value*. Chicago, IL: Chicago University Press.

Morton, I. (ed.) (1999) *Person-Centred Approaches to Dementia Care*. Bicester: Winslow Press.

Moustakas, C. (1990) Heuristic research: Design and methodology. *Person-Centered Review*, 5(2), 170–90.

Naess, A. (1989) *Environment, Community and Lifestyle: Outline of an Ecosophy* (D. Rothenberg, trans.). Cambridge: Cambridge University Press.

Naess, A. (1994) In C. Johnstone (ed.) *The Lens of Deep Ecology: A Systems Approach to Deep Ecology and Despairwork*. London: Institute for Deep Ecology.

Nash, R. F. (2003) Wild world. *Resurgence, 216,* 36–8.

Natiello, P. (1987) The person-centered approach: From theory to practice. *Person-Centered Review*, 2(2), 203–16.

Natiello, P. (1990) The person-centered approach, collaborative power, and cultural transformation. *Person-Centered Review*, 5(3), 268–86.

Natiello, P. (2001) Collaborative power: Can it succeed in the world of work? In *The Person-Centred Approach: A Passionate Presence* (pp. 75–85). Llangarron: PCCS Books. (Original work published 1990.)

Natiello, P. (2001) From group to community. In *The Person-Centred Approach: A Passionate Presence* (pp. 121–40). Llangarron: PCCS Books. (Original work published 1991.)

Natiello, P. (2001) A person-centered training program. In *The Person-Centred Approach: A Passionate Presence* (pp. 97–108). Llangarron: PCCS Books. (Original work published 1998.)

Natiello, P. (2001a) From the intern's point of view. In *The Person-Centred Approach: A Passionate Presence* (pp. 109–17). Llangarron: PCCS Books.

Natiello, P. (2001b) Preparing to practice. In *The Person-Centred Approach: A Passionate Presence* (pp. 89–95). Llangarron: PCCS Books.

Natiello, P. (2001c) *The Person-Centred Approach: A Passionate Presence*. Llangarron: PCCS Books.

National College for School Leadership. Website: www.ncsl.org.uk

National Society for the Prevention of Cruelty of Children. (1998) *Parenting: A Rough Guide. Group Activities*. London: NSPCC.

Naydler, J. (1996) *Goethe on Science*. Edinburgh: Floris Books.

Newell, T. (2000) *Forgiving Justice: A Quaker Vision for Criminal Justice*. Swarthmore Lecture 2000, Quaker Home Service, London.

Newton, K. (1996) Response to J. Bozarth article. *Renaissance, 13,* 2,3, 4.

Newton, K. (1997) Response to J. Bozarth article. *Renaissance, 14,* 1.

Oberst, U. E. and Stewart, A. E. (2003) *Adlerian Therapy: An Advanced Approach to Individual Psychology*. London: Brunner-Routledge.

Office for National Statistics. (2002) *Health Statistics Quarterly (England and Wales), Vol. 19*. London: ONS.

O'Hara, M. M. (1989) Person-centered approach as conscientização: The works of Carl Rogers and Paulo Freire. *Journal of Humanistic Psychology, 29*(1), 11–36.

O'Hara, M. M. and Wood, J. K. (1983) Patterns of awareness: Consciousness and the group mind. *The Gestalt Journal, 6*(2), 103–16.

O'Leary, C. (1999) *Couple and Family Counselling: A Person-Centred Approach.* London: Sage.

Onions, C. T. (ed.) (1973) *The Shorter Oxford English Dictionary* (two vols). Oxford: Clarendon Press. (Original work published 1933.)

Orr, D. W. (1992) *Ecological Literacy: Education and the Transition to a Postmodern World.* Albany, NY: SUNY Press.

Oxford Research Group. (undated) *Everyone's Guide to Achieving Change.* Oxford: Oxford Research Group.

Pally, R. (2000) *The Mind-Brain Relationship.* London: Karnac.

Panskepp, J. (1998) *Affective Neuroscience: The Foundations of Human and Animal Emotions.* Oxford: Oxford University Press.

Parry, G. (1988) Mobilizing social support. In F. N. Watts (ed.) *New Directions in Clinical Psychology, Vol. 2* (pp. 83–104). Chichester: Wiley/British Psychological Society.

Patterson, C. H. (2000) Foundations for a systemic eclectic psychotherapy. In *Understanding Psychotherapy: Fifty Years of Client-Centred Theory and Practice* (pp. 87–101). Ross-on-Wye: PCCS Books. (Original work published 1989.)

Patterson, C. H. (2000) Outcomes in counselor education. In *Understanding Psychotherapy: Fifty Years of Client-Centred Theory and Practice* (pp. 208–15). Ross-on-Wye: PCCS Books. (Original work published 1993.)

Patterson, C. H. (2000a) On being non-directive. In *Understanding Psychotherapy: Fifty Years of Client-Centred Theory and Practice* (pp. 181–4). Llangarron: PCCS Books.

Patterson, C. H. (2000b) Resistance in therapy: A person-centered view. In *Understanding Psychotherapy: Fifty Years of Client-Centred Theory and Practice* (pp. 185–7). Llangarron: PCCS Books.

Patterson, C. H. (2000c) *Understanding Psychotherapy: Fifty Years of Client-Centred Theory and Practice.* Llangarron: PCCS Books.

Peck, S. (1987) *The Different Drum.* London: Rider and Co.

Peck, S. (1990) *The Road Less Travelled: A New Psychology of Love, Traditional Values and Spiritual Growth.* New York: Arrow Books.

Peevey, F. (1986) *Heart Politics.* Philadelphia, PA: New Society Publishers.

Perls, F. S., Hefferline, R. and Goodman, P. (1973) *Gestalt Therapy: Excitement and Growth in the Human Personality.* Harmondsworth: Penguin. (Original work published 1951.)

Phillips, A. (1994) *On Flirtation.* London: Faber and Faber.

Piaget, J. (1964) *Six Psychological Studies.* New York: Random House.

Pink Therapy. Website: www.pinktherapy.com

Piontelli, A. (1992) *From Fetus to Child: An Observational and Psychoanalytic Study.* London: Routledge.

Plas, J. M. (1996) *Person-Centered Leadership: An American Approach to Participatory Management.* Thousand Oaks, CA: Sage.

Pörtner, M. (2000) *Trust and Understanding: The Person-Centred Approach to Everyday Care for People with Special Needs.* Llangarron: PCCS Books.

Pratt, J. (2003, March) Community meetings and the person-centred approach. *Person to Person*, 3.

Pratt, J., Gordon P. and Plamping, D. (1999) *Working Whole Systems: Putting Theory into Practice in Organizations.* London: King's Fund.

Prouty, G. F. (1976) Pre-therapy, a method of treating pre-expressive, psychotic and retarded patients. *Psychotherapy: Theory, Research and Practice, 13*(3), 290–5.

Prouty, G. F. (1990) Pre-therapy: A theoretical evolution in the person-centered/experiential psychotherapy of schizophrenia and retardation. In G. Lietaer, J. Rombauts and R. Van Balen (eds) *Client-Centered and Experiential Psychotherapy in the Nineties* (pp. 645–58). Leuven: Leuven University Press.

Prouty, G. F. (1994) *Theoretical Evolutions in Person-Centered/Experiential Therapy: Applications to Schizophrenic and Retarded Psychoses.* Westport, CT: Praeger.

Prouty, G. F., Van Werde, D. and Pörtner, M. (2002) *Pre-Therapy: Reaching Contact-Impaired Clients.* Llangarron: PCCS Books.

Provence, S. and Lipton, R. C. (1962) *Infants in Institutions: A Comparison of their Development with Family Reared Infants during the First Year of Life.* New York: International University Press.

Psychotherapists and Counsellors for Social Responsibility. Website: www.pcsr.org.uk

Raeburn, J. and Rootman, I. (1998) *People-Centred Health Promotion.* Chichester: Wiley.

Rank, O. (1907) *Art and the Artist: Creative Urge and Personality Development.* New York: W. W. Norton.

Raskin, N. J. (1948) The development of non-directive psychotherapy. *Journal of Consulting Psychology, 13*, 154–6.

Raskin, N. J. (1987) From spyglass to kaleidoscope [Review of R. F. Levant and J. M. Shlien (eds) *Client-centered Therapy and the Person-centered Approach: New Directions in Theory, Research and Practice*]. *Contemporary Psychology, 32*, 460–1.

Raskin, N. J. (2004, in press) *Contributions to Client-Centered Therapy and the Person-Centered Approach.* Llangarron: PCCS Books.

Raskin, N. J. and van der Veen, F. (1970) Client-centered family therapy: Some clinical and research perspectives. In J. T. Hart and T. M. Tomlinson (eds) *New Directions in Client-Centered Therapy* (pp. 387–406). Boston, MA: Houghton Mifflin.

Reber, A. S. (1985) *The Penguin Dictionary of Psychology.* London: Penguin.

Redfield, R. (1960) *The Little Community and Peasant Society and Culture.* Chicago, IL: Chicago University Press.

Reed, E. (1975) *Women's Evolution: From Matriarchal Clan to Patriarchal Family.* New York: Pathfinder Press.

Registrar General of Marriages, Divorces and Adoptions. (2001) *Marriages, Divorces and Adoptions (England and Wales).* London: ONS.

Reich, W. R. (1961) *Character Analysis* (M. Higgins and C. M. Raphael, eds and V. F. Carfagno, trans.), third edition. New York: Farrar Strauss and Giroux. (Original work published 1933.)

Rennie, D. L. (1998) *Person-Centred Counselling: An Experiential Approach.* London: Sage.

Rennie, R. and Landreth, G. (2000) Effects of filial therapy on parent and child behaviors. *International Journal of Play Therapy, 9*(2), 19–37.

Robertson, J. (1952) *A Two-Year-Old Goes to Hospital* [Video]. London: Robertson Centre/Ipswich: Concord Video and Film Council.

Robinson, K. (2001) *Out of our Minds: Learning to be Creative.* Oxford: Capstone.

Robinson, P. A. (1969) *The Freudian Left.* New York: Harper and Row.

Robson, K. (1967) The role of eye-to-eye contact in maternal infant attachment. *Journal of Child Psychology and Psychiatry, 8,* 13–25.

Rogers, C. R. (1939) *The Clinical Treatment of the Problem Child.* Boston, MA: Houghton Mifflin.

Rogers, C. R. (1942) *Counseling and Psychotherapy: Newer Concepts in Practice.* Boston, MA: Houghton Mifflin.

Rogers, C. R. (1951) *Client-Centered Therapy.* London: Constable.

Rogers, C. R. (1957) The necessary and sufficient conditions of therapeutic personality change. *Journal of Consulting Psychology, 21,* 95–103.

Rogers, C. R. (1959) A theory of therapy, personality and interpersonal relationships, as developed in the client-centred framework. In S. Koch (ed.) *Psychology: A Study of Science, Vol. 3: Formulation of the Person and the Social Context* (pp. 184–256). New York: McGraw-Hill.

Rogers, C. R. (1961) Two divergent trends. In R. May (ed.) *Existential Psychology* (pp. 85–93). New York: Random House.

Rogers, C. R. (1963) The actualizing tendency in relation to 'motives' and to consciousness. In M. R. Jones (ed.) *Nebraska Symposium on Motivation, 1963* (pp. 1–24). Lincoln, NE: University of Nebraska Press.

Rogers, C. R. (1967a) Some of the directions evident in therapy. In *On Becoming a Person* (pp. 73–106). London: Constable. (Original work published 1953.)[1]

Rogers, C. R. (1967b) 'This is me'. In *On Becoming a Person* (pp. 3–27). London: Constable. (Original work published 1953.)

Rogers, C. R. (1967a) Some hypotheses regarding the facilitation of personal growth. In *On Becoming a Person* (pp. 31–8). London: Constable. (Original work published 1954.)

Rogers, C. R. (1967b) The characteristics of a helping relationship. In *On Becoming a Person* (pp. 39–58). London: Constable. (Original work published 1954.)

---

[1] A number of Rogers' books comprise previously published material. For historical interest and accuracy, we refer to separate chapters in these books, citing them in the text, for example, as Rogers (1955/1967, 1957/1967) and so on. Where two papers were published in the same year we adopt the convention: Rogers (1953/1967a, 1953/1967b) and so on.

Rogers, C. R. (1967c) Toward a theory of creativity. In *On Becoming a Person* (pp. 347–59). London: Constable. (Original work published 1954.)

Rogers, C. R. (1967) Persons or science? A philosophical question. In *On Becoming a Person* (pp. 199–224). London: Constable. (Original work published 1955.)

Rogers, C. R. (1967) A therapist's view of the good life: The fully functioning person. In *On Becoming a Person* (pp. 183–96). London: Constable. (Original work published 1957.)

Rogers, C. R. (1967) A process conception of psychotherapy. In *On Becoming a Person* (pp. 125–59). London: Constable. (Original work published 1958.)

Rogers, C. R. (1967) Significant learning: In therapy and in education. In *On Becoming a Person* (pp. 279–96). London: Constable. (Original work published 1959.)

Rogers, C. R. (1967) 'To be that self which one truly is': A therapist's view of personal goals. In *On Becoming a Person* (pp. 163–82). London: Constable. (Original work published 1960.)

Rogers, C. R. (1967a) A tentative formulation of a general law of interpersonal relationships. In *On Becoming a Person* (pp. 338–46). London: Constable. (Original work published 1961.)

Rogers, C. R. (1967b) *On Becoming a Person*. London: Constable. (Original work published 1961.)

Rogers, C. R. (1967c) The implications of client-centered therapy for family life. In *On Becoming a Person* (pp. 314–28). London: Constable. (Original work published 1961.)

Rogers, C. R. (1967d) What we know now about psychotherapy – objectively and subjectively. In *On Becoming a Person* (pp. 59–69). London: Constable. (Original work published 1961.)

Rogers, C. R. (1969) *Freedom to Learn*. Columbus, OH: Charles E. Merrill.

Rogers, C. R. (1973) *Carl Rogers on Encounter Groups*. Harmondsworth: Penguin. (Original work published 1970.)

Rogers, C. R. (1973) *Becoming Partners: Marriage and its Alternatives*. London: Constable.

Rogers, C. R. (1978a) A person-centred workshop: Its planning and fruition. In *Carl Rogers on Personal Power* (pp. 143–85). London: Constable.

Rogers, C. R. (1978b) *Carl Rogers on Personal Power*. London: Constable.

Rogers (1978c) The emerging person: Spearhead of the quiet revolution. In *Carl Rogers on Personal Power* (pp. 255–82). London: Constable.

Rogers, C. R. (1980) The foundations of a person-centered approach. In *A Way of Being* (pp. 113–36). Boston, MA: Houghton Mifflin. (Original work published 1963 and 1978.)

Rogers, C. R. (1980) In retrospect: Forty-six years. In *A Way of Being* (pp. 46–69). Boston, MA: Houghton Mifflin. (Original work published 1974.)

Rogers, C. R. (1980) Empathic: An unappreciated way of being. In *A Way of Being* (pp. 137–63). Boston, MA: Houghton Mifflin. (Original work published 1975.)

Rogers, C. R. (1980) Beyond the watershed: And where now? In *A Way of Being* (pp. 292–315). Boston, MA: Houghton Mifflin. (Original work published 1977.)

Rogers, C. R. (1980) Do we need 'a' reality? In *A Way of Being* (pp. 96–108). Boston, MA: Houghton Mifflin. (Original work published 1978.)

Rogers, C. R. (1980a) *A Way of Being.* Boston, MA: Houghton Mifflin.

Rogers, C. R. (1980b) Growing old: Or older and growing? In *A Way of Being* (pp. 70–95). Boston, MA: Houghton Mifflin.

Rogers, C. R. (1980c) The world of tomorrow, and the person of tomorrow. In *A Way of Being* (pp. 339–56). Boston, MA: Houghton Mifflin.

Rogers, C. R. (1983) *Freedom to learn for the 80's.* Columbus, OH: Charles E. Merrill.

Rogers, C. R. (1985) Toward a more human science of the person. *Journal of Humanistic Psychology, 25*(4), 7–24.

Rogers, C. R. (1986) The dilemmas of a South African white. *Person-Centred Review, 1*, 15–35.

Rogers, C. R. (1990) A note on the 'Nature of Man'. In H. Kirschenbaum and V. L. Henderson (eds) *The Carl Rogers Reader* (pp. 401–8). London: Constable. (Original work published 1957.)

Rogers, C. R. (1990) A therapist's view of personal goals. In H. Kirschenbaum and V. L. Henderson (eds) *The Carl Rogers Reader* (pp. 436–8). London: Constable. (Original work published 1960.)

Rogers, C. R. (1990) Toward a modern approach to values: The valuing process in the mature person. In H. Kirschenbaum and V. L. Henderson (eds) *The Carl Rogers Reader* (pp. 168–85). London: Constable. (Original work published 1964.)

Rogers, C. R. (1990) The Rust workshop. In H. Kirschenbaum and V. L. Henderson (eds) *The Carl Rogers Reader* (pp. 457–77). London: Constable. (Original work published 1986.)

Rogers, C. R. (1991) An open letter to participants of European workshops. In E. McIlduff and D. Coghlan (eds) *The Person-Centered Approach and Cross-Cultural Communication: An International Review, Volume I* (pp. 11–13). Dublin: Center for Cross-Cultural Communication.

Rogers, C. R., Gendlin, E. T., Kiesler, D. J. and Truax, C. B. (eds) (1967) *The Therapeutic Relationship and its Impact: A Study of Psychotherapy with Schizophrenics.* Madison, WI: University of Wisconsin Press.

Rogers, C. R. and Hart, J. T. (1970) Looking back and ahead: A conversation with Carl Rogers. In J. T. Hart and T. M. Tomlinson (eds) *New Directions in Client-Centered Therapy* (pp. 502–33). Boston, MA: Houghton Mifflin.

Rogers, C. R. and Roethlisberger, F. J. (1952) Barriers and gateways to communication. *Harvard Business Review, 30*(4), 46–52.

Rogers, C. R. and Russell, D. E. (2003) *Carl Rogers: The Quiet Revolutionary, An Oral History.* Roseville, CA: Penmarin Books.

Rogers, C. R. and Stevens, B. (1973) *Person to Person: The Problem of Being Human: A New Trend in Psychology.* London: Souvenir Press. (Original work published 1967)

Rogers, C. R. and Wallen, J. L. (1946) *Counseling with Returned Servicemen.* New York: McGraw-Hill.

Rogers, N. (1993) *The Creative Connection: Expressive Arts as Healing.* Palo Alto, CA: Science and Behavior Books.

Rogers, N. (2002) *Carl Rogers: A Daughter's Tribute*. CD-ROM. Mindgardenmedia. Available from www.mindgardenmedia.com

Rothwell, W. J., Sullivan, R. and McLean, G. N. (1995) *Practicing Organization Development: A Guide for Consultants*. San Francisco, CA: Jossey Bass.

Rowan, J. (1990) *Subpersonalities; The People Inside Us*. London: Routledge.

Ruskin, J. *Modern Painters, Vol. 4*. London: Dent. (Original work published 1856.)

Rutter, M. (1998) Developmental catch-up and deficit following adoption after severe global early privation. English and Romanian adoptees (ERA) Study Team. *Journal of Child Psychology and Psychiatry, 39*(4), 465–76.

Samuels, A. (2001) *Politics on the Couch*. London: Profile Books.

Sanders, P. (2000) Mapping person-centred approaches to counselling and psychotherapy. *Person-Centred Practice, 8*(2) 62–74.

Sanders, P. and Wyatt, G. (2002) *Contact and Perception*. Llangarron: PCCS Books.

Sanford, R. (1999) Experiencing diversity. In C. Lago and M. MacMillan (eds) *Experiences in Relatedness: Groupwork and the Person-Centred Approach* (pp. 77–91). Llangarron: PCCS Books.

Schein, E. H. (1980) *Organizational Psychology*. Upper Saddle River, NJ: Prentice-Hall.

Schein, E. H. (1985) *Organizational Culture and Leadership*. San Franciso, CA: Jossey-Bass.

Schmid, P. F. (1996) Probably the most potent social invention of the century: Person-centered therapy is fundamentally group therapy. In R. Hutterer, G. Pawlowsky, P. F. Schmid and R. Stipsits (eds) *Client-Centered and Experiential Psychotherapy*. Frankfurt am Main: Peter Lang.

Schmid, P. F. (1998) 'Face to face' – The art of encounter. In B. Thorne and E. Lambers (eds) *Person-Centred Therapy: A European Perspective* (pp. 74–90). London: Sage.

Schmid, P. and Wascher, W. (eds) (1994) *Towards Creativity: A Person-Centered Reading and Picture Book*. Linz: Sandkorn.

Schore, A. N. (1994) *Affect Regulation and the Origin of the Self: The Neurobiology of Emotional Development*. Hillsdale, NJ: Lawrence Erlbaum.

Schore, A. N. (2002) *Pain to Violence; Disrupted Attachment* (Video). Available from: R. Bowlby, Boundary House, Wyldes Close, London NW11 7JB.

Schumacher, E. F. (1973) *Small is Beautiful*. New York: Harper.

Schutz, W. (1973) *Elements of Encounter*. Big Sur, CA: Joy Press.

Schwartz, J. (2000) *Cassandra's Daughter: A History of Psychoanalysis*. London: Penguin.

Seeman, J. (1959) Toward a concept of personality integration. *American Psychologist, 14*, 633–7.

Seeman, J. (1983) *Personality Integration: Studies and Reflections*. New York: Human Sciences Press.

Seeman, J. (1988) Self-actualization: A reformulation. *Person-Centered Review, 3*(3), 304–15.

Segrera, A. S. (1984) Becoming Being: Reflections from the perspective of the therapeutic scales. In A. Segrera (ed.) *Proceedings of the First International Forum on the Person-Centered Approach*. Oaxtepec, Morelos, Mexico: Universidad Iberoamericana.

Semler, R. (1993) *Maverick! The Success Story Behind the World's Most Unusual Workplace*. London: Century.

Senge, P. M. (1990) *The Fifth Discipline: The Art and Practice of the Learning Organization*. London: Century Business.

Shaffer, J. B. P. and Galinsky, M. D. (1974) *Models of Group Theory and Sensitivity Training*. Englewood Cliffs, NJ: Prentice-Hall.

Shand, J. (1994) *Philosophy and Philosophers: An Introduction to Western Philosophy*. Harmondsworth: Penguin.

Sharpe, S. (1998) *Restorative Justice: A Vision of Healing and Change*. Edmonton, Alberta: Edmonton Victim-Offender Mediation Society.

Shields, K. (1991) *In the Tiger's Mouth: An Empowerment Guide for Social Action*. Newtown, New South Wales: Millenium Books.

Shlien, J. (1984) A countertheory of transference. In R. Levant and J. Shlien (eds) *Client-Centered Therapy and the Person-Centered Approach: New Directions in Theory, Research and Practice* (pp. 153–81). New York: Praeger.

Shlien, J. (1989) Boy's person-centered perspective on psychodiagnosis. A response. *Person-Centered Review*, 4(2), 157–62.

Shlien, J. (2003) *To Lead an Honourable Life: Invitations to Think about Client-Centered Therapy and the Person-Centered Approach* (P. Sanders, ed.). Llangarron: PCCS Books.

Shweder, R. A. (1990) Cultural psychology – What is it? In J. W. Stigler, R. A. Shweder and G. Herdt (eds) *Cultural Psychology* (pp. 1–43). Cambridge: Cambridge University Press.

Silverstone, L. (1997) *Art Therapy: The Person-Centred Way*. London: Jessica Kingsley.

Singh, J. and Tudor, K. (1997) Cultural conditions of therapy. *The Person-Centered Journal*, 4(2), 32–46.

Sivanandan, A. (1985) RAT and the degradation of black struggle. *Race and Class*, XXVI(4), 1–33.

Smith, B. and Tudor, K. (2003) Oppression and pedagogy: Anti-oppressive practice in the education of therapists. In. C. Lago and B. Smith (eds) *Anti-Discriminatory Counselling Practice* (pp. 135–50). London: Sage.

Snyder, W. U. (1945) An investigation of the nature of non directive psychotherapy. *Journal of General Psychology*, 33, 193–223.

Soloman, L. N. (1987) International tension reduction through the person-centered approach. *Journal of Humanistic Psychology*, 27, 337–47.

Solms, M. (1994) *The Limbic System and the Internal World*. Unpublished lecture delivered at the New York Psychoanalytic Institute, 2 April 1994.

Solms, M. (1998) Preliminaries for an integration of psychoanalysis and neuroscience. *Bulletin of the British Psycho-Analytic Society*, 34(9), 23–38.

Sommerbeck, L. (2003) *The Client-Centred Therapist in Psychiatric Contexts: A Therapist's Guide to the Psychiatric Landscape and its Inhabitants*. Llangarron: PCCS Books.

Spears, L. C. and Lawrence, M. (eds) (2002) *Focus on Leadership: Servant-Leadership for the 21st Century*. New York: John Wiley.

Speierer, G.-W. (1990) Toward a specific illness concept of client-centered therapy. In G. Lietaer, J. Rombauts and R. Van Balen (eds) *Client-Centered and Experiential Psychotherapy in the Nineties* (pp. 337–59). Leuven: Leuven University Press.

Speierer, G. (1996) Client-centered therapy according to the Differential Incongruence Model (DIM). In R. Hutterer, G. Pawlowsky, P. F. Schmid and R. Stipsits (eds) *Client-Centered and Experiential Psychotherapy: A Paradigm in Motion* (pp. 299–311). Frankfurt am Main: Peter Lang.

Stamatiadis, R. (1990) Sharing life therapy. *Person-Centered Review, 5*(3), 287–307.

Stein, M. and Hollwitz, J. (eds) (1992) *Psyche at Work: Workplace Applications of Jungian Analytic Psychology*. Wilmette, IL: Chiron Publications.

Steiner, C. (1984) Emotional literacy. *Transactional Analysis Journal, 14*(3), 162–73.

Steiner, C. (1997) *Achieving Emotional Literacy*. London: Bloomsbury.

Stern, D. N. (1985) *The Interpersonal World of the Infant*. New York: Basic Books.

Stillwell, W. (2000) *Three Voices: Interviews into Person-Centered Approaches with Ernie Meadows, Maria Bowen, Bob Lee*. La Jolla, CA: Center for Studies of the Person.

Stockwell, D. (1984) An attempt at an ongoing, person-centered community. In A. Segrera (ed.) *Proceedings of the First International Forum on the Person-Centered Approach*. Oaxtepec, Morelos, Mexico: Universidad Iberoamericana.

Stonewall. (1998, March) *Same Sex Couples and the Law*. Factsheet. Available from: Stonewall, 16 Clerkenwell Close, London, EC1R 0AA.

Sturdevant, K. (1995) Classical Greek 'koinonia': The psychoanalytic median group, and the large person-centred community group: Dialogue in three democratic contexts. *The Person-Centered Journal, 2*(2), 64–71.

Suhd, M. M. (ed.) (1995) *Positive Regard: Carl Rogers and Other Notables He Inspired*. Palo Alto, CA: Science and Behavior Books.

Swimme, B. and Berry, T. (1992) *The Universe Story*. San Francisco, CA: Harper.

Taft, J. (1933) *The Dynamics of Therapy in a Controlled Relationship*. New York: Macmillan (now Palgrave Macmillan).

Tannen, D. (1990) *You Just Don't Understand: Women and Men in Conversation*. London: Virago.

Teich, N. (ed.) (1992) *Rogerian Perspectives: Collaborative Rhetoric for Oral and Written Communication*. Norwood, NJ: Ablex Publishers.

Thomas, D. (1952) *Collected Poems: 1934–1952*. London: Dent.

Thorne, B. (1991) *Person-Centred Counselling: Therapeutic and Spiritual Dimensions*. London: Whurr.

Thorne, B. (1992) *Carl Rogers*. London: Sage.

Thorne, B. (1998a) *Person-Centred Counselling and Christian Spirituality*. London: Whurr.

Thorne, B. (1998b) *Person-Centred Counselling: Christian Spiritual Dimensions*. London: Whurr.

Thorne, B. (2002) *The Mystical Power of Person-Centred Therapy*. London: Whurr.

Thorne, B. (2003) *Carl Rogers*, second edition. London: Sage.

Thorne, B. and Lambers, E. (eds) (1998) *Person-Centred Therapy: A European Perspective*. London: Sage.

Tolan, J. (2003) *Skills in Person-Centred Counselling and Psychotherapy*. London: Sage

Tolstoy, L. (2000) *Tolstoy as Teacher* (R. and B. Blaisdale, eds and C. Edgar, trans.). New York: Teachers and Writers Collaborative. (Original work published 1852.)

Truax, G. B. and Carkhuff, R. R. (1967) *Toward Effective Counseling and Psychotherapy*. Chicago, IL: Aldine.

Tuckman, B. W. (1965) Developmental sequence in small groups. *Psychological Bulletin*, *63*, 384–99.

Tuckman, B. W. and Jenson, K. (1977) Stages of small-group development revisited. *Group and Organization Studies*, *2*(4), 419–27.

Tudor, K. (1996) *Mental Health Promotion: Paradigms and Practice*. London: Routledge.

Tudor, K. (1997) Being at dis-ease with ourselves: Alienation and psychotherapy. *Changes*, *22*(2), 143–50.

Tudor, K. (1999) *Group Counselling*. London: Sage.

Tudor, K. and Embleton Tudor, L. (1999) The philosophy of Temenos. *Self and Society*, *27*(2), 32–7.

Tudor, K. and Hargaden, H. (2002) The couch and the ballot box: The contribution and potential of psychotherapy in enhancing citizenship. In C. Feltham (ed.) *What's the Good of Counselling and Psychotherapy?: The Benefits Explained* (pp. 156–78). London: Sage.

Tudor, K. and Merry, T. (2002) *Dictionary of Person-Centred Psychology*. London: Whurr.

Tudor, K. and Worrall, M. (1994) Congruence reconsidered. *British Journal of Guidance and Counselling*, *22*(4), 197–206.

Tudor, K. and Worrall, M. (2004) *Freedom to Practise: Person-Centred Approaches to Supervision*. Llangarron: PCCS Books.

Tudor, K. and Worrall, M. (2004, in preparation) *Clinical Philosophy: Advancing Theory in Person-Centred Therapy*. London: Brunner/Routledge.

Turnbull, O. (2003) Emotions, false beliefs, and the neurobiology of intuition. In J. Corrigall and H. Wilkinson (eds) *Revolutionary Connections: Psychotherapy and Neuroscience* (pp. 135–62). London: Karnac.

Umbreit, M. S. (2000) *Restorative Justice Conferencing: Guidelines for Victim Sensitive Practice*. Document. Center for Restorative Justice and Peacemaking, School of Social Work, University of Minnesota. Available online at: http://ssw.che.umn.edu/njp/

United Kingdom Council for Psychotherapy. Website: www.ukcp.org.uk

University of the Third Age. Website: www.u3a.org.uk

Uzzell, L. (1999) The psycho-spatial dimensions of global environmental problems. *Journal of Environmental Psychology*, *20*, 307–18.

Valdés, L. F., Barón, A. and Ponce, F. Q. (1987) Counseling Hispanic men. In M. Scher, M. Stevens, G. Good and G.A. Eichenfeld (eds) *Handbook of Counselling and Psychotherapy with Men* (pp. 203–17). Newbury Park, CA: Sage.

Van Werde, D. (1994) An introduction to client-centred pre-therapy. In D. Mearns (ed.) *Developing Person-Centred Counselling* (pp. 121–5). London: Sage.

Van Werde, D. (1998) 'Anchorage' as a core concept in working with psychotic people. In B. Thorne and E. Lambers (eds) *Person-Centred Therapy* (pp. 195–205). London: Sage.

Van Werde, D. (2002) The falling man: Pre-therapy applied to somatic hallucinating. *Person-Centred Practice, 10*(2), 101–7.

Villas-Boas Bowen, M. C. (1986) Personality differences and person-centered supervision. *Person-Centered Review, 1*(3), 291–309.

Walker, A., Rabin, R and Rogers, C. R. (1960) Development of a scale to measure process changes in psychotherapy. *Journal of Clinical Psychology, 16*, 79–85.

Wann, T. W. (ed.) (1964) *Behaviorism and Phenomenology: Contrasting Bases for Modern Psychology*. Chicago, IL: University of Chicago Press.

Ware, P. (1983) Personality adaptations (Doors to therapy). *Transactional Analysis Journal, 13*, 11–19.

Warner, M. S. (1991) Fragile process. In L. Fusek (ed.) *New Directions in Client-Centered Therapy: Practice with Difficult Client Populations (Monograph Series I)* (pp. 41–58). Chicago, IL: Chicago Counseling and Psychotherapy Center.

Warner, M. S. (1998) A client-centered approach to therapeutic work with dissociated and fragile process. In L. Greenberg, J. Watson and G. Lietaer (eds) *Handbook of Experiential Psychotherapy* (pp. 368–87). New York: The Guilford Press.

Warner, M. S. (2000) Person-centered psychotherapy: One nation, many tribes. *The Person-Centered Journal, 7*(1), 28–39.

Warnock, M. (1967) *Existentialist Ethics*. London and Basingstoke: Macmillan (now Palgrave Macmillan).

Waterhouse, R. (1993) 'Wild women don't have the blues': A feminist critique of 'person-centred' counselling and therapy. *Feminism and Psychology, 3*, 55–71.

Watson, J. C., Goldman, R. N. and Warner, M. S. (eds) (2002) *Client-Centered and Experiential Psychotherapy in the 21st Century: Advances in Theory, Research and Practice*. Llangarron: PCCS Books.

Weare, K. (2000) *Promoting Mental, Emotional and Social Health: A Whole School Approach*. London: Routledge.

Westman, J. (1994) *Licensing Parents: Can We Prevent Child Abuse and Neglect?* New York: Insight Books.

Wexler, D. A. and Rice, L. N. (eds) (1974) *Innovations in Client-Centered Therapy*. New York: Wiley.

Wheatley, M. J. (1994) *Leadership and the New Science: Learning about Organization from an Orderly Universe*. San Francisco, CA: Berrett-Koehler.

Wheatley, M. J. and Kellner-Rogers, M. (1996) *A Simpler Way*. San Francisco, CA: Berrett-Koehler.

Wibberley, M. (1988) Encounter. In J. Rowan and W. Dryden (eds) *Innovative Therapy in Britain* (pp. 61–84). Milton Keynes: Open University Press.

Wilkins, P. (1997) Congruence and countertransference: Similarities and differences. *Counselling, 8*(1), 36–41.

Wilkins, P. (2003) *Person-Centred Therapy in Focus*. London: Sage.

Wilson, A. and Beresford, P. (2000) Anti-oppressive practice: Emancipation or appropriation? *British Journal of Social Work, 30,* 553–73.

Winnicott, D. W. (1952) Anxiety associated with insecurity. In *Collected Papers: Through Paediatrics to Psycho-Analysis.* London: Hogarth.

Winnicott, D. W. (1957) Support for normal parents. In *The Child and the Family: First Relationships* (J. Hardenberg, ed.) (pp. 137–40). London: Tavistock Publications. (Original work published 1944.)

Winnicott, D. W. (1957a) *The Child and the Family: First Relationships* (J. Hardenberg, ed.). London: Tavistock Publications.

Winnicott, D. W. (1957b) *The Child and the Outside World* (J. Hardenberg, ed.). London: Tavistock Publications.

Winnicott, D. W. (1971) *Playing and Reality.* Harmondsworth: Penguin.

Wolf, A. (1949) The psychoanalysis of groups. *American Journal of Psychotherapy, 3,* 525–58.

Wood, J. (1990) Children discover how it feels to be disabled. *Therapy Weekly, 16*(40), 10.

Wood, J. K. (1982) Person-centered group therapy. In G. Gazda (ed.) *Basic Approaches to Group Psychotherapy and Group Counselling* (pp. 235–75). Springfield , IL: Charles Thomas.

Wood, J. K. (1984) Communities for learning. In R. F. Levant and John M. Shlien (eds) *Client-Centered Therapy and the Person-Centered Approach: New Directions in Theory, Research and Practice.* New York: Praeger.

Wood, J. K. (1994) The person-centered approach's greatest weakness: Not using its strength. *Person-Centered Journal, 1*(2), 96–105.

Wood, J. K. (1995) The person-centered approach: Toward an understanding of its implications. *The Person-Centered Journal, 2*(2), 18–35.

Wood, J. K. (1996) The person-centered approach: Towards an understanding of its implications. In R. Hutterer, G. Pawlowsky, P. F. Schmid and R. Stipsits (eds) *Client-Centered and Experiential Psychotherapy: A Paradigm in Motion* (pp. 163–81). Frankfurt am Main: Peter Lang.

Wood, J. K. (1997) Notes on studying the large group workshops. *The Person-Centered Journal, 4,* 65–77.

Wood, J. K. (1999) Toward an understanding of large group dialogue and its implications. In C. Lago and M. MacMillan (eds) *Experiences in Relatedness: Groupwork and the Person-Centred Approach.* Llangarron: PCCS Books.

Wood, J. K. (2003a) *Genius Loci* [The Spirit of the Place]. Unpublished manuscript.

Wood, J. K. (2003b) *The Effect of Group, Sensible Dialogue, and Innovative Learning.* Unpublished manuscript.

World Association for Person-Centered and Experiential Psychotherapy and Counseling. Website: www.pce-world.org

Worrall, M. (1997) Contracting within the person-centred approach. In C. Sills (ed.) *Contracts in Counselling* (pp. 65–75). London: Sage.

Worsley, R. (2002) *Process Work in Person-Centred Therapy: Phenomenological and Existential Perspectives.* Basingstoke: Palgrave (now Palgrave Macmillan).

Wyatt, G. (ed.) (2001) *Congruence*. Llangarron: PCCS Books.

Wyatt, G. and Sanders, P. (eds) (2002) *Contact and Perception*. Llangarron: PCCS Books.

Yablonsky, L. (1965) *The Tunnel Back: Synanon*. New York: Macmillan (now Palgrave Macmillan).

Yalom, I. D. (1995) *The Theory and Practice of Group Psychotherapy*, fourth edition. New York: Basic Books.

Zimring, F. M. and Raskin, N. J. (1992) Carl Rogers and client/person-centered therapy. In D. K. Freedheim (ed.) *History of Psychotherapy: A Century of Change* (pp. 629–56). Washington, DC: American Psychological Association.

About the Authors

Louise Embleton Tudor began her career as a secondary school teacher and a Lecturer in Further Education before moving into the field of mental health. For seven years she managed a local authority mental health project for people diagnosed with psychiatric illnesses, following which she was a Development and Training Officer (Mental Health) in a local authority social services department. She has qualifications in art, education, psychotherapy and biodynamic massage and is a UKCP registered Integrative Psychotherapist. Louise is in independent practice offering psychotherapy, supervision and training in Sheffield where she is also a Director of and Course Tutor and Facilitator at Temenos. She is also a Proprietor of the Sheffield Natural Health Centre. She is the author of a number of publications in the field of mental health and psychotherapy, and is particularly interested in infant and child development, politics in general and, specifically, the politics of therapy.

Keemar Keemar worked in the hospitality industry before making a major career change to the field of counselling and human development. He worked for five years in the hospice movement where he managed a Day Hospice, linked to an inpatient unit, for young adults with terminal disease. After gaining extensive counselling experience in the voluntary sector, Keemar now works part-time in a staff counselling service in the NHS and has a private practice in central and south London, offering counselling, clinical and organisational supervision. He also works with a national youth charity doing intensive therapeutic residentials, both with local communities and within the prison service. As well as being a Director of Temenos, Keemar is a Course Tutor and Facilitator and is the Head of Responsibility for the Person-Centred Psychotherapy and Counselling Diploma Course.

Keith Tudor is a qualified Social Worker and Psychotherapist, registered with the UKCP both as a Humanistic Psychotherapist and as a Group Psychotherapist and Facilitator. He has worked for over 25 years in the helping professions in a number of settings including probation, shelters, youth counselling and psychiatry, in voluntary agencies and statutory social work. He has a small private/independent practice offering therapy, supervision, training and consultancy in Sheffield where he is a Director of Temenos and a Proprietor of the Sheffield Natural Health Centre. He is

304

a widely published author in the field of social policy, mental health and therapy including five books, the most recent of which are, with Tony Merry, the *Dictionary of Person-Centred Psychology* (Whurr, 2002) and, with Mike Worrall, *Freedom to Practice: Person-Centred Approaches to Supervision* (PCCS Books, 2004). Keith is an Honorary Fellow in the School of Health, Liverpool John Moores University.

Joanna Valentine works in the National Health Service as an internal Organisational Development and Leadership Development Consultant and Facilitator. A professional member of the Institute of Personnel and Development, she has over 20 years' experience within her field in the public, private and voluntary sectors, and holds a Masters Degree in Management Learning. Originally trained in gestalt approaches to organisational consulting, she began training in the person-centred approach with Temenos in order to enhance her facilitation skills, and stayed to complete her Diploma in the Person-Centred Approach to Organisations because she was inspired by her experience of using the approach with teams. Following a training in Deep Ecology with Joanna Macy, she was for a while involved with environmental education and training, which is still a deep concern. She is currently actively involved in a Quaker Peace Education charity.

Mike Worrall read English at Oxford and worked in the Probation Service before training as a counsellor at Metanoia Psychotherapy Training Institute, London, where subsequently he was a Primary Tutor on the BACP Recognised Person-Centred Counselling Course. He has a private practice in Oxford offering person-centred counselling and supervision, is a BACP Accredited Senior Practitioner and a UKCC Registered Independent Practitioner. He was for seven years a Director of the Person-Centred Counselling Course at Temenos, where he remains a Trainer and Facilitator.

About Temenos
Temenos is an independent organisation, based in Sheffield, providing quality training in the person-centred approach. Founded in 1993, and under new partnership since 2002, Temenos is now a limited company. Temenos is committed to training therapists (psychotherapists and counsellors) to a high level of professional competence, grounded in one particular, coherent approach, whilst taking account of other philosophical and therapeutic approaches. The design of the courses (in counselling skills, psychotherapy and counselling, supervision and training, as well as professional development workshops) is intended to offer students maximum flexibility in terms of entry level, exit qualification and access to professional accreditation and

registration, as well as academic validation, and graduate and postgraduate degrees. At the same time we promote independence of thought in relation to theory and practice and to the processes of education/training, accreditation, registration and validation. For further details about the history and philosophy of Temenos, its courses and staff, see our website at www.temenos.ac.uk or contact us at 289 Abbeydale Road, Sheffield S7 1FJ. Tel: 144 (0)114 258 0058. E-mail:admin@temenos. ac.uk.

Author Index

Subject Index